**Harvard Business School
Finance Club**

Career Guide:
Finance 1996

Edited by

**Linda A. LaGorga and
Vijay Krish**

Harvard Business School
Class of 1996

Distributed by
Harvard Business School Publishing

ISBN 0-87584-679-3
ISSN 0899-7098

Contents

Companies Profiled

Preface

When we began our job search last fall, we craved for any and all information on the finance industry. With widely varying degrees of knowledge and exposure to finance, both of us found the *Harvard Business School Finance Club Career Guide* to be an invaluable resource. To those of us attempting a career change, the insights and company profiles were extremely helpful in guiding us through the initial stages of the recruiting process. To those of us who have been in the industry before, a cursory glance revealed opportunities of which we were not previously aware.

In this fourth edition of the guide, we have attempted to maintain the level of intimate professionalism while updating the knowledge base. This guide covers numerous sectors of finance: investment banks, commercial banks, Fortune 500 companies, and many other international and regional firms. Descriptions detail how each firm differentiates itself, the opportunities and career paths each offers, as well as the recruiting process practiced by the firm.

We have also attempted to leverage the knowledge base inherent within the Harvard Business School community. Professors Samuel L. Hayes III and Joshua Lerner share their insights about careers in finance, and two 1993 graduates from the Harvard Business School candidly report on their experiences in finance and describe what job seekers can expect to encounter during their search. Additional alumni perspectives are provided by three seasoned HBS graduates, who share some of their experiences and secrets to success. Also included are a helpful glossary of finance terms, a mailing list of contacts for the companies described in the guide, and a selective bibliography of relevant books and directories.

We thank the individuals at all the firms who contributed to this book. Thanks are also due to Professors Samuel L. Hayes III and Joshua Lerner, Vikram Gandhi, Girish Nadkarni, Joel Peterson, Seth Rosenblatt, and Brian Webber for giving us their time so that we could learn from their personal experiences. Sue Marsh at Baker Library was most helpful in compiling the bibliography. Furthermore, this book would not have come to fruition were it not for the efforts of Eileen Marks and Nindy LeRoy at HBS Publishing.

Compiling this book has been a great pleasure for us, and we sincerely hope you find the *Harvard Business School Finance Club Career Guide* as helpful in your job search as we did in ours. Best of luck!

VIJAY KRISH
NEW YORK
AUGUST 1995

LINDA LAGORGA
NEW YORK
AUGUST 1995

Introduction

Samuel L. Hayes III
Jacob H. Schiff Professor of Investment Banking
Harvard Business School

Joshua Lerner
Assistant Professor
Harvard Business School

Business school faculty have many occasions to counsel students gearing up for the post-MBA job market. It is, to be sure, a time of high expectations. At the same time, the post-MBA job search can be daunting, even for those who have been through a search before.

Identifying and landing a job in the field of finance presents many of the same challenges of other functional areas: identifying promising potential employers, evaluating and discriminating among various job possibilities, assessing the long-term potential of a particular entry-level job, and so forth. At the same time, a finance job search poses certain special challenges. This book will give you a head start in the investigatory "due diligence" effort we all go through in the course of a job campaign.

The word *financial* in a job description usually reveals very little about the work content. One business school student took a summer job between the first and second years of his MBA program that seemed to promise opportunities for financial analysis within a large corporation. He had in mind the sort of strategic decision-making process that had dominated his first-year finance course. The actual job content turned out to be bread-and-butter accounting. Thankfully, the job was only temporary; he gamely did the work as competently as possible and then gracefully withdrew at the end of the summer.

Although it is difficult to categorize financial jobs, they can be broken down into those that take place within a corporate organization and those whose setting is a particular financial institution. The structure of finance functions within a corporation is easier to articulate. Typically, there is a chief financial officer (CFO) under whom internal financial (controllership) and external financial (treasurer) activities are grouped. In many companies, strategic and long-range planning have considerable finance content and may also report to the CFO, if only on a dotted-line basis.

Jobs concerned with the collection, measurement, and evaluation of financial data generated from internal operations are typically placed under the controller's super

vision. In these jobs, training in accounting (and possibly auditing) comes in very handy. An organization's relations with financial markets and institutions are often grouped under the supervision of the treasurer. These include management of bank lines and other credit facilities to ensure that the company can pay its bills in a timely fashion, communication with shareholders, and oversight of offshore financing arrangements. (The increasing frequency of foreign activities reflects the growing integration of national economies into a large, interdependent global market.) Evaluation of external acquisitions, or the sale of parts of the company's own operations, could be grouped under the treasurer's umbrella or within a separate office.

Most ambitious MBA graduates are eager to be at the heart of the real action in a company. In many ways, this is what they have been trained for. If you are of this disposition, it is important to determine the center of financial action within a prospective company.

Many graduating MBAs are immediately attracted to the treasury function and to strategic financial planning. These seem glamorous and represent activities that are closely related to the newly minted MBAs' training. In some companies, primarily those serving essentially as holding companies for a number of decentralized operating units, the financial focus may be on the company's relations with external capital markets. But despite the glitz associated with strategic planning and the treasurer's contacts with Wall Street and other external organizations, the real guts of the financial function for most firms—the site of the real action—is internal control.

Among financial vendors—commercial banks, investment banks, insurance companies, and money management firms—the array of job possibilities is extremely broad:

> Corporate finance
> Investment analysis
> Portfolio management
> Trading
> Private equity investing
> Institutional and retail sales
> "Financial engineering," or the application of
>   quantitative methods to the construction of
>   financial products
> General management

Corporate finance in the context of a financial vendor typically involves the basket of products, services, and counsel marketed to nonfinancial companies. This is an elastic definition. For investment banks, it encompasses the structuring and issuance of new securities to the public. For finance companies, such as GE Credit, corporate finance has a different meaning. GE Credit does not itself underwrite securities but does offer a broad variety of services to corporate customers, including secured financing and general counsel on corporate financial strategy.

Investment analysis is usually associated with the role of the analyst of publicly traded securities. Typically focusing on only one category of securities (e.g., the auto industry, "junk" bonds), analysts are employed by many different vendors. These may be on either the buy side (investment management firms or other institutional investors such as insurance companies and pension managers) or the sell side (securities firms and commercial banks). Sell-side analysts typically focus on products that they and their institutional sales colleagues think can be sold to portfolio managers responsible for the investment of large pools of savings. Buy-side analysts generally play the role of thoughtful skeptics in evaluating ideas generated by vendor firms.

Portfolio managers are often veteran security analysts, although some vendors hire young people for direct assignment as portfolio managers. Some portfolio managers describe their field as the place "where the buck stops." While the analyst recommends actions on certain securities, the portfolio manager makes the ultimate decisions and is evaluated on the consequences.

If portfolio managers are under the gun to demonstrate quarter-by-quarter quality performance, traders of particular categories of stocks, bonds, and derivatives live minute-by-minute. The consequences of their judgments are usually priced out each day for everyone to see. This is an exciting, "white-knuckle" business that attracts certain types of personalities.

At the opposite extreme are private equity investors. Their investments in venture capital and leveraged buyout deals can take years to mature to the point of being harvested, typically through the sale of stock to the public. Many MBAs are attracted to such private equity investing, which combines the satisfaction of building companies during their formative years with the potential for impressive capital gains. Unfortunately, the number of job openings each year in this area is modest, typically under 100 nationwide. Those interested in a career in private equity investing should bear in mind the stern odds against them and remember that many of the most successful investors first had experience as operating managers or in other financial sectors.

Institutional sales people work closely with traders and security analysts and create a bridge between them and the big institutions whose investment activities dominate modern public markets. They sell products that their firms have either developed or acquired for resale, and they must be conversant with the details of these products and how they serve the objectives of their institutional customers. The days of the "gentleman bond salesman" immortalized by F. Scott Fitzgerald are long gone. This is a demanding business—and the rewards for success are extraordinary.

Retail securities sales involves the marketing of stocks, bonds, and other financial products to individual investors. These investors are, on the average, likely to be less sophisticated than institutional investors and therefore are dependent on their brokers for more comprehensive counsel. Building a retail customer base takes time, but these customers tend to be loyal to their individual brokers and often follow them if they move from one brokerage house to another in search of a more lucrative deal or better support. Retail brokerage is one of the last bastions of relationship-based financial business.

Derivative securities—the disaggregation and reconstruction of securities with features specifically tailored to particular types of investors or issues—have become big business for some financial vendors and their clients. For vendors possessing the proprietary quantitative techniques used to construct and price out these hybrid securities, derivatives have been very profitable.

Jobs focusing on the *management* of financial service firms have gotten much more attention in recent years. More than a decade of acquisitions, mergers, and internally generated growth has made these firms larger and more complex; they no longer lend themselves to the informal managerial oversight long characteristic of the business. Back-office jobs are a case in point. After a variety of securities vendors became overloaded by the trading volume in the late 1960s and 1970s, the firms' leadership realized that the fate of their organizations was tied to their ability to get their internal paperwork and controls better organized. This change has raised the stature of professionals opting for internal management careers. Similarly, commercial banks discovered that a secret to successful expansion and profitability in the contemporary marketplace lies in the management of their own information systems. John Reed, CEO of Citibank, owes his leadership post, at least in part, to his successful mastery of this area.

It should be cautioned, however, that many general managers of financial service organizations have come up through the ranks as specialists in a product or service rather than through an initial career entry into the vendor's internal management structure. Many of these organizations still hold the highest places of honor for top business getters and revenue producers. However, an appreciation for professional management skills is gradually developing.

Students seeking to enter the finance profession must grapple with several challenging decisions. A crucial issue is whether finance is the right occupation. A finance career almost invariably involves long hours, stress, and often great uncertainty. If the field itself does not genuinely excite you or stimulate your curiosity, it is unlikely to be a happy choice, no matter how generous the compensation.

The next question is the appropriate subfields of finance on which to focus the job search. The demands of various subfields vary considerably. Some areas, such as trading and selling complex derivative securities, place a premium on quantitative abilities. In others, such as retail brokerage, the ability to communicate clearly and persuasively is paramount. The time demands of these positions also vary considerably. For instance, while corporate finance demands a considerable amount of time—to the point of serious conflicts between family and work—trading positions have traditionally been less demanding from an hours-per-week perspective.

A third decision relates to the institutions on which to focus job-searching efforts. Each organization has a distinctive personality. Finding a good match between an employer's personality and your own is an important prerequisite to long-run success. The descriptions contained in this book and the promotional material you will receive during the interviewing process should provide some indication of these firm-by-firm differences. Important insights can also be gathered through conversations with peers who have worked or are currently working for these organizations. But ultimately it is very difficult for others to point you toward the best match; it is a personal choice and an issue to which you should be particularly sensitive during the interviewing process.

Concerning the job search itself, several thoughts may be helpful. One frequent source of concern of students relates to the résumé. What résumé features, students wonder, will pique the interest of a financial services vendor? How do you avoid either overselling or underselling your credentials? How should the "job objective" section be handled? Although there is no single answer to these questions, among the key things potential employers look for is evidence of your purpose and direction. Do you appreciate the demands of the position that you are seeking? Do you understand the characteristics of the firm that you are pursuing? Are you serious about a finance career, or is this just one more option along with consulting, marketing, and other industries? The importance of thorough preparation for the job search process cannot be overestimated. This same concern applies to the interview process, only more so.

The successful completion of a job search is just a beginning. To translate the promise of a new job into long-run success requires the same careful thought and planning that won the job. A sure prerequisite is unmistakable enthusiasm for the work, which manifests itself as energy and personal innovation.

As you take your first position, be aware of several pitfalls that have derailed promising careers. The first relates to workload. Finance jobs tend to be high pressure and demand long hours. Giving the job the best you have is essential. But it is also necessary to pace yourself and ensure that the office does not entirely dominate your life. Without outside interests and time to enjoy them, it will be only a question of when, not if, you burn out.

A second mistake can be to move too quickly toward specialization. One objective of your initial position should be to illuminate the variety of potential career opportunities. Limiting your early career experience to a narrow focus on a particular product or a single industry, for instance, may limit your ability to move on to other opportunities as they present themselves.

A final point concerns the very nature of "opportunities." Our natural tendency, when faced with an uncertain future, is to plan our way out of it. But developing too precise a plan, and sticking rigidly to it, is likely to be a mistake. Career opportunities have a way of surfacing when one least expects them. Be alert for new and unanticipated opportunities that will almost surely come along. As Disraeli warned, "What we anticipate seldom comes; what we least expected generally happens."

Good luck!

Jobs in Investment Banking

Seth A. Rosenblatt
Harvard Business School, Class of 1993

What Is Investment Banking?

Investment banking denotes and connotes a number of different ideas. For those who have not worked in the industry before and are considering a summer or full-time position in investment banking, the job search can bring confusion and frustration.

In a very general sense, the term *investment bank* is broadly used to describe any financial institution that provides services in the areas of security issuing and brokering, financial advisory, or asset management. From the smallest boutiques to the large full-service firms, the term *investment bank* is far too often used. Large investment banks such as the "bulge-bracket" firms engage in many arenas outside traditional commercial banking or insurance underwriting. However, the function of investment banking requires a narrower industry definition. Investment banking generally encompasses four functions, all interrelated. Some firms may engage in all of these functions, while some may specialize in one or more of these areas:

1. Corporate finance.

2. Mergers and acquisitions.

3. Merchant banking.

4. Advisory/financial consulting.

In addition, many firms may specialize in one or two industry groups. The largest firms tend to have many functional and/or industry groups to serve their client base fully. Although many of the terms used here are fairly universal, the terminology in different countries does vary. If you are looking for an investment banking job outside the United States, become familiar with specific terminology used there (exact translations do not necessarily apply).

Corporate Finance
Corporate finance is the process of raising money for corporate clients (or public institutions) in the form of equity,

debt, convertible, or other derivative security. This process involves two steps: (1) determining the funding needs of the client (type, amount, and structure) and (2) finding investors to supply those funds. This second step can generally be accomplished through either of two methods: a public issue or a private placement. A public issuance of a security involves the investment bank's acting as an underwriter of the securities, purchasing the securities from the issuer and then reselling them on the public market. For larger investment banks, this process will involve other areas of the firm, such as sales and trading, research, and a syndicate function (sharing the underwriting responsibilities with other investment banks). A private placement, on the other hand, calls for the investment bank to act solely as an agent, matching the issuer of the security with one or a handful of potential investors in an offering not made available to the public.

Mergers and Acquisitions
For investment bankers the much publicized "M&A" business has the banker acting as an advisor to a company in transactions involving the sale of a whole company, a division, or just certain assets. The investment banker acts as an advisor to the client (on either the buy side or sell side), determines an appropriate valuation range, and negotiates terms most favorable to the client. The investment bank may also take a more active role by participating as a principal in the transaction. From an auction to a negotiated sale, from a stock swap to an LBO, the form and structure of an M&A transaction vary widely.

Merchant Banking
Merchant banking is the process whereby an investment bank acts as a principal in a transaction, either by purchasing newly issued securities of a firm or by purchasing (or selling) a stake in an M&A transaction. Some firms specialize only in merchant banking, while the largest investment banks tend to have a separate group to perform this function. Merchant banking is closely tied to the functions of corporate finance and M&A, and bankers from different industry or functional groups normally work on a merchant banking transaction together.

Advisory
Advisory work is linked to corporate finance, M&A, and merchant banking. It is generally performed as part of the overall service given to clients, or it may be tied to a specific transaction. Advisory or consulting work can take an infinite number of forms, including capital structure

analysis, comparable analysis, and industry research. Much of the specific work is dependent on the particular client's industry. In addition, the past few years have seen a dramatic growth in advisory work related to corporate restructurings and reorganizations.

Looking for a Job in Investment Banking

For those who have not previously worked in the industry, a lot of anxiety arises in the investment banking job search. For first-year students who are seriously considering making a career switch into investment banking, I strongly recommend that you work in the field for the summer. Not only will this make it easier to find a job with an investment bank after your second year, but you will learn what the industry is all about. Investment banking is such a unique field that it is difficult to understand the work, the environment, and the culture without experiencing it.

When beginning your self-assessment and your job search, first speak to as many people as you can who are or have been in the industry. In your class, you will probably find at least a dozen people who worked in an investment bank for at least two years. Your peers will be your greatest resource. Ask a lot of questions; you will get a good cross-section of various experiences, good and bad.

Many of your business school classmates have been former "analysts." *Analyst* is the usual entry-level title for undergraduates. Understand, that if hired, you will probably enter at the associate level (or equivalent). Although the long hours may be similar, the responsibilities may be very different. Try to understand the general career path in investment banking and the specific one in each firm.

Your next stops should be at the placement center and the library. Try to research each firm in which you may be interested. Understand which firms are full-service broker-dealers and investment bankers, which are middle-market firms, and which are boutiques. What appears to be the corporate culture and reputation of each firm? Does a firm specialize in a particular industry, function, or geographic region? Does it match your interests? Try to discover, through speaking with peers and research, which firms are the leaders in each of the areas (industries or functions) in which you are interested. There are a number of specific places where you can look for information on each firm that you are researching. Your career resource center will have the following information:

- Annual reports, 10-Ks, 10-Qs, prospectuses (if it is a public company)

- Recruiting brochures

- Company files

- Industry file/packet

- Summer job reports

- Current and previous job descriptions

- Lotus One Source/Other online services

- Alumni career advisor list

- Book of job search and salary statistics

Additionally, check these sources:

- Company recruiting briefings and dinners

- *Wall Street Journal*

- Business magazines (*Business Week, Forbes, Fortune, Economist*)

- LEXIS/NEXIS news searches (available on-line)

- Job Search Guide (available from your career center)

- Career fairs

- Friends, relatives, classmates, professors

- This book

Most of the larger investment banking firms, although they may have offices throughout the country and the rest of the world, tend to be based in New York City and do all recruiting from there. Regardless of which office you may be interested in, you may have to go through a general interviewing process based in New York. Be sure to understand each firm's policies and procedures for hiring outside the main office, particularly internationally. Many firms have a bias toward hiring nationals of a particular country to work in an office located there. If you are unsure, ask. During the correspondence and interviewing process, make your geographic preferences clear. If you can work only in city X, you will find it very frustrating to go through the entire process and be offered a job, only to find that the firm is not hiring this year in city X. Try to understand office placement policies before the interview.

Attend as many recruiting briefings as you can to get an idea of each firm's strategy, focus, and culture. Compare the people who have been successful in each firm to your own track record and where (or who) you would like to be in 5, 10, or 20 years. Finally, make it a practice to read the newspaper (the *Wall Street Journal* in particular) to get a good sense of what is going on in the industry and with specific firms.

If you have done sufficient researching and querying, the interview should be the easiest part of the process. These interviews are generally not like "stress" consulting interviews. You will probably not be asked the implications of an inverted yield curve or queried as to the number of restaurants in New York City. This, of course, varies by firm (and there are stories of difficult interviews), but in general investment banks are looking to see if you:

- Are a hard worker and detail oriented.

- Have leadership skills and enjoy working in groups.

- Have a genuine interest in the industry and are excited about it.

- Show good judgment and demonstrate responsibility.

- Are analytically inclined and comfortable with numbers and computers.

- Understand the lifestyle and are willing to make the sacrifices required.

- Are a fun person to be around. ("Would I like to go to dinner with you?")

Conclusion

You must determine what methods of research work best for you. Speak to people whose advice you value, and then draw your own conclusions. Two issues that need to be addressed are the money and the hours. Much time has been spent talking about both of these subjects.

All in all, I found investment banking to be a great experience. It was stimulating and challenging, and I got to work with some fascinating people. If you decide to make a career of it, do it for reasons like this. If you find,

through talking to peers or through a summer job, that you do not expect to get the same kind of fun, challenge, or excitement that I did, do not go into the industry. You will be miserable. Investment banking is not for everybody. Where I worked, there were a few of my peers who thought that it was the greatest experience of their lives, while others, doing the exact same job, were miserable. In other words, the money should *not* be the deciding factor. There is little doubt that investment banking is one of the best-paying positions (in the short run) that you can take, and money is certainly not unimportant. Although compensation is always a consideration in any job decision, the people I knew who regretted the job the most were the ones who took it solely for the cash.

As for the hours, this is something also that has sparked quite a legend on Wall Street—and throughout the rest of the business world. Stories of all-nighters and ruined weekends plague the minds of former analysts. While it is true that investment bankers work very long hours, the variance within and among firms is so large that it defies most generalizations. Nevertheless, there usually is some lifestyle sacrifice that particularly a junior banker will have to make in investment banking. The only way to get an accurate sense of the hours is for you to talk to friends or classmates who worked for a particular firm. Even then, their information may not be accurate because different departments in the same firm may require much different hours. Additionally, changes in the business cycle and season can dramatically affect the work load in any firm.

Only through asking a lot of questions and through a little soul searching can you determine if the investment banking lifestyle is indeed right for you.

Finance Careers in Manufacturing Companies

Brian M. Webber
Harvard Business School, Class of 1993

A variety of career opportunities are available to students interested in finance other than well-known financial services jobs. Manufacturing companies have positions in strategic planning, product development, and division controllers' offices. I worked as a financial analyst in product development at Ford Motor Company prior to attending HBS.

In the controller's office of product development, I worked on various product development teams associated with the development of new models of Taurus and Sable. Product development teams consist of engineers, marketing people, planning people, and a finance person. My main responsibility was to perform the financial analysis required by the team when making product decisions, but I was also exposed to a wide array of team decisions and problems and to the team strategies and solutions employed throughout the development process. I met daily with team members to review, update, and discuss the progress of the new product. The requirements of this assignment were to visit the plants of small suppliers, assist with cost control and financial projections, and work closely with development engineers and designers to report the financial status of the program to senior management. Since each team member is encouraged to contribute and to assume responsibility where feasible, I quickly gained a reasonable knowledge of the entire development process. Interaction with engineering, marketing, planning, and outside suppliers was extremely interesting and helped me to understand the engineering and marketing functions. Often the various functional areas are faced with conflicting goals, and compromises among team members are required. Frequently team meetings are held at supplier locations, where the team analyzes specific product proposals, or meetings are held in the prototype plant next to a prototype vehicle so that decisions can be implemented in real time. Finance positions in product development allow a finance person to work closely with the manufacturing process. Every member of the product development team provides input for decisions that affect the outcome of the product.

The environment in product development finance is intense, and the hours are demanding. The hours do not compare to investment banking hours but are considerably longer than other positions within the company. A great deal of responsibility is heaped on finance representatives with respect to reporting to senior management the financial status of the

new product, preparing financial models to analyze the impact of various proposals, and assuming team leadership at times when financial analysis has a major impact on a product decision. Analysts may also evaluate future marketing programs and compare competitors' products from a financial perspective. Analysts perform business analyses for new programs that include profitability, return on capital, evaluation of alternatives, and presentations to senior management.

Product development is only one aspect of finance within a manufacturing company. Other areas requiring financial expertise are sales and marketing, capital markets, and manufacturing.

Sales and marketing finance positions require analysts to evaluate and develop appropriate strategies for retail pricing and various incentive programs. With recent developments in automobile pricing, such as cash back and low interest financing, a great deal of analysis is required to recommend appropriate pricing levels. Analysts also evaluate competitors' pricing strategies and form arguments for an appropriate counterresponse.

Capital market finance positions exist both within credit areas, such as Ford Motor Credit, and in various treasury areas. Analysts provide financial support for issuance of commercial paper, long-term debt, common and preferred stock, and sale leaseback transactions. Analysts act as buyers of various investment banking services. Analysts recommend strategies for capital structure and dividend policies, manage daily cash flow, and perform analyses for acquisitions and divestitures.

Manufacturing finance positions involve developing capital budgets and analyzing specific capital spending projects. Analysts are involved with site analysis and evaluate new plant proposals. They also analyze financial and operating results of manufacturing plants.

A finance background can often open doors for international assignments depending on the size and needs of the company. Many of my colleagues planned to work internationally, and I saw doors open up for them to do so.

There are many things to consider when choosing a summer job or a career, including location and corporate environment. The best source of information is often individuals who have worked in the industry or have worked for the specific company you are considering. Do not hesitate to contact someone who has worked for a company or in an area you are considering.

Interviews: Three Harvard Business School Alumni Reflect on Careers in Finance

Vikram Gandhi

Harvard Business School, Class of 1989
Vice President, Mergers and Acquisitions
Morgan Stanley & Company

Describe the stages of your career path and changes in responsibility.

During the first couple of years, my career developed along a diversified set of experiences. I worked in Capital Markets, the Natural Resource Area, and the Merger and Acquisitions/Restructuring Area. These two years served as a time to build a network of relationships and access pockets of knowledge throughout the firm. In addition to being exposed to new functional and industry arenas, this stage enabled me to develop and refine my teamwork skills further. My role was primarily to complete modules of a large project and to contribute to the team's efforts in executing transactions.

The opportunity to move around in the first two years was a valuable experience for two reasons. First, given the nature of the investment banking industry and flux of the business, you should not expect to have a "home" for good, and so it is worthwhile to share in multiple experiences in case you need to shift specialties in the future. Second, given the importance of working with a variety of people, the more people you meet, the better you will be positioned later in your career.

My first two years emphasized agenda execution; my current career stage emphasizes agenda setting as a team manager in the M&A group. I now work more directly with the principals and managing directors, am responsible for ensuring the quality of the team's work, and manage analysts and new associates. A critical junction in my role as team manager is to manage upward and across specialty areas to ensure that the necessary expertise is brought to bear to solve client problems.

What have been the obstacles and challenges of your career progression?

Three challenges in my career have been managing up, coordinating resources, and motivating down. First, since I am now responsible for ensuring the quality of work yet lack many years of experience, it is imperative that I seek the perspective of senior people, and getting their time is not

easy. Therefore, it is critical to get them to focus, and one must manage and communicate effectively to accomplish this feat.

Second, a key success factor in investment banking is bringing various resources of the firm to bear on a project. This requires a healthy dose of coordination, especially since I work on six to seven projects at a time. Achieving cooperation in a firm with many egos is a challenge. One must massage egos when coordinating to ensure that what colleagues and senior people say is intelligently articulated to the client.

A third challenge is motivating down. We work hard at Morgan Stanley, and it is vital to maintain a good experience for the analysts and new associates. I must position the work as a valuable and fun experience so that junior people do not mind being at work until 1 A.M. I need to motivate them so they feel involved and they have a high degree of job satisfaction.

Can you describe an experience that has significantly influenced your career?

I enjoy my job, but I cannot point to any one experience that has significantly influenced my career.

What strengths have helped you excel in your career?

A strength that has helped me in my career is being analytically oriented. This should come as no big surprise, but it is especially relevant to M&A given the abundance of valuation and creative structuring required. Another strength is being involved in many extracurricular activities while at school. This involvement was valuable for enabling me to obtain a better understanding of how people think and work. The key to success at Morgan Stanley is teamwork, and my extracurricular activities enhanced my ability to manage my time, to motivate, and to keep people interested in what they are doing while getting the most out of them.

Where do you see your career going over the next ten years? How will you prepare for such changes?

I'm happy in investment banking. I enjoy what I do because it builds on my strengths, and there is a fair degree of variety in the projects I work on. Yes, investment banking is tiring and difficult, but it's also fun. Hence, I'd like to continue for at least the next few years as I transition from a team manager to a team leader. Yet over the long haul, I can see myself getting involved on the principal side of the business.

To prepare for the future, I focus on my interactions with senior firm officials and senior client officials. Eventually, it will be important for me to secure clients if I hope to transition to a team leader. Therefore, I make sure I know current clients well and build those relationships while establishing others. Preparing for the future means that when a client has a problem, he or she will call on me.

To what extent did your HBS degree prepare you for the day-to-day life of Morgan Stanley?

HBS definitely prepares you for investment banking. One works on six to seven projects at a time in different industries, and the work requires creative problem solving. At Morgan Stanley, I might be considering a joint venture for a natural resource client, a buying opportunity for an auto client, and a selling opportunity for a telecommunications client. This might be only half of the projects on my plate at any given time. And like HBS, even though I had less time to think about the business situation, I would have to grasp key issues of three business situations each evening. So, similar to the requirements for being an exceptional investment banker, HBS prepares one to handle a lot of stuff in a short amount of time and effectively deal with the intensity of work.

The second way HBS prepared me was in the exercise of analytics. Every day I have to go through thick documents or consider complicated situations and come up with three key issues. The client describes a problem, and it's my job to figure out some options and decide which makes the most sense for the client. This type of work is not too different from discussions that occurred every day in Aldrich Hall.

Finally, a third way that HBS prepared me was with regard to people. The people at HBS are the same type that I work with at Morgan Stanley; they're smart and hard working, but they often have large egos. HBS prepared me well for those types of people.

Is there anything else you would recommend to future HBS graduates entering the finance industry?

First, teamwork is critical to success and should not be underestimated. HBS makes some people think they can be a solo star, but it just doesn't work that way.

Second, don't try to run before you can walk. Coming out of HBS, you may think there's not much more to learn. Nothing could be further from the truth. A place like Morgan Stanley can humble you. Consider your first couple of years as an opportunity where you are being paid to learn. I strongly recommend that you demonstrate an eagerness to learn.

Third, recognize that investment banking is a cyclical industry. You must anticipate that while today the equity product might be hot while M&A is slow, the situation could reverse itself very quickly. Given this industry nature, you should be flexible to change as it may become necessary to shift to different industry or function groups during your career. But the good thing to remember is that the HBS education enables you to be flexible because of the exposure to many industries, functions, people, and business situations.

Girish V. Nadkarni
Harvard Business School, Class of 1988
Vice President, Strategic Transactions
The Prudential Insurance Company of America

Describe the stages of your career path and changes in responsibility.

Before attending HBS, I practiced law on Wall Street: three years with Coudert Brothers and three years with Shearman & Sterling. Hence, my first job after HBS is not typical for MBAs straight out of school. After graduating from HBS, I was hired as Vice President and Assistant to the Vice Chairman of The Prudential Insurance Company of America, responsible for handling a variety of special projects for the Vice Chairman. I also was "on loan" to the heads of several business units throughout The Prudential. The work I was assigned often pertained to strategic initiatives and gave me wide exposure to Prudential's businesses. For instance, one of the special projects required me to work on a task force to assess the sensitivity of Prudential's leveraged buyout (LBO) portfolio to recession.

Fourteen months later, I was promoted to Corporate Vice President in the Central Financial Services Group of Prudential Capital Corporation, responsible for new product development. One of the products I created was Pru-Shelf, a proprietary medium-term note program. Our first Pru-Shelf transaction was a $200 million financing with Toys R Us. To date, The Prudential has executed approximately 24 Pru-Shelf transactions totaling $1.6 billion. The product was featured in articles in *Corporate Finance*, *Investment Dealers Digest*, and *Investors Daily* and was also included in a *Business Week* cover story on innovative financial instruments. I also led a team that helped Prudential Capital's 14 regional offices manage complex transactions, such as LBOs and cashouts.

In 1990, I transferred to the work-out area of Prudential Capital and assumed a portfolio of 16 troubled companies. No other job has stretched me so much physically, emotionally, and intellectually. Every day was a crisis. Extensive negotiating and posturing skills were critical in this job, and when I was reassigned to my current position 18 months later, I knew my strengths and weaknesses.

For a number of reasons that range from Hurricane Andrew to the new risk-based capital requirements imposed on insurance companies, The Prudential has embarked on a reassessment of its main lines of business. Consequently, in my current position as Vice President, Strategic Transactions with the Prudential Investment Corporation, I help with the strategic assessment of different businesses and carry out the decisions to eliminate or expand a business unit. If we decide to expand a business or acquire companies, then I might lead an effort to raise external capital. If, on the other hand, we decide to exit a business, then I will execute a sale of our operations in that business.

What have been the obstacles and challenges of your career progression?

I have faced three challenges: diversity, politics, and a line versus staff trade-off. I was born and raised in India and therefore am different from most of the other people at The Prudential. I have independent opinions, and I tend to state them. There is the natural challenge of being different from the status quo and the challenge of peers resisting someone like me who does not always agree with their decisions, analyses, and opinions.

Entering an organization at a high level has its own challenges. People often resent you for not having paid your dues. It therefore takes a lot of effort and time to establish your credibility.

I also have been challenged by my lack of roots to a home unit within The Prudential. This has come about because of my constant transfers from one area of the company to another—wherever the action is hot. I'm not really complaining, though, because putting out fires has been exciting. But movements between line and staff positions can be difficult. It's especially hard to move back into a line assignment after having been in a staff position. But, unfortunately, I am not considered part of the family by any group or senior person and there is no one other than myself who looks after my career.

Can you describe an experience that has significantly influenced your career?

Our business is fraught with legal issues; if we take the wrong step, we'll be sued. And though I am not trained in bankruptcy law, my legal background provides me with the ability to understand most of the intricacies of the workout business. I also know how to make the most of our own lawyers. In fact, because of my legal experience, the synergy between our legal counsel and me is fantastic. Between us, we make one and one equal six.

A second significant experience is my assignment in the workout area, where I honed my negotiating skills and learned and practiced the art of diplomacy, often facing people with diverging interests and constantly shifting alliances. I developed a better understanding of finance and strengthened my structuring skills. And I achieved better credit analysis as I saw what can and does go wrong in companies. I also learned that you cannot underestimate the critical need and value for good management and should not analyze a company without considering the probable significant changes imminent within the industry.

What strengths have helped you excel in your career?

My legal background has been a remarkable strength. Another strength is my generalist experience at The Prudential. Although it sometimes hurts not to have a home, transferring throughout the organization has given me wide exposure and a holistic view of Prudential's business. It also taught me to get up to speed quickly. The problems with diversity are synthesizing experiences that will make me an excellent senior manager in the long run. Other strengths include creative problem solving, structuring, and negotiating skills.

Where do you see your career going over the next ten years? How will you prepare for such changes?

I honestly have no clue where my career will be in ten years. The Prudential is experiencing a major transition. Its business is already very different than it was just five years ago. Uncertainty is a big problem. Like most other Harvard Business School alumni, I wouldn't mind being on my own one day, maybe with my own fund. And perhaps unlike most other HBS alumni, I have a strong interest in politics and am likely to run for some type of office one day. The future is definitely uncertain but exciting.

Preparing for uncertainty is a challenge. Often it's not what you know that is important but who you know. It is very important to know the right people—those who make the decisions and not those who make the most noise. It is valuable to adopt a mentor and build credibility.

To what extent did your HBS degree prepare you for the day-to-day life of The Prudential?

I loved my two years at HBS. They gave me tremendous analytical and problem-solving capabilities, as well as frameworks and paradigms to guide my thinking. The education forced me to understand the economics of a business. I graduated appreciating that there are times when the process of making decisions is more important than the substance; that achieving commitment, involvement, and organizational buy-in is not easy; that getting the rank and file to adopt and implement plans is about applying the right process; and that treating customers and employees well is critical to survival.

Nevertheless, HBS failed to prepare me for many of the soft issues that one deals with every day. Perhaps I wasn't listening, but it didn't teach me how to manage my career in a political organization. HBS taught me how to manage others but not how to be managed. It's like expecting one to be a parent before he or she has finished being a child. Furthermore, HBS fell short of enabling me to handle entering an organization at a high-profile level and to fight the stereotypes of an "HBS Baker Scholar type."

Is there anything else you would recommend to future HBS graduates entering the finance industry?

First, make sure you know why you want to be in finance. Too many people think it's a stepping-stone to bigger and better things. For instance, many people think investment banking or mergers and acquisitions is a stepping-stone to running your own business one day. Nothing in investment banking prepares you for running your own business. If you want to operate a business, then consider marketing. Investment banking teaches one only how to process transactions. Make sure you know what working life will be like on a day-to-day basis. Don't choose money management because you want your photograph in the newspaper as the next Peter Lynch. Make sure you understand what Peter Lynch did at Fidelity on a daily basis.

Know your strengths and play to them, and don't forget soft issues both inside and outside your company. Remember that judgment is more important than technical skills. It's critical to reach a judgment based on what the numbers say and not just crunch them. Don't hesitate to push the envelope. Too many people think they are pushing the envelope, but often they don't know where the envelope really is, or they define it too narrowly. Finally, to succeed at the top, it's helpful to be a generalist. Yet there's a trade-off, because to get to the top you need to be a specialist and the risk is obsolescence of your specialty; so be careful to follow industry dynamics constantly, and if they change, manage your career accordingly.

Joel W. Peterson
Harvard Business School, Class of 1983
Managing Director, Utilities
CIBC, a subsidiary of Canadian Imperial Bank of Commerce

Describe the stages of your career path and changes in responsibility.

I would describe my career in five stages: the Learning Stage, "Just Another Banker" Stage, "Not Just Another Banker" Stage, People Manager Stage, and "Not Just Another Manager" Stage.

- *The Learning Stage* (about one year): This is the period right after business school, when I tried to absorb as much information as possible, figure out who's who, and simply do my best even though I was not sure what specific career benefit would accrue from a particular work matter.

- *"Just Another Banker" Stage* (about two years): In this stage I sought valuable personal contacts and team-building opportunities. I knew enough to be dangerous yet not enough to be noticed or have too much impact.

- *"Not Just Another Banker" Stage* (about three years): At this point in my career, I had real impact. This was manifested in specific transactions in which I could differentiate myself through personal excellence and organizational team-building skills.

- *People Manager Stage* (about two years): Although I have always managed projects and people to some extent in my career (you have to manage people up, down, and sideways throughout a successful career), it was during this stage about three years ago that I had responsibility for ten direct reports.

- *"Not Just Another Manager" Stage:* Finally, in the fifth stage, I now differentiate myself by fostering a culture of productivity and compatibility, hiring sincere and motivated people and setting high standards that are consistently met.

It's important to note that throughout the five stages it has been personal knowledge and abilities that enabled me to be successful. At the beginning of my career, technical, industry, and job knowledge were important, but my progression is rewarded and will continue to be rewarded due to personal knowledge and organizational abilities, which are competencies honed at HBS.

What have been the obstacles and challenges of your career progression?

The biggest challenge has been managing up. I didn't realize the critical importance of managing up, especially with respect to making sure my manager understands what I'm doing. I'm not promoting brown-nosing but rather the notion of effective communication of one's ideas. What good is the world's best idea if you can't effectively communicate it? Upward management through effective communication yields believability, credibility, and promotability. It is especially important and challenging to manage up when personal rapport with the manager is not ideal. I think that talking to unbiased parties and bouncing ideas off them— mentors or peers—is a great way to assess whether you're seeing the big picture and test how such should be communicated to your superiors.

Another challenge to keep in mind is that there are advantages and disadvantages to being in your company's corporate headquarters. In fact, I think there are better reasons for *not* being at headquarters, which is contrary to what many people usually believe. People often want to be located at headquarters because they feel they will reap benefits of greater visibility to the chairman. However, so much time at headquarters is spent gossiping and not enough on business. A satellite office operates as if it were running its own business. Being in a satellite office is liberating.

The other two challenges involve people. First, don't be surprised when the seemingly most neutral colleague backstabs you. The people who openly disagree are at least willing to talk about it; however, it's the people who are quiet who are plotting their actions against you and preparing for guerrilla warfare. Never expect to win every battle. Take the long-term view. Second, career advancement requires successful people management. It requires a lot of time and attention. Don't patronize and don't ignore your people because it may come back to haunt you. People management is more time intensive and critical than technical problems. Take care of people problems first.

Can you describe an experience that has significantly influenced your career?

The experience that significantly influenced my career is when I left First Chicago to pursue a long-term management opportunity at CIBC, where I would be more than just a banker. I took a long-term perspective regarding my career and took a risk in pursuit of this long-term opportunity because I was confident in my abilities to make another move if the CIBC opportunity did not materialize. As the saying goes, "No risk, no return."

What strengths have helped you excel in your career?

Three strengths that have enabled me to excel in my career are communicating persuasively, having a long-term perspective, and completing tasks I set out to perform. With regard to the first strength, anyone can run a computer or regression analysis, but those who excel can also communicate the analysis into a coherent strategy to follow. And to the strength of always completing tasks I set out to perform, I call this "consistent integrity"— doing what I promised. I will not make commitments I cannot keep; everyone is watching everything I do.

Where do you see your career going over the next ten years? How will you prepare for such changes?

Right now I'm at a juncture. I could continue my career per the status quo, but the limiting factor is the trend of flattening organizations, and hence increasing responsibility becoming limited. I like what I do, especially with respect to managing people, and I would not mind moving into more senior management levels, which suggests that I strongly consider broadening my horizons and perspective. But doing my own thing could be fun as well. I also think about working for a client.

Preparing for the future means continuing to develop and refine my skills, talking to a lot of people, and building a network of contacts and a broad knowledge base. It would be great to have a guardian angel, but it just doesn't work that way. In fact, mentor time is limited, and career development is usually nonexistent except for the first couple of years. Advice can be expected but is often unorganized and from many sources. In short, preparing for the future is difficult.

To what extent did your HBS degree prepare you for the day-to-day life of CIBC?

HBS attracts leaders and hones those skills. Personal values, knowledge, and abilities are extremely important, and I think HBS excels at developing and refining these personal attributes. Any smart person can learn technical, industry, and job knowledge, but it's the general, broad knowledge base and personal values that enable excellence, and HBS is distinguished at developing them. Because of my HBS education, I am well organized and see the big picture. These attributes are important in the day-to-day life at CIBC. Also, HBS made me sensitive to other cultures and international differences. This is especially important in the increasingly global world and has made a significant difference in my career.

Is there anything else you would recommend to future HBS graduates entering the finance industry?

I recommend that you set short-term, mid-term, and long-term goals. Evaluate these goals for yourself and your company. Ask yourself questions and ponder answers. Are you compatible with your job and the people around you at work? Do you enjoy your job? If not, then leave, because life is too short. But to a certain extent, you also have to put up with some things you don't like.

A helpful analogy is to think of your career as an investment. You would not put money in a stock and let it sit for 50 years. You would probably look at that investment every six months. Do the same for your career; HBS is an investment in yourself. Don't keep doing something you don't like. If you're unhappy, it will be obvious in your work and in your life.

Firm Descriptions

During the spring of 1995, a variety of firms that typically hire MBAs for positions in finance were contacted and asked to respond to the questionnaire that appears on page 132. The firms contacted include investment banking firms, commercial banks, Fortune 500 firms, and international and regional companies. Responses from firms in this section are printed, for the most part, as received.

A.G. Edwards & Sons, Inc.

One North Jefferson
St. Louis, MO 63103
(314) 289-3000

MBA Recruiting Contact(s):
Barbara H. Boyle, Vice President
(314) 289-3691

Company Description

Describe your firm's business and the types of clients served by your finance group(s).

Founded in 1887, A.G. Edwards is the largest securities firm headquartered off Wall Street; it is one of the few firms described as a "national full-line" firm by the Securities and Exchange Commission and the Securities Industry Association. For over 100 years, the firm has played a major role in providing financial services to a variety of clients nationwide. From its headquarters in St. Louis, the firm and its subsidiaries provide securities and commodities brokerage, asset management, insurance, real estate, and investment banking services. Our departments provide investment banking services in the areas of Corporate Finance, Mergers and Acquisitions, and Valuations.

Public and Structured Finance, a department that is separate and distinct from those discussed below, is also part of A.G. Edwards's investment banking services. While the Public and Structured Finance department does not currently recruit on college campuses, inquiries can be made to Jon Savage, (314) 289-3849, at the address listed above.

Describe your ownership structure.

A.G. Edwards, a publicly owned corporation for over 20 years, is traded on the New York Stock Exchange under the symbol AGE.

How does your approach to finance differ from that of other firms, and what do you consider to be your strengths and distinctive capabilities?

Our success has been built in large part on our orientation toward relationship banking. Rather than emphasizing individual transactions, we provide a variety of services that meet our clients' needs and further our long-term relationships with them. Although our clients range from Fortune 500 corporations to small private companies, we consider our niche to be middle-market companies. We serve clients coast to coast and compete with other national, as well as regional, investment banks.

The close attention we provide clients gives A.G. Edwards the distinction of being the nation's only retail brokerage firm to be included in both editions of *The Service Edge: 101 Companies That Profit from Customer Care* and both editions of *The 100 Best Companies to Work for in America*. We attribute the firm's success to our emphasis on consistently maintaining the customers' success as a primary focus, creating value with the services we deliver, and treating employees "like members of the family."

According to *Institutional Investor*, at year-end 1994, A.G. Edwards was the fourth largest securities firm in the United States based on the number of offices (over 500 in 48 states), and the sixth largest based on the number of registered representatives (over 5,400). Well known within the industry for our national distribution network, our distribution of securities in small amounts to a large number of investors results in a large, geographically dispersed shareholder/bondholder base for the issuer.

Discuss changes in your firm's revenues (both domestic and international) and professional staff over the past year; over the past five years.

Although most of A.G. Edwards's revenues are derived from commissions generated by selling securities to individual investors, our departments' revenues are derived from a diversified base of business that includes underwritings of equity and debt, mergers and acquisitions, valuations, and financial advisory projects. Our departments have significantly expanded both the breadth and depth of our capability over the past decade. The rapid growth of our departments affords a motivated individual the opportunity to make a meaningful contribution to A.G. Edwards. The number of professionals in the Corporate Finance, Mergers and Acquisitions, and Valuations departments has grown from 7 professionals in 1983 to over 50 professionals in 1995. All associates are hired for our St. Louis headquarters, where over 2,600 of our over 11,000 employees work.

The Finance MBA's Job Description

Describe the career path and corresponding responsibilities for an MBA at your firm.

A.G. Edwards's Corporate Finance, Mergers and Acquisitions, and Valuations departments are rapidly developing areas of the company that afford talented, hardworking individuals recognition and responsibility early in their career development. A generalist program for an associate's development is strongly emphasized, and new associates in investment banking are given a wide variety of projects in corporate finance, mergers and acquisitions, and valuations.

A.G. Edwards emphasizes teamwork. Teams are small, and new associates can expect to work directly on client assignments with senior investment banking professionals, ensuring the associates' visibility and responsibility on projects. In addition, we have developed a system of semiannual and annual reviews, as well as specific project reviews, to provide individuals with feedback on their development.

Describe the opportunities for professional mobility between the various departments in your firm.

We expect associates to be generalists in corporate finance, mergers and acquisitions, and valuations in the early stage of their careers. Because there are no rigid boundaries separating these areas, new associates will be involved in projects in all of these areas. Associates are allowed to develop areas of expertise and specialization as they gain experience in investment banking.

Discuss the lifestyle aspects of a career with your firm (i.e., average hours per week, amount of travel, flexibility to change offices, corporate culture, etc.).

Demands and expectations at A.G. Edwards are very high. The firm, however, tries to maintain a reasonable balance between work and personal interests, which is reflected by a low turnover rate for our employees. St. Louis offers a very affordable and pleasant quality of life. The city consistently rates in the top ten of U.S. metropolitan areas in terms of quality of life. St. Louis provides an array of dance, theater, music, art, leisure activities, and sports and includes many nationally recognized landmarks. The city is also home to a significant number of Fortune 500 companies.

The Recruiting Process

Describe your recruiting process and the criteria by which you select candidates. Is prior experience necessary?

Our strategy for selecting new investment banking associates is to employ those whom we feel have the skills and compatibility to build long-term careers at A.G. Edwards. We have avoided the cutbacks common in our industry because we do not initially overhire. Instead, the number of new positions is commensurate with the firm's steady growth. Each new associate is carefully chosen to assume a role in which long-term dedication and a commitment to manage increasing responsibility are expected.

Leadership, personal integrity, academic success, and demonstrated success in other areas are some of the criteria we use to judge individual candidates. A commitment to investment banking, shown by summer internships or relevant experience prior to graduate school, is also an important criterion.

How many permanent associates and analysts do you hire in a typical year? How many summer interns do you expect to hire? If you have a formal summer program, please describe it. Please be sure to indicate whether the summer program is in place for all offices or just some.

We add new associates and analysts according to the quality of individual candidates and the compatibility of those candidates with A.G. Edwards. Therefore, we do not set yearly quotas for hiring. We have retained a very high percentage of the associates we have hired over the past ten years.

We currently do not offer a summer program.

What international opportunities does your firm offer for U.S. citizens? For foreign nationals?

While A.G. Edwards does participate in the international marketing of underwritings to a limited extent, all of our operations, including investment banking, are located in the United States.

Alex. Brown & Sons, Inc.

135 East Baltimore Street
Baltimore, MD 21202
(800) 638-2596

MBA Recruiting Contact(s):
Anne Ford

Company Description

Describe your firm's business and the type of clients served by your finance group(s).

Alex. Brown & Sons Incorporated is a national specialty investment bank based in Baltimore. It is also the nation's oldest investment banking firm, founded in 1800. The firm's main objective is to provide value-added financing and investment advice to its clients—corporate, institutional, municipal, and individual—regardless of the market environment. This commitment to client service and high ethical standards is fundamental to the firm's corporate culture.

The firm's services are based primarily on industry knowledge, and its resources are concentrated on six dynamic industry sectors with attractive long-term fundamentals. These sectors are consumer, financial services, industrial, health care, media/communications, and technology.

Alex. Brown operates in two general business areas which capitalize on our industry knowledge and technical competence: Capital Markets and Private Investor Services. Capital Markets includes Research, Investment Banking, Equity Sales and Trading and High Yield Sales and Trading. Private Investor Services includes Private Client Services, Asset Management, and Fixed Income.

The firm has significant global capabilities, yet remains highly focused on the areas in which it can leverage its industry knowledge and technical competence. Today, Alex. Brown has more than 2200 employees in 22 offices in the United States, Europe, and Asia.

Describe your ownership structure.

Alex. Brown Inc. is a public company. Its common stock trades on the New York Stock Exchange under the symbol "AB."

How does your approach to finance differ from that of other firms, and what do you consider to be your strengths and distinctive capabilities?

We believe that industry knowledge and technical competence, more than any other factors, distinguish our ability to provide differentiated, value-added, and superior advice and service. The dynamic nature of the investment world requires knowledge of many areas, including markets, individual securities, types of transactions, and economic and societal trends. Because of the focused nature of our business and the consequent accumulation of experience, we feel that our technical competence in each of these areas is substantial. We believe, however, that our most valuable and distinctive competence is industry knowledge.

By concentrating our resources on a limited number of industries and encouraging a teamwork approach to communicate our collective knowledge efficiently throughout the firm, we are able to develop valuable insights and bring them to bear in each client relationship. Over the years, we have invested heavily in the human and technological resources necessary to build this knowledge base into a substantial corporate asset. The cumulative effect of this investment provides us with the "intellectual capital" to compete favorably with other entities, some of whose overall resources are much greater than our own. Most important, it is our commitment to long-term relationships and our constantly expanding resources that serve our clients well, even as the markets change.

Discuss changes in your firm's revenues (both domestic and international) and professional staff over the past year; over the past five years.

Over the past five years, the firm's revenues have grown 122% from $272 million in 1990 to $605 million in 1994. The growth in revenues is attributable, in part, to equity and fixed income market conditions conducive to the firm's particular mix of business. The firm has also succeeded in leveraging its industry knowledge and technical competence to expand its services and its global presence.

The Finance MBA's Job Description

Describe the career path and corresponding responsibilities for an MBA at your firm.

Investment Banking
Associates in the Investment Banking Division work in either industry groups or product groups where they are usually part of small project teams consisting of a managing director or principal, a vice president, and one or

more analysts. An associate may work on several assignments simultaneously. In one of our six industry groups, this may include working on public offerings, mergers and acquisitions, or private placements. In product groups, such as mergers and acquisitions, high yield, or private equity placements, an associate may work simultaneously on several assignments with different industry groups. By the end of the first year, associates are expected to assume a high degree of responsibility for project management and client maintenance.

Public Finance

Associates initially rotate through product groups within the division and are then placed in a group depending on where the associates are needed and on individual interest. During the first year, an associate is exposed to all aspects of a transaction, from getting the business to selling and closing a bond issue. Working closely with senior bankers on each project, the associate will write proposals and organize presentations. As the public finance associate develops, he or she will become more involved in various phases of client contact and presentations.

Equity Research

The associate analyst is teamed with a senior analyst to cover a specific industry sector. The position entails development of specialized industry and analytical skills, frequent interviews with senior corporate management, company visits, primary research, and ultimately intensive interpersonal marketing to the investment community and companies. Analysts are expected to build a franchise with the institutional investment community and companies through published research and client interaction.

Institutional Sales

Sales professionals are responsible for marketing research recommendations and investment banking products to buy-side analysts and portfolio managers at institutional investment firms. Sales associates are teamed with senior institutional salespeople to cover specific institutional accounts. An associate will have daily contact with research analysts and clients, frequent client visits, and interaction with corporate management teams. By the end of the first year, associates are expected to assume a high degree of responsibility for client relationships.

Trading

Trading professionals are responsible for trading securities, with a focus on industries that are covered by the firm's research analysts. The firm is one of the leading OTC market makers and has significantly increased its listed securities trading activity over the last five years.

Trading associates are teamed with senior traders and work with institutional and retail sales, research, and other traders within the firm.

Describe the opportunities for professional mobility between various departments in your firm.

Alex. Brown recruits associates and analysts directly into the various departments described above. Professional mobility between departments is handled on a case-by-case basis.

Discuss the lifestyle aspects of a career with your firm (i.e., average hours per week, amount of travel, flexibility to change offices, corporate culture, etc.).

A career at Alex. Brown is challenging and rewarding and requires a significant commitment of time and energy. The firm's emphasis on teamwork creates a very positive working environment, particularly for new professionals who want to benefit from the firm's distinctive industry and technical competence. The lifestyle aspects of a career with Alex. Brown vary from department to department, particularly when market conditions are conducive to a department's particular industry or product expertise. Associates are encouraged to make their lifestyle decisions within the context of doing the best job possible for the firm and its clients.

The Recruiting Process

Describe your recruiting process and the criteria by which you select candidates. Is prior experience necessary?

The recruiting process involves a series of interviews, initially on campus and ultimately in one of the firm's offices. We strongly believe in building consensus within the firm regarding any new hire and, as a consequence, try to have each candidate meet as many people as possible. Alex. Brown has no predetermined criteria in evaluating candidates. We look for individuals whose work experience and academic record emphasizes initiative, excellence, and creativity in a team-oriented environment.

How many permanent associates and analysts do you hire in a typical year? How many summer interns do you expect to hire? If you have a formal summer program, please describe it. Please be sure to indicate whether the summer program is in place for all offices or just some.

Alex. Brown's philosophy is to concentrate hiring at the entry level, seeking each year to attract a small number of MBA candidates to fill openings on an as needed basis. We have no immediate plans to initiate a summer intern program.

What international opportunities does your firm offer for U.S. citizens? For foreign nationals?

Alex. Brown has offices in Europe and Asia which support investment banking and institutional sales efforts. The typical career path for a new associate or analyst with an interest in international opportunities is to start with Alex. Brown in the United States and transfer to one of the foreign offices after a suitable indoctrination period within the firm.

Banco Pactual

Av. Rep. do Chile, 230/29° andar
Rio de Janeiro, RJ 20031-170
(55-21) 272-1100
Fax: (55-21) 533-1661

MBA Recruiting Contact(s):
Andre Barbosa or Kevin Coogan

Company Description

Describe your firm's business and the types of clients served by your finance group(s).

Banco Pactual S.A. is an investment banking firm based in Rio de Janeiro, Brazil, that specializes in proprietary trading of Brazilian and other Latin American securities, portfolio management, and corporate finance activities.

The firm has subsidiaries and affiliates in both Rio de Janeiro, São Paulo, as well as in the Cayman Islands, the Bahamas, Uruguay, and New York. Pactual has consistently produced high returns on investment, both for its own account and for its clients. The firm is managed in an entrepreneurial spirit, with a lean and flat organizational structure focusing on opportunities that will offer potentially significant margins while seeking to reduce downside risk.

Describe your ownership structure.

Pactual is a limited partnership, currently with 19 partners. Furthermore, it is a requirement that all partners must be active executives of the bank. All professionals at Pactual work in a highly entrepreneurial environment and everyone is encouraged to become a partner of the firm.

How does your approach to finance differ from that of other firms, and what do you consider to be your strengths and distinctive capabilities?

If there is one key factor for Pactual's success over the past 10 years it is the firm's ability to remain flexible and to adapt to Brazil's ever changing market conditions. Pactual believes Brazil is undergoing a transformation toward a more open, competitive, and internationally integrated economy, although many political obstacles still remain to be overcome. A truly international perspective and understanding of events not only in Brazil but in other countries and markets is imperative. Pactual

is firmly committed to ensuring that both our professionals and the structure of the firm enable it to stay at the forefront of these changes.

Discuss changes in your firm's revenues (both domestic and international) and professional staff over the past year; over the past five years.

Pactual was founded in 1983 as a securities dealer with US$600,000 of capital, focusing principally on proprietary trading and financial intermediation. Since then, Pactual has grown at an impressive rate to become one of the most successful investment banks in Brazil. Net income has increased 1,200% over the period 1990–94 and from US$33 million in 1993 to US$48 million in 1994. Over the same five-year period, the number of employees has increased 160% and, more specifically, from 239 in 1993 to 279 in 1994.

The Finance MBA's Job Description

Describe the career path and corresponding responsibilities for an MBA at your firm.

Hired candidates start at the associate level. Candidates may start at any of the bank's main business divisions (Sales and Trading, Corporate Finance, Research, Portfolio Management) and will work under the supervision of one of the firm's partners. We tend to emphasize performance in determining compensation. The semiannual bonus is usually a substantial part of overall compensation.

Discuss the lifestyle aspects of a career with your firm (i.e., average hours per week, amount of travel, flexibility to change offices, corporate culture, etc.).

Lifestyles vary significantly from one business division to another, being in line with typical investment banking conditions. Pactual's corporate culture is also comparable with that of other successful investment banks—entrepreneurial, aggressive, intense, fast changing, and demand driven.

The Recruiting Process

Describe your recruiting process and the criteria by which you select candidates. Is prior experience necessary?

We have a strong commitment to recruiting the best people, with emphasis given to individuals with independent thinking, drive, aptitude for numbers, and initiative to work without constant supervision. No prior banking experience is needed, but proficiency in Portuguese is essential. We are strongly committed to promoting a working environment that places a premium on internal cooperation.

Selected candidates will be interviewed in New York, Miami, or Brazil. Interviews are expected to start in late December (Brazil) and January (New York and Miami).

How many permanent associates and analysts do you hire in a typical year? How many summer interns do you expect to hire? If you have a formal summer program, please describe it. Please be sure to indicate whether the summer program is in place for all offices or just some.

Pactual actively recruits students graduating from prestigious foreign institutions. In 1993 and 1994, Pactual hired, on average, 10 graduates from top American and European schools. Typically, two summer interns are hired per year and are normally taken on by the Rio de Janeiro or São Paulo offices.

What international opportunities does your firm offer for U.S. citizens? For foreign students?

For students proficient in Portuguese, we offer full-time and summer positions in Rio de Janeiro or São Paulo.

Bankers Trust

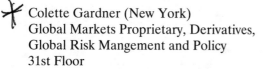

130 Liberty Street
New York, NY 10006

MBA Recruiting Coordinator:
Debbie Barry (New York)
Global Investment Management
12th Floor

MBA Recruiting Contact(s):
Susan Markell (New York and Chicago)
Corporate Finance, Latin America, Real Estate
12th Floor

Colette Gardner (New York)
Global Markets Proprietary, Derivatives,
Global Risk Mangement and Policy
31st Floor

Jennifer B. Lemaigre (New York)
Technology
31st Floor

Karen McCartney (New York)
Management Consulting Group
15th Floor

Elizabeth Wood-Snell (Los Angeles)
Global Investment Bank
300 South Grand Avenue, 41st Floor
Los Angeles, CA 90071

Liz Lieberman (Asia)
New York, 12th Floor

Anne Peach (London)
One Appold Street
Broadgate
London EC2A HE England

Company Description

Describe your firm's business and the type of clients served by your finance group(s).

Bankers Trust New York Corporation, with headquarters in New York City, is a registered bank holding company incorporated in 1965. Its principal banking subsidiary, Bankers Trust Company, began business in 1903 as a trust company and became a commercial bank in 1917. In the early 1980s it sold its retail branch network and redirected its resources toward investment banking, focusing its businesses on major corporations, financial institutions, governments, and high net worth individuals worldwide.

Today, Bankers Trust is a global financial services company that operates in the world's financial markets to deliver tailored financial solutions to its clients and to provide superior returns to its shareholders. All of the human and financial resources of Bankers Trust are committed to preeminence in the strategic management of risk for its clients and for the firm.

Consistent with this business strategy, the firm is organized globally into five major business units. The Global Investment Bank combines the firm's financing, derivative, and advisory capabilities. Global Emerging Markets delivers a full range of financial services to clients in the Pacific Rim and Latin America. The firm's funds management activities are performed by Global Investment Management. Global Assets consists of the trust, securities processing, cash management, and private banking businesses. And finally, proprietary trading and positioning activities are undertaken by Global Markets Proprietary.

Within and across these businesses there are five business functions that represent the fundamental roles that are performed in the marketplace: Client Finance, Client Advisory, Client Financial Risk Management, Client Transaction Processing, and Trading & Positioning. These functions provide earnings diversity during all phases of the market cycle.

The success of Bankers Trust's business strategy has been demonstrated by its strong financial performance. Since 1979, our return on average common equity has increased from 13% to an average of 22% since 1990, making Bankers Trust one of the most profitable major financial services companies in the world.

Describe the opportunities for MBAs interested in finance.

Global Investment Bank

Bankers Trust Investment Banking Division combines the firm's capital markets and finance business with the strategic risk management products and strategic advisory capabilities. Bankers Trust is able to provide underwriting, distribution, and trading services to its corporate, institutional, and investor clients. Bankers Trust combines global expertise and local finance presence in over 30 countries making BT a recognized leader in international investment banking. Associates joining the Global Investment Bank may work in the **Derivatives, Corporate Finance,** or **Advisory businesses.**

The **Derivatives** group at Bankers Trust is responsible for medium and long-term financing, investments, and hedging transactions for the bank's customers. At Bankers Trust the Derivatives Group is not product oriented;

rather we make a fundamental distinction between origination/marketing and risk management. The marketing function is structured parallel to the different customer groups. The risk management function is organized around five key market risks: interest rate, foreign exchange, equity, commodity, and securities (bonds and mortgage backed).

Interested students should contact Colette Gardner, Liz Lieberman, or Anne Peach

Bankers Trust's **Corporate Finance Group** is one of the leading underwriting/investment banking groups serving global corporate, institutional, and investor clients. BT is a leader in the non-investment grade companies serving top-tier leveraged buyout firms and non-investment grade companies. Bankers Trust is the only firm with a major presence in both the high yield bond market and the leveraged loan market. We've been consistently rated in the top two in the High Yield Finance lead tables. BT ranks as the top issuer of B- rated issues and is the largest underwriter of zero coupon securities.

Associates begin as generalists, gaining both diverse product, industry and relationship management expertise. Associates take on a high level of responsibility early on in both transactions and business development. Positions are available in New York, Chicago, Los Angeles, Europe, and Asia.

Bankers Trust's **Advisory** groups are collectively known as The Risk Merchant Bank and include Mergers and Acquisitions, Asset Finance, Risk Management Advisory, and the Transactional Development Group. Bankers Trust offers a full range of advisory services including divestitures and corporate sales, recapitalizations, defense advisory, restructuring and reorganizations, and privatizations. The Mergers and Acquisitions Group ranked 12th in advisory deal rankings for the first half of 1995 with over $7.1 billion in completed deal volume. The Transaction Development Group provides expertise in M&A, equity risk management, dollar and non-dollar interest rate hedging, structured notes, and capital raising. Associates are hired into one of the specific advisory groups.

Interested students should contact Susan Markell, Elizabeth Wood-Snell, Liz Lieberman, or Anne Peach

Real Estate Investment Bank
The Real Estate Investment Bank provides client financial advisory services, performs debt placements and syndications, structures innovative real estate securities and real estate investment trusts, and completes equity investments and placements. With a real estate debt and equity position valued at more than $1 billion, Bankers Trust has extensive hands-on experience with real estate investment and asset management. Associates rotate through three main departments: Finance and Origination, Direct Investment, and Positioning and Distribution.

Interested students should contact Susan Markell.

Latin America Merchant Bank
The Latin America Merchant Bank (LAMB) is comprised of several functional specializations, including Client Advisory (country-specific), Capital Markets (Debt/Equity/Hybrids), Derivative Products, M&A, Structured Finance, Real Estate, and Trading and Distribution. Associates work on a variety of projects simultaneously, including writing proposals, analyzing companies, monitoring capital markets pricing and trends, and meeting with clients. The majority of the positions are available in New York; select positions are available in Latin America.

Interested students should contact Susan Markell.

Global Risk Management and Policy Business
The Global Risk Management department is responsible for overseeing the worldwide market risks of Bankers Trust's proprietary and client-driven businesses. The department defines risk management policy, sets and approves market risk limits, and sets uniform standards for market risk assessment. This is accomplished by determining market risk limits, using a uniform standard for market risk assessment (RAROC), identifying, evaluating, and reporting market risk in all business lines and performing strategic planning. The GRM&P Group also conducts fee-based market risk consulting for external clients.

During the first year, MBA associates can expect to generate models, participate in new product development, create market strategies, execute trades, and prepare client presentations. MBA associates in Global Trading's Funds Management Group have helped determine that the Portuguese Escudo represented excellent value, enabling BT to accumulate sizable positions in the currency before its EMR entry and subsequent appreciation. MBA associates in the Global Portfolio Group worked on fixed-rate cross currency swaps to help extend the maturity of the firm's foreign exchange hedges during a period of divergent yield curves in the United States (steeply positive) versus Europe (slightly inverted).

Interested students should contact Colette Gardner.

Global Markets Proprietary Business
The Global Markets Proprietary business is comprised of the Global Trading and Global Portfolio groups as well as the trading, capital markets, funds management, and merchant banking businesses in the Australia/New Zealand markets.

The Global Trading Group trades liquid instruments including U.S. Treasury and Federal Agency Securities, Foreign Government Securities, Foreign Exchange, and Currency Options. Global Trading also manages a fund for a performance-based fee and foreign exchange funds for institutional clients.

The Global Portfolio Group is responsible for the funding of the corporation worldwide, capital and liquidity management, the management of the corporation's investment portfolio, and the intermediate and longer term proprietary trading of liquid securities, foreign exchange, and derivative products.

The traditional trading businesses consist of foreign exchange, sovereign bonds, and U.S. government securities. The Foreign Exchange Group is responsible for capturing risk and market opportunities through spot trading, cross currency trading, interest rate differentials, and currency options. The Sovereign Bond Group is responsible for capturing risk and market opportunities through liquid trading, arbitrage activity, and intermediate-term risk taking. The U.S. Government Securities Group is responsible for capturing risk through primary market participation and secondary market trading. The proprietary business is responsible for maintaining and enhancing the financial structure of the corporation. The group focuses on managing the bank's balance sheet, maintaining liquidity and low-cost funding for all bank transactions.

During the first year, MBA associates can expect to generate models, participate in new product development, create market strategies, execute trades, and prepare client presentations. Officer trainees in Global Trading's Funds Management Group have helped determine that the Portuguese Escudo represented excellent value, enabling BT to accumulate sizable positions in the currency before its EMR entry and subsequent appreciation. Officer trainees in the Global Portfolio Group worked on fixed-rate cross currency swaps to help extend the maturity of the firm's foreign exchange hedges during a period of divergent yield curves in the United States (steeply positive) versus Europe (slightly inverted).

Interested students should contact Colette Gardner, Liz Lieberman, or Anne Peach.

Global Investment Management Business

The Global Investment Management (GIM) business brings together all of the resources dedicated to asset management at Bankers Trust. With a network of global investment offices, more than $180 billion in assets under management, and over 50 years of investment management experience, Bankers Trust's GIM business offers institutions and individuals a range of products that span the investment spectrum. GIM employs over 400 individuals in New York, London, Tokyo, and Hong Kong.

In contrast to the Global Markets Proprietary business at Bankers Trust which operates as a principal in markets and advises client origination of securities (the "sell" side), GIM is a fiduciary asset manager, investing client assets (the "buy" side). GIM portfolio managers also invest proprietary capital in high-performing strategies in separate accounts from client funds.

The GIM business has integrated the Bank's risk management and investment management talent and is leading the way in introducing new forms of specialization and dynamic asset allocation methods to the industry. By working regularly with our customers on identifying, asset allocating, and thoughtfully executing a client-driven investment strategy, GIM is able to deliver superior performance-driven products that precisely fit the needs of our clients.

The scope of GIM's capabilities is unique, covering advanced trading and derivative strategies as well as traditional active and indexed products. GIM manages over 66 investment strategies, roughly equal amounts in equities and fixed income, and equal amounts in active and quantitative strategies. Although GIM is large in terms of assets under management, it is an organization comprised of small teams of talented specialists who focus on a particular market niche. This type of organization structure fosters entrepreneurial initiative within a large organization.

GIM's proven traditional investment management capabilities include active equity management, active fixed income management, cash management, and equity index management. In addition to our traditional investment management capabilities, GIM also has a dedicated Hedge Funds and Derivative Products team. This team has been continuously engaged in structuring derivatives for asset managers in world securities, commodities, and foreign exchange markets, providing unique advantages in altering return and risk exposures and lowering overall transaction costs. The Hedge Funds and Derivative Product team uses advanced analytical models developed in our Proprietary Trading Group to measure and manage diversified portfolios to achieve the highest return per unit of risk for our clients.

GIM's extensive investment capabilities are sold by GIM product specialists and Private Advisory Services relationship managers. While historically our clients have been primarily U.S. corporate pension funds, GIM has established a solid presence in managing assets for governments, central banks, insurance companies, and high net worth individuals. Bankers Trust's goal is to become the global leader in asset management and is aggressively expanding its domestic and international base significantly by focusing on performance and risk management. We intend to achieve this goal by continuing to attract and retain talented individuals, encouraging an entrepreneurial business environment, and developing innovative investment solutions for our clients.

During the first year an associate with the group can expect to participate in and contribute to all aspects of the business, from generating models, marketing the group's capabilities and products, tailoring and structuring investment vehicles for clients, to selecting and trading for the group's portfolios.

Interested students should contact Debbie Barry.

Technology

Bankers Trust views technology as key to its competitive success. The Bank relies on a combination of application development units embedded in each business and a central technology organization. Developers are part of their respective businesses, participating in the creation of new products and responding quickly to shifts in the market. The central organization provides architectural strategy and standards as well as "economies of scale" functions like telecommunications and systems engineering. This approach is uniquely successful for Bankers Trust in large part due to the understanding and commitment it receives from all levels of management.

The result is a technology function that is responsive to the business, yet consistent in architecture and direction. This powerful combination has been cited by industry analysts and regulators as giving us a position of true leadership in the effective leveraging of information technology.

As Technology associates, MBAs work in partnership with their respective businesses or with the technologists who provide engineering and infrastructure support throughout the firm. The specific role associates play depends on their experience and interests, not just their position in the organization. Bankers Trust Technology encourages employees to take initiative and to work as a team to help the business evolve and improve.

Typical technology assignments include:

- designing and implementing a new interest rate swap processing system;

- building a fully object-oriented trading support system;

- conceptualizing and implementing "groupware" for the front-office professionals of a business on a worldwide basis, including PC-based market data feeds, filtered news feeds, document management capabilities, and retrieval engines with links to a variety of internal and external databases;

- rebuilding Bankers Trust's worldwide telecommunications infrastructure with next-generation technology; and

- marketing and then delivering an integrated customer workstation for a large new fiduciary and trust services customer.

Interested students should contact Jennifer Lemaigre.

Management Consulting Group

The Management Consulting Group can be your introduction to Bankers Trust. Here you will be immediately exposed to many of the key issues facing the bank today. As an MCG consultant, you will work closely with the senior managers who lead Bankers Trust's businesses. Our clients and project work span the entire spectrum of BT's business portfolio: Global Investment Management, Global Investment Banking, Global Emerging Markets, Global Institutional Services, the Private Advisory Services Group (our Private Bank), the Risk Merchant Bank, Global Markets Proprietary, and the Office of the Chief Financial Officer.

The MCG is a unique, respected, and truly innovative consulting practice. Our senior professionals have joined us from the world's leading consulting firms. We offer something no other external organization can match—after learning about BT's products, culture and major initiatives, and raising the value of key businesses, you will rotate into a key line or staff position and assume significant management responsibilities.

As a professional with the MCG, you will deliver a diverse range of advisory services. Your client activities will include projects focused on new product introduction, core business process re-design, competitive bench marking, systems and MIS enhancement initiatives, and market/financial analysis. Working on these projects requires you to negotiate initial proposals with prospective clients, structure the problem solving effort, complete a comprehensive analysis, and present our final recommendations. In addition, MCG professionals participate directly in the execution and implementation of our recommendations, further preparing you for a line position.

Considering BT's flat organizational structure, performance-based management style, and distinct institutional culture, you will be able to direct your own career into areas where your talents are continually enhanced and your interests are matched to the bank's most important challenges.

Interested students should contact Karen McCartney.

The Finance MBA's Job Description

Describe the career path and corresponding responsibilities for an MBA at your firm.

Global Investment Bank/Real Estate Investment Bank/Latin America Merchant Bank/Global Risk Management and Policy/Global Markets Proprietary/Global Investment Management

All MBA associates in the Global Investment Bank, Real Estate Investment Bank, Latin America Merchant Bank, Global Risk Management and Policy, Global Market Proprietary, and Global Investment Management groups attend a two-month Financial Services Training Program.

The objective of the program is to provide an overview of each group's fast-paced, ever-changing environment. The program includes presentations on foreign exchange, trading, long- and short-term origination, trading and distribution, mortgage-backed securities sales and trading, liabilities/positioning, derivative products, client advisory, as well as financial strategies and arbitrage. All course work is developed and taught by our internal line managers.

Upon completion of the training program:

Global Investment Bank trainees are placed in one of the GIB businesses based upon their individual interests, aptitude, and current needs of the business groups.

Real Estate Investment Bank associates receive on-the-job training in essential real estate concepts and practices.

Latin America associates participate in a two-week Latin America training program addressing more regionally specific issues such as inflationary accounting, bond math, and valuation techniques.

Global Risk Management and Policy trainees are placed in one of the businesses based upon their individual interests, aptitude, and current needs of the business groups.

Global Markets Proprietary trainees are placed in one of the businesses based upon their individual interests, aptitude, and current needs of the business groups.

Global Investment Management training also includes an introduction to various areas within GIM, including High Yield Fixed Income, Derivative Products, Hedge Funds, and Passive and Active Equity funds.

Technology

Bankers Trust believes in staying flexible with a solid technical architecture as a foundation. Therefore, the firm does not pre-program your assignments, ongoing skills development, or career. Instead, associates are allowed to progress at their own pace, quickly assuming responsibility for increasingly demanding assignments.

Management Consulting Group

MBA's entering the MCG receive a combination of formal and informal training on a wide range of disciplines including analytical and conceptual problem solving, influence management, core process re-design, derivatives, and communications and presentation skills. The emphasis is on skills development through direct client interaction, project work, and immediate responsibility.

The Recruiting Process

Describe your recruiting process and the criteria by which you select candidates. Is prior experience necessary?

Global Investment Bank/Global Risk Management/Global Markets Proprietary

The successful candidate will be an MBA with outstanding academic achievement, proven leadership ability, drive, and motivation to succeed. We are seeking individuals who possess flexibility, a strong analytic and quantitative background, and demonstrate a risk orientation. The successful candidate is bright, outgoing, creative, flexible, and aggressive, possessing the ability to perform optimally in a high-pressure environment.

Real Estate Investment Bank

The ideal candidate has an MBA in finance and/or real estate. We are seeking MBAs who possess strong analytical and communication skills, along with the ability to prioritize tasks and work as part of a team. Successful candidates will have a strong command of accounting and financial modeling using a PC. Prior professional experience in finance or real estate is preferred.

Latin America Merchant Bank

The successful candidate is an MBA with strong analytic and quantitative ability and excellent communication skills both in English and the relevant foreign languages (Spanish and/or Portuguese, Hebrew, Arabic and Asian dialects).

Global Investment Management

The successful candidate will be an MBA with outstanding academic achievement, proven leadership ability, drive, and motivation to succeed. We are looking for individuals who possess strong analytical and quantitative skills. The successful candidate is creative, aggressive, and performs optimally in a dynamic and constantly changing environment.

Technology

A successful candidate's qualifications will include technical depth and breadth, well-developed interpersonal and communicative skills, and the ability to manage several projects simultaneously. Experience in the financial services industry is valuable but not required.

Management Consulting Group

We hire individuals who are challenged by the project-oriented, rapidly changing environment of a professional consulting firm and who, at the same time, express a longer-term interest in moving into line positions in one of BT's businesses. Successful candidates will demonstrate very strong problem solving skills—at both the pure analytical and more conceptual levels—and will be able to develop, recommend, and execute insightful solutions with confidence. We require self-starters with high energy and motivation who can come up the learning curve quickly across a broad range of business issues.

We look forward to meeting many of you.

Bear, Stearns & Co. Inc.

245 Park Avenue
New York, NY 10167
(212) 272-2000

MBA Recruiting Contact(s):
Jennifer Rolnick, MBA Recruiting Coordinator
(212) 272-7749

Investment Banking
John Kilgallon, Vice President
(212) 272-3045

Debt and Equity Markets
Barry Cohen, Senior Managing Director, Equity
(212) 272-4502

Bruce Yablon, Senior Managing Director, Debt
(212) 272-8117

Company Description

Describe your firm's business and the types of clients served by your finance group(s).

Bear, Stearns & Co. Inc. ("Bear Stearns") is a leading global investment banking and securities firm with over $5.8 billion in total capital and more than 7,600 employees worldwide. The firm's primary businesses are the Investment Banking Department and the Debt and Equity Markets groups. In addition, Bear Stearns provides professional and correspondent clearing services to over 350 securities firms.

Over the past 10 years, Bear Stearns has grown rapidly in size and capital base. Bear Stearns has built its reputation as an aggressive and innovative investment banking and trading firm by carefully matching its capital and underwriting commitments with disciplined and sustained growth, and since its founding over 70 years ago, Bear Stearns has never had an unprofitable year. The combination of rapid growth, disciplined management, and an entrepreneurial culture creates tremendous opportunities for those people with the talent and desire to excel in investment banking.

Bear Stearns is headquartered in New York City. In addition to nine domestic offices, Bear Stearns maintains offices in Beijing, Frankfurt, Geneva, Hong Kong, Karachi, London, Madrid, Manila, Paris, São Paulo, Shanghai, and Tokyo.

Investment Banking Department

Bear Stearns' Investment Banking Department offers a full range of advisory and underwriting services to a broad array of public and private sector clients. These services include:

- Mergers and Acquisitions
- Corporate Finance
- Emerging Markets Finance
- Debt and Equity Capital Markets
- High Yield Finance
- Financial Restructuring
- Project Finance
- Asset-backed Finance
- Public Finance
- Principal Investments

Bear Stearns' investment banking capabilities are enhanced by a focus on certain specialized industries including retail, media, telecommunications, technology, energy, forest products, financial institutions, health care, aerospace/defense, chemicals, utilities, and gaming.

Bear Stearns' commitment to the global markets has made the firm a recognized leader in international investment banking. In 1994, Bear Stearns lead-managed a $480 million equity offering for USIMINAS, the second largest steel producer in Brazil; the transaction was named "Deal of the Year" by *International Financing Review, Euromoney, Latin Finance,* and *World Equity.* The firm is at the forefront in assisting public and private sector entities with innovative financing and advisory services in connection with acquisitions, privatizations, recapitalizations, and restructurings throughout Asia, Latin America, and Eastern Europe. Bear Stearns' emerging markets expertise dates back over a decade to its Latin American origins. From the beginning of 1991 through 1994, Bear Stearns ranks as a leading underwriter of Latin American equity and fixed income securities, ranking number one in equity issuance.

Bear Stearns' mergers and acquisitions group provides a full range of advisory services to acquirers and sellers of businesses. Bear Stearns recently acted as financial advisor in a number of large and highly publicized transactions, including Viacom's acquisition of Paramount Communications, the merger of Martin Marietta and Lockheed, and ITT's acquisition of both Caesar's World and a 50% interest in Madison Square Garden. Other major clients in recent financial advisory assignments include American Home Products, Warner Lambert, Bell Atlantic, Rhône-Poulenc Rorer, and Unisys.

Bear Stearns is also a leading underwriter of investment grade and high yield debt securities, specializing in high yield securities rated B or lower. Since 1993, Bear Stearns has managed over 100 high yield debt offerings raising almost $20 billion.

Bear Stearns remains a major presence in the public finance/municipal markets and is a recognized industry leader in financing infrastructure development projects, such as highways, bridges, tunnels, mass transit, airports, and electric and water utilities. The firm's experience working with state and local housing finance agencies had enabled it to continue to develop new products and maintain its leadership position in single family and multifamily housing finance.

Debt and Equity Markets

Fixed Income
Bear Stearns is a leader in all fixed income markets, including corporate, derivative, government, high yield/bankruptcy, mortgage, asset-related, and municipal securities. The firm's recognized position in these markets is enhanced by product innovation, unique systems technology, and fixed income research. Trading positions in all of these markets average $50 billion, and during 1994 the firm raised over $64 billion in taxable fixed income issues for its corporate, government, agency, and sovereign clients.

Bear Stearns is recognized by the Federal Reserve Bank of New York as a primary dealer of U.S. government securities. The firm has ranked in the top three for lead-managing mortgage-backed issues for the past six years and offers a full line of mortgage and asset-related products in U.S. and Euromarkets. Domestically, Bear Stearns accounted for 18% of the public issuance of asset-backed securities in 1994, with transactions totaling $14 billion out of a $76 billion market.

Underpinning the firm's success in the fixed income markets in the Financial Analytics and Structured Transactions (F.A.S.T.) Group, a firmwide resource providing financial engineering and securitization capabilities, investment research, fixed income portfolio management and analytical systems, trading technology, and general financial expertise. This group has developed one of the most advanced fixed income analytical capabilities in the securities industry and serves as a primary tool in facilitating the trading and sales of all the firm's fixed income products.

Institutional Equities
Bear Stearns is a leader in the trading and distribution of equity securities for institutional customers. Through the combined efforts of the equity sales force and equity research and trading professionals, the Institutional Equities Department offers premier sales and trading services to its clients.

Providing value-added ideas to Bear Stearns' client base is essential to a successful institutional equities business. The Equity Research Department focuses on over 40 specific industries and categories of stocks representing over 800 companies, comprising almost 90% of the companies in the S&P 500 index.

The Over-the-Counter Department is an important component of Bear Stearns' institutional equities business. With a customer-driven approach, Bear Stearns has developed a major presence in the secondary trading of NASDAQ-listed stocks. Utilizing a state-of-the-art trading system, the firm focuses on a high-quality universe of approximately 450 over-the-counter stocks.

The Finance MBA's Job Description

Describe the career path and corresponding responsibilities for an MBA at your firm.

Investment Banking
Associates work on a wide variety of corporate finance and merger and acquisition transactions in a variety of different industries. Often, an associate will be working on three to five different transactions in project teams that typically consist of three to four people.

Job responsibilities include detailed financial analysis and modeling; due diligence with respect to a client's business, industry, financial results, and projects; creation of new business proposals/presentations; and preparation of internal memoranda for the various committees that review and approve transactions.

After a three-week training program, associates begin working either as generalists or in a product or industry specialty group. Associates are typically eligible for promotion to vice president after three years. The timing of future promotions is based entirely on performance.

Debt and Equity Markets

Sales and trading associates are provided with an opportunity to rotate among the firm's various product areas during the first two to six months while also receiving classroom instruction on the firm's debt and equity products. Following this, the associate will focus on a specific product area. The timing and frequency of promotions are based entirely on an individual's performance.

The Recruiting Process

Describe your recruiting process and the criteria by which you select candidates. Is prior experience necessary?

Bear Stearns endeavors to hire individuals who have demonstrated outstanding academic achievement and a proven track record of performance excellence. In addition, a candidate should possess strong oral and written communications skills, attention to detail and concern for accuracy, the ability to work well with others under pressure, and a willingness to work long hours. No specific academic major is a prerequisite; however, a strong finance and accounting background is desired and candidates must be proficient with financial and mathematical concepts.

Do you have a summer program for associates or analysts? If so, please describe.

Bear Stearns has a summer associate program in which MBA candidates are hired as generalists in Investment Banking and Debt and Equity Markets. Over the course of the summer, Investment Banking summer associates will have the opportunity to work on a variety of projects in the mergers and acquisitions, capital markets, and corporate finance areas. Debt and Equity Markets summer associates have the opportunity to work with the firm's sales and trading professionals in variety of different product areas. Bear Stearns views the summer associate program as an important part of its overall hiring process and recruits summer associates to aid in providing the firm with the best possible assessment of an individual's long-term potential.

Bowles Hollowell Conner & Co.

227 West Trade Street
Charlotte, NC 28202
(704) 348-1000

MBA Recruiting Contact(s):
John W. Pollock
(704) 348-1092

Mark Swartzberg
(704) 348-1081

Company Description

Describe your firm's business and the types of clients served by your finance group(s).

Bowles Hollowell Conner & Co. is a national investment banking firm specializing in corporate finance services for middle-market companies. From its Charlotte headquarters, the firm assists corporations, private investment firms, and middle-market companies with mergers and acquisitions; divestitures; structured financing, including private placements of senior and mezzanine debt and equity securities; and valuations. Transaction values typically range from $15 million to $200 million.

Describe your ownership structure.

Bowles Hollowell Conner & Co. is a private corporation owned by its employees.

How does your approach to finance differ from that of other firms, and what do you consider to be your strengths and distinctive capabilities?

Bowles Hollowell Conner & Co. was founded in 1975 to provide middle-market companies with a level of corporate finance expertise generally not available to them. Although the nation's largest corporations have long had the benefit of expert consultation and assistance with complex corporate finance matters, this same expertise has not been readily available to smaller companies.

Our firm has been successful in helping to fill this void. A professional staff of approximately 50 employees provides clients with the high level of knowledge and experience in business, finance, accounting, law, and taxation needed for success with corporate finance transactions.

Bowles Hollowell Conner & Co. has demonstrated capability in a wide range of transactions in many different industries, from basic manufacturing to high technology and from consumer products to industrial commodities. In all of its services, the firm emphasizes thoroughness of preparation, professionalism in execution, and effectiveness in assisting clients in meeting business objectives.

A specialty of Bowles Hollowell Conner & Co. is in the area of mergers, acquisitions, and divestitures involving companies with values less than $200 million. Clients include large corporations, private investment firms, and public and private middle-market companies. The firm represents either the buyer or the seller in a typical transaction. In addition, Bowles Hollowell Conner & Co. provides valuation services to public and private companies for purposes such as fairness opinions, employee stock ownership plans, or individual estate and gift tax planning.

In the past several years, Bowles Hollowell Conner & Co. has increased its emphasis on assisting clients in the capital raising process and currently has four professionals devoted exclusively to this effort. The Private Financing Group is focused on raising capital for organizations for a variety of purposes, including financings, leveraged recapitalizations, and restructurings.

Discuss changes in your firm's revenues (both domestic and international) and professional staff over the past year; over the past five years.

Bowles Hollowell Conner & Co. has enjoyed tremendous growth over the past five years, and 1994 was a record year for the firm in terms of transactions completed, revenue, and profits. As such, Bowles Hollowell Conner & Co. offers a new associate the opportunity to develop corporate finance skills in a dynamic environment.

The Finance MBA's Job Description

Describe the career path and corresponding responsibilities for an MBA at your firm.

Bowles Hollowell Conner & Co. expects each MBA whom it hires as an associate to become a managing director and owner of the firm. The responsibilities of an associate revolve around working in a team environment on a variety of transactions and generally on several transactions at the same time. As a critical member of the team, the associate is responsible for managing the work of one or more analysts on the team, overseeing the preparation of qualitative and quantitative analyses, writing comprehensive business descriptions and other documents, ensuring the accuracy and quality of all the analytical work supporting the transaction, and relating the ideas of the firm to the client. The firm offers a flexible environment that rewards initiative and allows the associate to develop as quickly as he or she is capable.

Describe the opportunities for professional mobility between the various departments in your firm.

Because the firm is devoted exclusively to the corporate finance needs of middle-market companies, each new professional is developed as a generalist working on a variety of assignments and teams within the firm.

Discuss the lifestyle aspects of a career with your firm (i.e., average hours per week, amount of travel, flexibility to change offices, corporate culture, etc.).

The business of the firm requires a great deal of hard work, dedication, and sacrifice. A high level of commitment is necessary to deliver financial expertise of the highest quality in the timeliest manner. Because approximately two-thirds of our assignments are outside the southeastern United States, an associate will be required to travel regularly throughout the country on firm business. Nevertheless, the firm respects the requirement of each individual for personal time away from the office and the importance of developing interests outside the firm.

In addition, involvement in outside activities within the community is viewed as an important aspect of an associate's development, and members of the firm participate in a variety of external community activities.

The Recruiting Process

Describe your recruiting process and the criteria by which you select candidates. Is prior experience necessary?

The firm is looking for MBAs who have demonstrated the potential to analyze financial problems quickly and effectively. We look for academic achievement, intellectual ability, demonstrated leadership abilities, personal integrity, and the ability to communicate ideas and recommendations effectively, orally and in writing. Although not a strict requirement, we look for individuals with two to four years of meaningful work experience.

How many permanent associates and analysts do you hire in a typical year? How many summer interns do you expect to hire? If you have a formal summer program, please describe it. Please be sure to indicate whether the summer program is in place for all offices or just some.

Bowles Hollowell Conner & Co. expects to hire two to four associates and seven to nine analysts in the coming year. The firm has brief, formal training programs for both associates and analysts but strongly favors on-the-job training. Associates and analysts are expected to become productive members of the firm quickly.

The firm currently has no summer program for MBAs, but the initiation of such a program is under consideration.

What international opportunities does your firm offer for U.S. citizens? For foreign nationals?

Bowles Hollowell Conner & Co.'s Charlotte headquarters is currently the company's only office. However, since roughly one-quarter of its sell-side engagements are completed with foreign buyers, Bowles Hollowell Conner & Co. relies upon its professionals' knowledge of foreign languages and their ability to conduct business in an international arena. A good portion of an associate's international work is in the form of phone calls, conversations, and visits with parties who are candidates to purchase or finance a transaction for which Bowles Hollowell Conner & Co. has been engaged.

Broadview Associates, L.P.

One Bridge Plaza
Fort Lee, NJ 07024
(201) 346-9000
Fax: (201) 346-9191

MBA Recruiting Contact(s):
Wendy Chapman, Manager of Recruiting

Company Description

Describe your firm's business and the types of clients served by your finance group(s).

Broadview Associates, L.P. is the leading merger and acquisition (M&A) firm serving companies in the global information technology (IT) industry or seeking initial participation in the industry. Founded in 1973, Broadview dominates M&A within the principal sectors of the IT industry, which encompasses software, hardware, internetworking, telecommunications, marketing/processing services, and database publishing businesses. Broadview has completed over 200 transactions in the last 5 years and over 500 in its 20-year history. In addition to M&A, Broadview services include minority investments, private placement, and strategic alliances. The firm is also a general partner in Geocapital, a venture capital firm formed to make private equity investments in the IT industry.

Broadview represents both buyer and seller clients. Buyer clients include large IT suppliers as well as smaller, specialized IT companies. IT companies seek to secure a sustainable competitive advantage and boost shareholder value by adding technologies, products, operations, and access to markets. Frequently, their objectives can be satisfied by acquiring part or all of a niche player. On the other side, seller clients that want to manage the passage between early growth stages and sustainable, superior equity value seek to leverage the resources of a larger, more established enterprise. Typically, companies wishing to sell have developed new technologies and products, gained unique market positions, or marshaled unique human resource capabilities that they cannot fully exploit alone. An appropriate partner for a seller client can telescope market-product development cycles, provide required capital, shrink the associated risks, and gain an innovative and focused management team.

The interaction of these corporate supply and demand forces has made IT the most M&A-prone industry in the world. Given the complexity and rapid change in this industry, finding the right strategic fit can be a difficult task. As a result, buyers and sellers utilize Broadview to grasp the industry's strategic underpinnings, as well as to leverage our track record of transaction experience. Broadview has over 110 employees located in offices in Fort Lee (NJ), San Mateo (CA), and London (UK). Opportunities exist for career growth and development throughout the firm.

Describe your ownership structure.

Broadview Associates is structured as a limited partnership. Each of the firm's 12 managing directors is recognized by the IT industry as an expert and spokesperson in M&A.

How does your approach to finance differ from that of other firms, and what do you consider to be your strengths and distinctive capabilities?

Developed and seasoned for 20 years, Broadview's unique set of qualifications includes the following:

- *Transaction experience.* The managing directors and associates of Broadview know the IT M&A environment because of their strong roots in the IT industry. They have been founders of privately held IT companies, as well as corporate officers of public companies. Their hands-on knowledge and experience assure clients that highly informed analysis and judgment concerning the multiple aspects of an acquisition will be readily available throughout the acquisition process.

- *Concentration.* Through its experience and industry focus, Broadview offers its clients an exceptionally high degree of expertise in a dynamic and complex environment.

- *Commitment.* Broadview's deal activities mirror those of the overall IT industry. Broadview has participated in the industry's highly visible transactions, including the sale of Nextbase to Microsoft and FORE Systems' purchase of Applied Network Technology. However, given that the average deal in the IT industry has a value of under $20 million, Broadview also participates in many transactions whose size is typically outside the focus of the M&A departments of traditional investment banking firms. Thus, one of Broadview's greatest strengths is it depth of experience in these middle-market transactions.

- *Contacts.* Broadview enjoys relationships with managers and directors throughout the IT industry, as well as with other players seeking to participate in this segment. In addition, Broadview maintains close working relationships with the venture capital community, given the predominance of venture-backed IT companies. This network provides unparalleled insight into the external development needs and strategies of IT companies.

- *Proprietary information.* Broadview's research department maintains the industry's most comprehensive databases in support of the firm's M&A and minority investment activity. The firm maintains active files on over 30,000 companies, as well as a proprietary database of IT industry acquisitions. Since 1980, in partnership with the Information Technology Association of America (formerly ADAPSO), Broadview has published the semiannual *Broadview Merger Report,* which tracks and analyzes M&A activity and valuation benchmarks with the industry. This report is well recognized throughout the industry and serves as a valuable tool for both marketing to prospective clients and valuing companies engaged in transactions.

The Finance MBA's Job Description

Describe the career path and corresponding responsibilities for an MBA at your firm.

Associates are quickly given client management responsibility. The associate assists in the development of acquisition and divestiture strategies, identifies companies in relevant IT segments that represent potential partners, handles approaches to target companies, and ultimately helps to structure and negotiate deals between client and target companies. In managing the client relationship, the associate usually serves as part of a three-person team, joined by a managing director and an analyst. Each team member has unique responsibility and interacts daily. The associate manages daily client contact and assists in coordinating activities among the team members.

Discuss the lifestyle aspects of a career with your firm (i.e., average hours per week, amount of travel, flexibility to change offices, corporate culture, etc.).

Broadview attracts and seeks dedicated, self-motivated professionals who can generate a superior quality of work without sacrificing their lifestyles. Travel is required, but the extent varies by specific assignment.

The Recruiting Process

Describe your recruiting process and the criteria by which you select candidates. Is prior experience necessary?

Broadview seeks individuals with excellent written and oral communication skills, transaction experience, and demonstrated interest or experience in the IT industry. The ideal candidate must also be a highly motivated self-starter and possess interpersonal skills.

Do you have a summer program for associates or analysts? If so, please describe.

The firm does not have a summer program.

What international opportunities does your firm offer for U.S. citizens? For foreign nationals?

Broadview's London office is staffed by U.S. citizens and foreign nationals from France, Germany, the U.K., and other European countries. Candidates for the London office typically have foreign language fluency.

Chemical Banking Corporation

270 Park Avenue
New York, NY 10017

MBA Recruiting Contact(s):
Annette Cuttley
(212) 270-7072

Company Description

Describe your firm's business and the types of clients served by your finance group(s).

Chemical Banking Corporation is a global financial services company and is one of the few financial institutions that has the position of leadership and scale in capital, products, and clients necessary to be a truly global competitor in the world financial markets.

A long-standing and well-recognized commitment to client relationships gives Chemical a leading position as banker, advisor, and trading and investment partner to large corporations, multinationals, financial institutions, and governments around the world. This commitment has been enhanced through an industry focus among the bank's corporate finance specialists, making Chemical a premier bank for the shipping, automotive, natural resources, energy, real estate, media, and telecommunications industries, as well as for financial institutions and the Wall Street community.

Chemical is ranked first in global loan syndications and is engaged as advisor, arranger, and agent by the world's largest and best-known companies to execute their most important bank financings. The bank has a recognized reputation for product leadership, expertise, and execution in global markets activities. It is a world leader in the derivatives market and the largest provider of U.S. dollar interest rate risk management products, and is ranked number one in interbank foreign exchange worldwide. The firm has experienced significant growth in underwriting and distributing corporate securities and is a leading player in the high yield and asset-backed markets.

Describe your ownership structure.

Chemical Banking Corporation is a publicly owned corporation and the third largest bank holding company in the United States. Its principal subsidiaries include Chemical Bank and Chemical Securities Inc. At year-end 1994, Chemical had total stockholders' equity of $10.7 billion, more than 53,000 stockholders, and 254 million common shares outstanding.

How does your approach to finance differ from that of other firms, and what do you consider to be your strengths and distinctive capabilities?

Chemical provides a truly integrated approach to global banking. It has built a powerful platform in credit, capital markets, corporate finance, and trading that underpins its ability to leverage core competencies, link products and resources, and seamlessly deliver financial solutions to clients worldwide. The firm's significant international network, with more than 60 offices in 35 countries, allows Chemical to meet client demands for global products, coverage, and execution.

Discuss changes in your firm's revenues and professional staff over the past year; over the past five years.

Chemical's 1994 core earnings were up 21% from 1993, and reported net income for the year was $1.3 billion. Net income for 1994 was approximately triple the $440 million reported in 1990. Over the past five years, total stockholders' equity has risen more than 50%, while the number of employees has decreased by approximately 7,000, to 41,567.

The Finance MBA's Job Description

Describe the career path and corresponding responsibilities for an MBA at your firm.

In 1995, Chemical's Global Bank hired a total of 47 MBAs: 19 for Domestic Corporate Finance, 17 for Sales & Trading, 7 for Asia & Europe Corporate Finance and Capital Markets, and 4 for Real Estate Finance.

New associates join Chemical in early August, and complete an intensive ten-week training program. In addition to the academic portion which includes case studies, team assignments, and trading modules, the program also provides extensive introduction to the business units within the Global Bank through presentations from senior practitioners.

The career path for a new associate at Chemical will vary depending upon the group the MBA joins. Following successful completion of the training program, Corporate Finance associates will be placed in three six-month assignments which typically will include two product and one client group, providing the associate with significant exposure to a variety of business units in the Global Bank.

Corporate Finance associates hired for our foreign nationals program will complete two to four six-month assignments prior to permanent placement in an overseas location.

Sales & Trading associates have the opportunity to join Chemical's Global Markets Group as either generalists or specialists. Generalists are exposed to a variety of product groups within Global Markets prior to permanent assignment. Specialists are hired directly into a product group, typically based on previous experience.

Describe the opportunities for professional mobility between the various departments in your firm.

New associates are encouraged to build relationships throughout Chemical. The success of the Global Bank in investment banking, capital markets, and client management is built upon teamwork and partnership. Movement among business units is supported, based upon business needs.

Discuss the lifestyle aspects of a career with your firm (i.e., average hours per week, amount of travel, flexibility to change offices, corporate culture, etc.).

Lifestyles and requirements vary depending upon which business unit an MBA joins but are typical for the investment banking and sales and trading industries.

The Recruiting Process

Describe your recruiting process and the criteria by which you select candidates. Is prior experience necessary?

Chemical invests substantial resources in identifying and recruiting high-quality candidates. Chemical hosts on-campus presentations and conducts on-campus interviews. Successful candidates are invited to New York for "Day in Bank" interviews. Selected candidates then par-

ticipate in "Final Round" interviews at which point an offer decision is made. Chemical observes individual school policies in its recruiting process.

The qualifications for a Chemical associate include superior quantitative and analytical abilities, excellent interpersonal and marketing skills, maturity, initiative, and a team approach. Strong academic performance is important. Previous work experience, while helpful, is not required.

How many permanent associates and analysts do you hire in a typical year? How many summer interns do you expect to hire? If you have a formal summer program, please describe it. Please be sure to indicate whether the summer program is in place for all offices or just some.

Recruiting goals are set early in the fall for the coming recruiting season based on the staffing needs of each business unit. In 1995, the Global Bank hired 47 MBAs for permanent associate positions and 25 MBA summer associates.

The MBA Summer Associate Program offers candidates an opportunity to work in Global Investment Banking and Client Management or Global Markets Sales & Trading. For corporate finance candidates, Chemical offers a unique two rotation program, exposing summer associates to both Client Management and Investment Banking Product units. Summer associates have significant responsibilities and participate directly as part of deal teams during their assignments. Sales & Trading candidates are assigned to a specific group for the summer and participate in a rotation program which introduces them to several capital markets and trading units.

In addition to the MBA Associate and Summer Associate Programs, the Global Bank recruits approximately 45 undergraduates each year for its two-year analyst program, which includes formal credit and corporate finance training.

Chevron Corporation

225 Bush Street
San Francisco, CA 94104-4289
(415) 894-2752

MBA Recruiting Contact(s):
Irene J. Melitas, Supervisor
Finance MBA Development Program

Company Description

Describe your firm's business and the types of clients served by your finance group(s).

Chevron Corporation is an international, integrated petroleum company consistently ranked among the leaders of the Fortune 500. Approximately 50,000 employees generate $40 billion in annual revenues and are responsible for nearly $35 billion in assets.

Headquartered in San Francisco, we are the largest producer of petroleum products and natural gas in the United States. Chevron has operations in over 100 countries and is pursuing worldwide ventures in petroleum exploration, production, refining, and marketing. Chevron is an industry leader that is positioned for international growth, building on a rich history of innovation and making the investments needed to provide the world with clean, safe, and economical energy.

In an age of accelerating globalization of the world's national economies, the petroleum industry was one of the first and remains one of the largest, truly global enterprises. The products of this industry can truly be said to drive the engine of our global economy, providing the energy to run our factories, fuel our transportation networks, and heat our homes. This industry vividly defines the risk/reward trade-off: only one multimillion-dollar well drilled out of nine has historically resulted in a commercially viable find, and capital-intensive developments often require investments of billions of dollars over time horizons of 10–50 years.

The Finance MBA's Job Description

Describe the career path and corresponding responsibilities for an MBA at your firm.

We are always seeking highly motivated individuals to help us achieve our goals. Chevron recruits MBAs to bring bright, highly skilled, and ambitious individuals with leadership and management potential into the finance function. Our goal is to develop senior financial management, including such positions as vice president of finance, comptroller, and treasurer, both at the corporate level and at any of our worldwide operating companies (predominantly headquartered in the Bay Area). Chevron pursues a deliberate policy to give top performers experience in many financial arenas in preparation for senior management.

In order to launch MBAs into this environment, Chevron maintains the Finance MBA Development Program, designed to give MBAs rapid exposure to the company and the finance function. This is a select, entry-level program that has been successfully developing financial and general managers for nearly 50 years. The program provides its members with four six-month assignments over a two-year period and is designed to give them broad exposure to financial and operating activities throughout the corporation. In addition, it provides MBAs with opportunities to apply the financial skills they acquired in business school to activities that contribute directly to the achievement of Chevron's business goals. These assignments are generally equal in responsibility to entry-level positions offered to graduating MBAs by other companies.

The assignments available to program members are located typically in organizations where financial skills are at a premium—corporate units such as the Comptroller's and Treasurer's Departments, plus finance, planning, and other functional positions at major operating companies such as Chevron U.S.A. Production, Chevron U.S.A. Products, Chevron Chemical, Chevron Shipping, and Chevron International Oil. There is no preestablished sequence of assignments. Instead, a balanced program is tailored to fit each individual's evolving needs and preferences while meeting the company's changing business requirements.

Having rapidly acquired expertise in many of Chevron's business areas and a wide range of company contacts, program members are placed in challenging positions at the program's conclusion. Many MBAs return to a group in which they had program assignments, while others undertake positions in areas new to them. An individual's personal preferences are considered in conjunction with company needs. By virtue of the high caliber of the participants and the broad experience they have gained in the program, MBAs are in great demand and are well positioned to pursue careers leading to senior financial and, often, general managerial positions.

The Recruiting Process

Describe your recruiting process and the criteria by which you select candidates. Is prior experience necessary?

Applicants must have authorization to work on a full-time basis in the United States (does not include practical training authorization). Although Chevron does not restrict candidates to specific majors or levels of work experience, the Finance MBA Development Program is considered to be most attractive to MBAs with a strong interest in finance who welcome the opportunity to gain rapid exposure to a wide variety of financial activities at Chevron. On average, program members have two to four years of work experience before obtaining their MBA.

How many permanent associates and analysts do you hire in a typical year? How many summer interns do you expect to hire? If you have a formal summer program, please describe it. Please be sure to indicate whether the summer program is in place for all offices or just some.

We hire four to six MBAs into the Finance MBA Development Program each year.

The Finance MBA Development Program sponsors an ongoing summer internship program. Similar to full-time Development Program members, summer interns are challenged by hands-on, meaningful work that provides an opportunity to experience the issues and actions of one of the world's leading corporations. Interns are placed within corporate groups (Treasury, Comptroller's, Planning) and operating companies (e.g., Chevron U.S.A. Products, Shipping, Chemical).

Internships are typically project oriented, utilizing strong analytical, organizational, and communication skills. Application of financial theory to actual business problem solving is encouraged. All positions are in the San Francisco Bay Area. Exposure to the company and managers outside each intern's particular work group is enhanced by a series of communications meetings, organizational presentations, and other activities. Interns usually have the opportunity to present their accomplishments and conclusions to finance managers at the end of the summer.

In recruiting summer interns, we look for individuals with strong interpersonal and analytical skills, leadership potential, and knowledge of a broad range of financial theory, from financial accounting to capital markets. Prospective interns should have long-term interests in careers in financial management. Again, applicants must have authorization to work on a full-time basis in the United States (does not include practical training authorization).

What international opportunities does your firm offer for U.S. citizens? For foreign nationals?

Although the domestic petroleum industry can certainly be characterized as mature, Chevron continues to pursue growth opportunities around the globe. We recently signed a joint venture petroleum production agreement with Kazakhstan that represents the largest commercial partnership between the West and what was formerly a republic of the Soviet Union.

MBAs can almost immediately gain exposure to our international operations with Bay Area assignments working in the worldwide headquarters of our international subsidiaries. Limited opportunities to work overseas are generally not available to our new hires until they have gained several years of domestic experience, largely a reflection of the complexities and scope of our business. We historically have not hired foreign national MBAs into our Development Program.

CS First Boston

55 East 52nd Street
New York, NY 10055
(212) 909-2000

MBA Recruiting Contact(s):
Sheila Cull, Sales & Trading Recruiting Manager
(212) 322-7758

Anne Hitchcock, Corporate Finance Recruiting
Manager
(212) 909-2420

Company Description

*Describe your firm's business and the types of clients served
by your finance group(s).*

CS First Boston is a leading global investment banking
and securities firm working in close cooperation with
Credit Suisse. The company serves both suppliers and
users of capital around the world. Through 32 offices in
21 countries, CS First Boston provides comprehensive
financial advisory and capital-raising services and develops and offers innovative financial products and services
for a broad range of clients.

The firm also employs its own capital resources to trade
and underwrite securities. Additionally, CS First Boston
has a 40% economic interest in Credit Suisse Financial
Products, a London-headquartered joint effort with
Credit Suisse and Swiss Reinsurance Company, providing derivative product services worldwide.

Describe your ownership structure.

CS First Boston is a privately owned company headquartered in New York. At year-end 1994, CS Holding held a
65% economic interest in the common stock of CS First
Boston, Inc. The firm's employees held a 20% interest
and financial institutions in Japan, the Middle East, and
North America held the remaining 15%.

The Finance MBA's Job Description

Investment Banking
CS First Boston's Investment Banking Department provides comprehensive financial advisory services and market executions in mergers and acquisitions and corporate

finance. Investment Banking is organized into groups of
product and industry specialists who work with client
officers to perform advisories and execute specific transactions.

Client services are delivered through CS First Boston's
client officers, who are organized according to industry
and geographic specialization. In addition to the Global
Corporate Finance Group, several of the industry groups
include Financial Institutions; Health Care; Media,
Transportation, and Telecommunications; Chemicals;
Natural Resources; and Retail.

CS First Boston's approach to client service involves the
carefully coordinated teamwork of client officers performing a variety of corporate finance and advisory assignments, and of specialists providing focused coverage
of specific financial product areas. The firm's many product specialists are called in as needed to work with clients,
and are organized by various kinds of corporate financing
activities. Several of CS First Boston's key financial advisory services include: Leveraged Finance, Global Power
and Project Finance, Private Placements, and Capital
Markets.

Upon joining CS First Boston, an Investment Banking
associate will have the opportunity to learn about every
department in the firm through a brief orientation program. Typically, an Investment Banking associate will
spend his or her early years working in a specific group or
geographic region on a broad range of client or product
assignments. The goal is to expose our professionals to a
rich variety of assignments so they may be especially well-
equipped to assume a higher level of responsibility.

Sales and Trading
CS First Boston's Sales and Trading activity is organized
into the Fixed Income and Equity Departments. The
breadth and complexity of the product offerings and trading activities in these departments have changed rapidly
in recent years in response to structural changes among
corporate finance clients, growing financial sophistica-
tion among institutional investors, and continued integration of the world's capital markets. CS First Boston is
a major market factor in all significant markets around
the world.

The Fixed Income Department at CS First Boston is well
known for its exceptional capabilities in fixed income and
foreign exchange. With our strong regional presence and
our integrated product groups, our global sales, trading
and research, and underwriting capabilities are at the top
tier of the industry. CS First Boston trades over US$100
billion of securities per day and makes markets in over

6,000 different fixed income securities. One of the keys to the success of the Fixed Income Department has been its ability to manage risk for our customers and adapt to the volatile environment of our world marketplace.

The Equity Department at CS First Boston has a preeminent position in the structuring, execution, secondary market trading, and research coverage of equity instruments in the global equity market. Our presence in the international developed markets combined with our significant involvement in privatizations in newly developing countries make us particularly adept at meeting investor's needs as they search for better returns and greater diversification. Equity sales and trading professionals provide investors with original investment ideas and timely market execution. In addition, our creative hedging strategies enable institutions and corporations to effectively manage both their risk and investment goals.

Upon joining CS First Boston, a Sales and Trading associate goes through a formal training program that lasts approximately three months. Both the Fixed Income and Equity training programs consist of intensive classroom instruction, reading assignments, and special projects. The program is designed to develop the associates' product knowledge and understanding of worldwide sales and trading activities.

After successful completion of the training program, each associate is placed in a sales, trading, or research position in the Fixed Income or Equity Departments where he or she continues with an in-depth on-the-job training experience. Sales account packages or trading responsibilities are assigned as soon as the associate has demonstrated the ability to represent the firm.

The Recruiting Process

Describe your recruiting process and the criteria by which you select candidates. Is prior experience necessary?

CS First Boston seeks highly motivated individuals who have a demonstrated record of achievement and the ability to work effectively with others. CS First Boston professionals come from diverse backgrounds. They demonstrate initiative and relate well to both colleagues and clients. In addition, they enjoy working in an atmosphere that may be best described as collegial and constructive.

If you have a formal summer program, please describe it. Please be sure to indicate whether the summer program is in place for all offices or just some.

CS First Boston's Summer Associate Program gives students finishing their first year of business school an opportunity to learn about the investment banking industry. The Summer Associate Program is 10 weeks in duration.

Investment Banking summer associates are assigned to specific groups and will participate in new business presentations, financial advisory assignments, and the completion of transactions.

The Sales and Trading Summer Associate Program is rotational and allows summer associates to be exposed to as many functional areas as possible within Fixed Income and Equities. Sales and Trading summer associates are given the opportunity to remain in their product area of choice for the final week of the program.

D.H. Blair Investment Banking Corp.

44 Wall Street
New York, NY 10005
(212) 495-4000

MBA Recruiting Contact(s):
J. Morton Davis, Chairman
(212) 495-5000

Company Description

Describe your firm's business and the types of clients served by your finance group(s).

D.H. Blair is an independent investment bank based in New York City. The firm has a capital base of over $150 million. Blair specializes in financings of small- and medium-size growth companies, as well as early-stage venture financings. Established in 1904, D.H. Blair has a strong and growing track record of providing financing for these types of companies. Equity financings include initial public offerings, private placements, venture capital, merchant banking, and mergers and acquisitions. Leveraged buyout (LBO) debt financings are growing in number and size at Blair. As a result of our long-standing relationships built up over many years with these companies, Blair has the opportunity to provide many investment banking services to its clients.

Describe your ownership structure.

D.H. Blair is an independent, privately held investment bank.

How does your approach to finance differ from that of other firms, and what do you consider to be your strengths and distinctive capabilities?

D.H. Blair is a focused, well-capitalized investment bank. It does not attempt to provide services outside its specific niche. The firm provides private and public equity and debt financing for small- and medium-size emerging-growth and high-technology companies. D.H. Blair has purposely remained an agile, niche organization with a strong capital base and retail client base. This gives us the flexibility and strength to act very quickly on finding and funding significant investment opportunities. Due to the numerous client and portfolio companies served over many years, D.H. Blair has developed relationships with several of the largest industrial and service companies in the United States as well as overseas. These relationships have led to many acquisitions, joint ventures, and other forms of investment in these D.H. Blair companies.

Discuss changes in your firm's revenues (both domestic and international) and professional staff over the past year; over the past five years.

D.H. Blair is located in New York City. The Investment Banking Group includes approximately 25 individuals. The firm has grown rapidly over the past decade and is committed to maintaining this growth. Because D.H. Blair is an entrepreneurial firm serving this nation's entrepreneurs, the current national trend toward increased levels of this activity provides even greater demands for our services.

The Finance MBA's Job Description

Describe the career path and corresponding responsibilities for an MBA at your firm.

The Corporate Finance Department of D.H. Blair considers highly motivated and aggressive MBAs who have a great deal of initiative and desire to work in various areas of investment banking. Public and private placements of equity and debt securities, as well as merchant banking, venture capital, and LBOs, are areas of opportunity at D.H. Blair. Due to the firm's entrepreneurial flair and structure, there is a great deal of opportunity for the aggressive individual to assume primary responsibility at an early stage. Thinly staffed teams allow us to recruit people looking to take on responsibility quickly. The investment banker should be able to handle all aspects of a deal, as opposed to being a transaction specialist. The banker should be able to understand all areas of a client's business, including knowledge of product, market, financial, and other nonfinancial analyses. The banker should be able to assist in management presentation, negotiation, and sales. Also, the investment banker will be responsible for solicitation of new business opportunities. The speed at which the banker will grow in importance at the firm will depend on the banker's ability to assume responsibility and develop business opportunities.

Describe the opportunities for professional mobility between the various departments in your firm.

Career paths vary greatly depending on an individual's abilities and goals. There is not the rigid structure found in larger investment banks. D.H. Blair encourages individuals to experiment in new areas in order to seek out the best opportunities and further their career goals. Due

41

to the thin staffing structure, there is plenty of opportunity for the banker to be observed by and interact with the staff in order to determine which areas are the most appropriate for career growth.

Discuss the lifestyle aspects of a career with your firm (i.e., average hours per week, amount of travel, flexibility to change offices, corporate culture, etc.).

A career at D.H. Blair is challenging and requires dedication, hard work, and flexibility. Lifestyles vary depending on the individual's own goals as well as those of the group in which the banker works.

The Recruiting Process

Describe your recruiting process and the criteria by which you select candidates. Is prior experience necessary?

We seek people with a history of achievement and success. These candidates show a great deal of initiative and aggressiveness, as well as the requisite analytical skills and strong interpersonal skills. Many successful candidates have had previous work experience, although it is not required. Although grades are a meaningful criterion, each candidate is considered as a combination of many abilities, and no single one is dominant.

How many permanent associates and analysts do you hire in a typical year? How many summer interns do you expect to hire? If you have a formal summer program, please describe it. Please be sure to indicate whether the summer program is in place for all offices or just some.

D.H. Blair hires between two and four associates each year. Although D.H. Blair offers no formal training, there is very thorough on-the-job training.

D.H. Blair has no formal summer program. We hire summer associates, depending on availability and need, in investment banking and brokerage.

Donaldson, Lufkin & Jenrette

140 Broadway
New York, NY 10005
(212) 504-3000

MBA Recruiting Contact(s):
Elizabeth Derby
Investment Banking
(212) 504-3903

Andrea Byrnes
Equities, ISG, and Wood, Struthers & Winthrop
(212) 504-4965

Marguerite Haran
Taxable Fixed Income
(212) 504-3073

Company Description

Describe your firm's business and the types of clients served by your finance group(s).

Donaldson, Lufkin & Jenrette (DLJ) is a rapidly growing, top-ranked, full-service investment and merchant bank. Founded in 1959 by three entrepreneurial Harvard MBAs as a research boutique specializing in institutional equity analysis, DLJ has developed premier franchises in research, sales, trading, and underwriting of equity and fixed income securities. These franchises extend to all major sectors of the capital markets and complement the firm's expertise in merchant banking, high yield financings, initial public offerings, and mergers and acquisitions. Furthermore, DLJ has expanded its emerging markets presence, particularly in Latin America and Asia.

DLJ services a wide variety of clients, ranging from small start-ups to Fortune 500 companies. DLJ has successfully grown its businesses by focusing on transactions in which the quality of ideas and execution skills can make a difference in our clients' performance.

Describe your ownership structure.

In 1985, DLJ was acquired by The Equitable Life Assurance Society of the United States. In turn, the AXA Group, one of France's largest insurance concerns, owns 60% of The Equitable.

How does your approach to finance differ from that of other firms, and what do you consider to be your strengths and distinctive capabilities?

DLJ's approach to capital raising, merchant banking, and venture capital investing has yielded superior results for our clients and portfolio companies. We believe that no transaction is easy or routine; each requires the personal attention and commitment of senior professionals. DLJ encourages teamwork to leverage the diverse talents of our various departments. DLJ values close client relationships, innovative solutions, and high-quality transactions and utilizes the intelligent employment of capital, our distinctive research strength, and strong institutional distribution capabilities.

Discuss changes in your firm's revenues (both domestic and international) and professional staff over the past year; over the past five years.

By almost any measure, 1994 was the worst year in half a century for the securities industry. In a year when industry profits fell by 80% and one-third of the firms on Wall Street reported losses, DLJ fared exceptionally well, recording its third best year ever. With the exception of the slight decline in 1994, DLJ's revenues have been growing steadily over the past five years as have the number of employees. As of January of 1995, DLJ employed 4,660 people in 24 offices in 18 cities in the United States and abroad.

The Finance MBA's Job Description

Describe the career path and corresponding responsibilities for an MBA at your firm.

Investment Banking
Each associate's career path is largely a function of his/her unique strengths and talents. There is no predetermined, limiting time frame for advancement. Compensation and advancement are based solely on merit and achievement. Some associates work exclusively in an industry or product group from the start, but the majority are generalists. Associates naturally gravitate to specialized areas during their first three years. As an associate progresses to more senior ranks (vice president, senior vice president, or managing director), a primary focus is encouraged but not required.

Associates assume immediate responsibility working with DLJ's senior professionals and our clients' senior management. DLJ is committed to providing exposure to a wide range of transactions. Project teams are typically small, offering the associate high visibility, impact, and recognition on each transaction. An associate may work on four or five assignments simultaneously. By the end of the first year, associates are expected to assume a high degree of responsibility for both project management and client maintenance.

Institutional Equity Research

The entry-level analyst (MBA) is given immediate responsibility for coverage of a mutually agreed upon industry. The position entails development of specialized analytical skills, frequent interviews with senior corporate managers, company visits, secondary research, and ultimately intensive interpersonal marketing. A group of senior analysts will be fully accessible to, and will assist in the development of, the new analyst. Ultimately it is the individual's responsibility to build a franchise of authority and expertise within the investment community through his or her written product and client interaction.

Institutional Equity Sales

Sales professionals are responsible for transmitting research recommendations generated by analysts and banking products generated by the Investment Banking Division to analysts and portfolio managers at institutional firms. Sales associates will spend the first six months in an Equities Division training program that incorporates rotation on various desks; meetings with research analysts; a research department project; and weekly meetings with senior sales professionals. Following training, a new associate takes on direct account responsibility.

Taxable Fixed Income

The Taxable Fixed Income Division recruits MBAs for its sales and research areas. In the sales area, new MBAs are assigned to work closely with experienced professionals for the first six months to obtain product knowledge. They then assume responsibility for smaller accounts in order to build their own book. In research, new MBAs work directly with senior professionals in a specific product group (high yield, quantitative research, investment grade, or real estate). DLJ has the most respected fixed income research on Wall Street and earned more first place citations than any other Wall Street firm in *Institutional Investor* magazine's All-America Fixed-Income Research Team.

Describe the opportunities for professional mobility between the various departments in your firm.

DLJ hires associates directly into the various departments described above. There is no preplanned mobility among departments, but if interest is expressed and the individual has demonstrated competence, there is some opportunity to move to a different area of specialization. An associate who joined DLJ's Investment Banking Division in 1982 now heads the High Yield Department in the Taxable Fixed Income Division; a former banking associate is now an equity research analyst; and several former Public Finance professionals are now in Investment Banking.

Discuss the lifestyle aspects of a career with your firm (i.e., average hours per week, amount of travel, flexibility to change offices, corporate culture, etc.).

The lifestyle aspects of a career with DLJ vary from department to department. Nevertheless, some career choices place large demands on an individual's time and require much travel. There is some flexibility to change offices. DLJ's corporate culture emphasizes excellence, informality, and independent initiative. We want our associates to take pride in personal and corporate accomplishments, assuming early responsibility without losing sight of our traditional final corporate final objective: **to have fun!**

The Recruiting Process

Describe your recruiting process and the criteria by which you select candidates. Is prior experience necessary?

The recruiting process is centrally managed from New York with the participation of our regional offices. Students must submit a résumé to the appropriate contact previously listed. DLJ has a three-round interview process in most cases. New MBAs are hired principally into the Investment Banking Division, with additional opportunities in Equity and Fixed Income Research, and Equity and Fixed Income Sales and Trading. Investment Banking associates are hired either as generalists or specialists.

DLJ has no predetermined criteria in evaluating potential associates. While some departments may inquire about grades (if permissible under that school's guidelines), they are not the driving criteria. Prior experience in finance, while helpful, is not required. More important, we look for individuals whose work experience emphasizes initiative, excellence, and creativity.

How many permanent associates and analysts do you hire in a typical year? How many summer interns do you expect to hire? If you have a formal summer program, please describe it. Please be sure to indicate whether the summer program is in place for all offices or just some.

In a typical year, the Investment Banking Division hires 19–27 associates and 30–35 analysts. Equity Research hires 1 or 2 MBAs and 5 to 10 undergraduates, and Taxable Fixed Income hires 0 to 2 associates. We conduct a formal training program when people start, but most of the training is on-the-job experience.

Investment Banking is the only department with a formal summer intern program. We typically hire 15–21 summer associates and 15–20 summer analysts and have opportunities in New York, Los Angeles, and Chicago. For the most part, summer interns are generalists and work on a broad array of transactions. DLJ considers its summer analysts and associates to be integral and active members of the professional staff and strives to provide each with a summer experience truly reflective of full-time employment. Summer interns are exposed to banking's specialty product and industry groups through a weekly lunch series and to other departments through weekly breakfast meetings with senior executives.

What international opportunities does your firm offer for U.S. citizens? For foreign nationals?

There are growing international opportunities at DLJ. DLJ's work authorization is as follows: U.S. citizens, green card recipients, persons eligible for legal visa status, or foreign nationals for appropriate openings.

DLJ took important steps in 1994 and 1995 to build its presence in emerging markets, most notably in Asia and Latin America. Investment Banking opened its Asian regional headquarters in Hong Kong. In our Latin American business, DLJ participated in debt or equity offerings in every major Latin American country except Venezuela in 1994. We have opportunities for investment banking associates in both our Asian and Latin American efforts.

During 1994, our Equities Division hired senior sales professionals to augment our institutional capabilities in our international offices in Geneva, London, Lugano, and Paris in addition to several domestic offices.

DLJ's Taxable Fixed Income Department has offices in the United States, London, and Tokyo.

Enron Capital & Trade Resources

1400 Smith Street
Houston, TX 77002
(713) 853-6614

MBA Recruiting Contact(s):
Lucy Marshall, MBA Recruiting Coordinator

Locations of Offices:
Houston, Calgary, London

Total Number of Professionals (U.S. & Worldwide)
U.S.: 1,350
Worldwide: 1,600

Company Description

Describe your firm's business and the types of clients served by your finance group(s)

Enron Capital & Trade Resources (ECT), the merchant arm of the $12 billion Enron Corp., was formed in 1989 to provide a multitude of financial services to the parent and to the domestic and international energy industries. During its short existence, ECT has grown to be the largest buyer and seller of natural gas in North America, one of the largest traders of natural gas on the NYMEX and the Over-the-Counter Market, and the largest electricity marketer. ECT's aggressive and entrepreneurial staff has achieved this level of market presence through focusing on creating customized solutions to complex, energy-related problems.

ECT's success has been achieved through its focus on its key core businesses: cash and physical transactions (sales and trading), risk management products (derivatives), and innovative financing activities in natural gas, crude oil, liquids, and electricity. These businesses are described below:

Cash and Physical:
(1994: 50% of ECT earnings)

* Day-to-day buying, selling, and transporting of commodities using cash and the NYMEX

* Supported by ownership of or access to physical assets including major pipelines, storage facilities, and power generation facilities

Risk Management:
(1994: 40% of ECT earnings)

* Activities include long-term contracting (>1 year), commodity risk solutions, and contract restructuring

* Manage books in crude oil, natural gas, liquids, crude products, clean fuels, electric power, interest rates, and currencies.

* Extensive portfolio in each area allows ECT to provide its customers with a wide array of physical and financial hedging products

Finance:
(1994: approximately 10% of ECT earnings)

* Arranges debt and equity capital for the energy industry and develops capital funding vehicles that support its financial product offerings

* Since 1991, ECT's funding activity has arranged more than $1.6 billion of capital

These three core businesses support a wide array of domestic and international energy users and producers. ECT's businesses stress internal product and skill integration so that optimal and customized physical and financial solutions can be developed for our customers. ECT sources energy from gas, oil, and electricity producers and suppliers through a variety of financial techniques including long-term contracting, acquisition financing, and price hedging. ECT, using similar financial techniques, supplies energy to local gas distribution companies, cogeneration facilities, electric utilities, and industrials. ECT's upstream and downstream customers find the company's tailor-made products provide critical value in managing their purchase and sale of energy in a market of significant risk and volatility.

Describe your ownership structure.

ECT is a wholly owned subsidiary of Enron Corp. Enron Corp. is a publicly traded company on the New York Stock Exchange under the ticker ENE.

How does your approach to finance differ from that of other firms, and what do you consider to be your strengths and distinctive capabilities?

ECT is a leader in the natural gas and electricity industry in developing innovative physical and financial products for producers and end users.

There are two specific groups within ECT that rely heavily on finance skills and abilities.

Enron Finance Corp. (EFC) arranges for funding of reserves that provide ECT with long-term supply commitments. EFC has developed unique programs to provide acquisition capital and price hedging to independent gas producers. One product offered is the volumetric production payment (VPP). With the VPP, ECT receives a stated volume of the producer's oil and gas production over time. The producer, in exchange, receives cash up front as a purchase price for the production. With more than $950 million in production payments originated as of July 1995, EFC has solidified its position as one of the largest entities arranging for capital to the independent oil and gas sector in North America. The debt and equity raised to fund these products does not affect Enron's balance sheet. EFC forms special companies to fund asset acquisitions. Through these companies, EFC packages collaterized natural gas reserves and sells them to banks and institutional investors, much like a bank packages home loans and resells them. EFC continues to search for financing opportunities within the United States and abroad. In 1994, EFC created a funding vehicle to augment the growing need for producer capital in the Canadian market.

Enron Risk Management Services (ERMS) provides structured risk management products that are physical and/or financial in nature to producers, consumers, investors, and lenders in the energy industry. ERMS acts as principal in a wide variety of structured product transactions, such as swaps, caps, floors, collars, swaptions, participating swaps, product spreads, and product spread options. These products are an integral part of the long-term contracts offered to a wide range of ECT customers. Recently *Risk magazine,* a leading trade publication, ranked ERMS consistently first, second, or third among worldwide commodity traders in natural gas, crude, and gasoline swaps, options, and exotic products.

ECT's success and industry advantage has been due, in large part, to its clear vision and ability to anticipate coming regulatory change and market developments. ECT has been aggressive in capitalizing on developing opportunities and is extremely well-positioned in nearly all segments of the worldwide natural gas industry and in the developing electricity markets.

Discuss changes in your firm's revenues (both domestic and international) and professional staff over the past year; over the past five years.

Five years ago, Enron Corp. had the vision of becoming the world's first natural gas major—the most innovative and reliable provider of clean energy worldwide for a better environment. In 1994, Enron reached that objective and has now set its five-year sights on becoming the World's Leading Energy Company—creating innovative and efficient energy solutions for growing economies and a better environment worldwide.

To receive these accolades requires significant growth in market presence and earnings. Enron Corp.'s growth over the last five years has been substantial and has clearly outpaced our competitors. Over this period, Enron Corp.'s earnings per share have grown at a compound growth rate of 20% and a return to shareholders of 135%.

ECT is a significant contributor to the parent having provided 20% of operating income in just five years. ECT's EBIT reached $225 million in 1994, a 33% increase over 1993.

Enron has committed to a growth of 15% per year in earning per share for 1995 and beyond. Growth is primarily targeted in three areas: the international marketplace, domestic retail energy marketplace, and the domestic electric power industry.

Staff at ECT has increased in the last year to 1,600 today. This number also represents the growth over the last five years since ECT was formed in 1989.

The Finance MBA's Job Description

Describe the career path and corresponding responsibilities for an MBA at your firm.

MBAs are hired into ECT's Associate Program where they work for one to two years. At the completion of the program, the associate transitions into a commercial role with direct and specific customer responsibility.

The Associate Program is designed to give the MBA extensive exposure to all facets of ECT's innovative approach to marketing physical and financial products for the natural gas and electricity industries. While in the program, the associates will provide commercial and analytical support to different ECT profit centers during three- to six-month rotations. As contributing members of deal teams, associates' efforts will directly affect the company's financial success and future growth. Projects and deals could include structured finance, trading and risk management, and marketing for the natural gas and power industries. Opportunities exist for associates to work on international development and merchant projects while based domestically or in one of our international offices.

Describe the opportunities for professional mobility between the various departments in your firm.

As described above, an associate will typically make four to five rotations between the different commercial groups within ECT. These rotations give the Associate a robust understanding of the way that ECT works and how best to create integrated solutions. The associate has a great deal of input in deciding where these rotations will be and how best to craft a career path that takes advantage of individual skills and capabilities as well as company needs. As the associate graduates into the commercial ranks, it is not uncommon for people to move between groups as new opportunities arise.

Discuss the lifestyle aspects of a career with your firm (i.e., average hours per week, amount of travel, flexibility to change offices, corporate culture, etc.).

Individuals that are attracted to ECT are ones that thrive in a fast-paced, intellectual, and entrepreneurial environment. Furthermore, ECT employees are self-motivated, deal-oriented, and biased for action. The company accommodates these types of individuals through a flat, nonbureaucratic organization that gives individual employees a great deal of latitude in setting their own schedule and monitoring their own work.

While it is difficult to precisely categorize the average hours per week and the amount of travel that would be required of an associate, most find that they are able to achieve a diverse and quality lifestyle that combines challenging and stimulating work with substantial time for leisure activities.

The Recruiting Process

Describe your recruiting process and the criteria by which you select candidates. Is prior experience necessary?

ECT is seeking candidates for its associate program who have received an MBA degree and have at least two years of work experience. As has been previously discussed, ECT is looking for candidates who are self-motivated and have well-developed quantitative and interpersonal skills. These candidates must be creative thinkers and able to work in unstructured surroundings. Candidates are not required to have an energy background, although prior knowledge or work experience in this industry is helpful.

ECT conducts interviews for associates during the late winter and early spring of each year. The interviews are conducted first at the university and then a final round is held at the home office in Houston. Most associates begin work in middle to late summer.

How many permanent associates and analysts do you hire in a typical year? How many summer interns do you expect to hire? If you have a formal summer program, please describe it. Please be sure to indicate whether the summer program is in place for all offices or just some.

As ECT continues to grow domestically and internationally, the need for associates will continue to grow as well. ECT is committed to staff its commercial positions from the associate program. ECT plans to hire 35 to 40 associates a year for the next several years.

ECT also maintains a formal summer associate program for first-year MBAs. ECT typically hires 10 to 15 summer associates. The summer associates are assigned to specific profit centers where they are fully integrated into deal teams. Summer associates are expected to be fully contributing team members and able to apply newly learned business skills to real life situations. The summer associate program is run out of the home office in Houston.

What international opportunities does your firm offer for U.S. citizens? For foreign nationals?

ECT has targeted numerous international opportunities that are well-suited to the risk management and commercial skill set that ECT has so well utilized in the United States. ECT currently has international offices in Calgary, Buenos Aires, and London. ECT is, however, continuing to evaluate many other areas and the likelihood of new offices is very high. International opportunities exist for U.S. citizens and foreign nationals alike.

FMC Corporation

200 East Randolph Drive
Chicago, IL 60601
(312) 861-6000
Fax: (312) 861-5902

MBA Recruiting Contact(s):
FMC College Relations

Company Description

Describe your firm's business and the types of clients served by your finance group(s).

FMC is a New York Stock Exchange–listed, $4 billion, Chicago-based multinational corporation producing machinery and chemicals for industry, agriculture, and government. Our worldwide work force of 22,000 staffs 95 manufacturing facilities and mines in 18 countries.

Our competitive edge in manufacturing excellence, technological innovation, cost control, and customer satisfaction has made us a leader in the global markets we serve. Earning a consistently high real return on shareholder equity is a challenge and an imperative. At FMC, the finance function is committed to increasing value today while positioning the company for future profitable growth and strategic development.

FMC is a corporate leader in developing and implementing state-of-the-art analytical techniques for financial planning, performance measurement, and resource allocation. For example, FMC recapitalized in 1986, doubling shareholder value, while enabling FMC to continue its vigorous program of internal development, capital investment, and research and development. We have also adopted an innovative current cost accounting system to assist top management in evaluating performance and strategic investment decision making. At one of our plants, we are implementing a new activity-based costing, which will give our management a deeper understanding of our product costs.

This philosophy of financial innovation pervades the entire corporation. Financial managers are active leaders of the management team and are required to think and act strategically. They are involved in all facets of managing FMC's complex businesses, from product planning to international investment decisions. Therefore, we seek highly motivated individuals who will become both our future financial leaders and future general managers.

The Finance MBA's Job Description

Describe the career path and corresponding responsibilities for an MBA at your firm.

Financial Business analysts begin their careers in the Chicago Corporate Operations Analysis Department, where they are responsible for analyzing, monitoring, and tracking the performance of specific business segments. Analysts also work with line management on a variety of projects that affect management decisions and business performance. After 9–15 months, most analysts assume positions in financial management in one of our line organizations. It is also possible for analysts to pursue other functions at this point. Their choices often depend on their career focus: specializing in a functional discipline or taking advantage of FMC's opportunities for cross-functional career growth. In addition, Financial Business analysts are in demand for a wide variety of offshore opportunities.

The Recruiting Process

How many permanent associates and analysts do you hire in a typical year? How many summer interns do you expect to hire? If you have a formal summer program, please describe it. Please be sure to indicate whether the summer program is in place for all offices or just some.

FMC recruits at six to eight major business schools. Typically, we hire 15 to 25 full-time MBAs and 12 to 20 interns each year in the Planning, Manufacturing, Human Resources, and Finance functions.

Ford Motor Company

World Headquarters Building
11th floor—East Wing
The American Road
Dearborn, MI 48121
(313) 323-0850

MBA Recruiting Contact(s):
Malcolm Macdonald

Company Description

Describe your firm's business and the types of clients served by your finance group(s).

Ford is the world's fourth-largest industrial corporation and the second-largest producer of cars and trucks. It also ranks among the largest providers of financial services in the United States. Approximately 325,000 employees in our plants, offices, and laboratories serve the automotive and financial services needs of customers in more than 200 countries and territories.

Our two core businesses are the Automotive Group and the Financial Services Group, which consists of Ford Credit, The Associates, and U.S. Leasing. We also are engaged in a number of other businesses, including electronics, glass, electrical and fuel-handling products, plastics, climate control systems, service and replacement parts, vehicle leasing and rental, and land development.

Our Finance Organization serves a broad range of internal and external clients. The primary focus of Finance at Ford is on providing timely and accurate financial analysis to company management in order to support a wide range of business decisions.

Describe your ownership structure.

Ford Motor Company is a widely held, publicly traded corporation. Approximately 40% of the voting shares in the corporation are controlled by the Class B stock—controlled by the Ford family.

How does your approach to finance differ from that of other firms, and what do you consider to be your strengths and distinctive capabilities?

Historically, finance has played a very strong role in the automobile industry, particularly at Ford. In fact, in a recent survey conducted by *CFO* magazine, over 200 financial executives, executive recruiters, bankers, and consultants identified Ford Motor Company as one of the three companies that best prepares financial managers for the chief financial officer chair.

Finance professionals are involved in every aspect of the company's operations—product development, engineering, sales and marketing, customer service (sale of aftermarket parts), and financial services—as well as the traditional finance functions, such as treasury, financial planning, and operations analysis. Typically, finance professionals move frequently among the company's different components, developing into well-rounded managers who can fill top-level positions in the Finance Organization or in general management. The extensive roster of Finance alumni in senior management includes Wayne Booker, Executive Vice President of International Automotive; Kenneth Whipple, President of Ford Financial Services Group; and Jacques Nasser, Group Vice President of Product Development.

Finance MBAs at Ford can expect a wide variety of challenging assignments that expose them to all the functional areas of the corporation. At Ford, finance is not about abstract theories; it is about real decisions that affect the viability of a multi-billion-dollar new car platform, the investment in hundreds of millions of dollars' worth of plant and equipment, or the pricing strategy of a major product line.

The Finance MBA's Job Description

Describe the career path and corresponding responsibilities for an MBA at your firm.

The Career Foundation Development Program ensures an early diversity of experiences, with the following job rotations (and job responsibilities):

- Year 1: At a vehicle assembly plant or a component manufacturing plant, typically located in the Midwest (manufacturing cost analysis, operations analysis, and special projects)

- Years 2 and 3: At one of the following groups, generally located in Dearborn, MI:

    Product Development (develop proposals for new product programs, analyze product line profitability).
    Sales (establish pricing strategies and incentive programs for new and existing products, competitive analysis)

Treasury/Capital Markets (capital structure decisions for acquisitions/joint ventures, dividend policy for parent/foreign affiliates, issuance of debt/equity, foreign exchange)

Manufacturing General Offices (capital project analysis, e.g., review of plant expansion proposals and quality improvement actions)

Parts and Service (financial analysis related to sales of after-market parts)

Ford Motor Credit Company/Financial Services (funding of automotive receivables via asset-backed securities, commercial paper, and/or swaps)

- Year 4: Rotate to a new organization (one of the groups listed above). Future rotations could be expected about every two years.

After the Foundation Development Program, an MBA could become a supervisor and eventually a finance manager or plant controller. Longer term, a career path could lead an MBA to become controller of a division, to become treasurer of an affiliate, or to move into general management.

Discuss the lifestyle aspects of a career with your firm (i.e., average hours per week, amount of travel, flexibility to change offices, corporate culture, etc.).

The finance culture at Ford is reflective of the people we hire: highly analytical, aggressive, motivated, and career oriented—with a strong desire to win. Professional development is an integral part of our corporate culture. At Ford, we view our people as an investment, not an expense.

Ford world headquarters is in Dearborn, MI, located about 15 miles from downtown Detroit. Southeastern Michigan offers a wide variety of affordable housing and an easy commute to the office yet has access to all of the cultural amenities one would expect of the nation's sixth largest metropolitan area, including outstanding universities, world-class museums, and four professional sports teams.

The Recruiting Process

Describe your recruiting process and the criteria by which you select candidates. Is prior experience necessary?

Ford is looking for aggressive, intelligent, highly motivated men and women who are looking for a challenge in an exciting, highly competitive industry. As Ford enters the twenty-first century, we face many challenges: globalization, trade barriers, increased regulation, excess capacity, and stiff competition, to name a few. We are looking for people to help us meet these challenges.

Prior technical experience or education is helpful but certainly not essential. A healthy interest in, and a willingness to get close to, our products is more essential to long-term success at Ford.

Our recruiting process includes a recruiting briefing in the fall followed by on-campus interviews in the winter. On-site visits follow a successful on-campus interview. In addition we will arrange a visit for candidates to take a "Ford Finance Test Drive"—an opportunity to spend a day with an MBA who has worked at Ford for two or three years. He or she will show you what a typical day is like. The Ford Finance Test Drive provides an additional opportunity to decide if Ford is the right place to make your career.

How many summer interns do you expect to hire? If you have a formal summer program, please describe it. Please be sure to indicate whether the summer program is in place for all offices or just some.

Ford plans to continue to seek a limited number of talented individuals for a variety of summer positions. Summer positions are designed to provide a challenging short-term assignment that will give an accurate perspective on a full-time career at Ford. The process and qualifications for summer applicants are similar to those for full-time positions.

What international opportunities does your firm offer for U.S. citizens? For foreign nationals?

Ford derives about 40% of its revenues from international operations, offering abundant opportunities for international experience. Overseas assignments, if desired, are possible after completion of the Foundation Development Program. Many Ford executives have had international experience at some point in their careers.

Ford recruits MBAs who are U.S. citizens or are authorized to work full time in the United States.

Furman Selz, Inc.

230 Park Avenue
New York, NY 10169
(212) 309-8382

MBA Recruiting Contact(s):
Diane Kopyscianski, Investment Banking Coordinator

Lillian Rinchiuso, Equity Research/Fixed Income Coordinator

Company Description

Describe your firm's business and the types of clients served by your finance group(s).

Furman Selz is a full-service investment banking firm, headquartered in New York with offices in Boston, San Francisco, Los Angeles, Chicago, London, and Tokyo. We employ over 600 people in the areas of investment banking, institutional equities and fixed income, institutional services, and investment management.

Describe your ownership structure.

The firm was founded in 1973 as a research boutique. It has grown consistently and today has over $100 million in capital and over $25 billion in assets under management and administration. The firm is privately owned by its employees and has been profitable in every year since its inception.

How does your approach to finance differ from that of other firms, and what do you consider to be your strengths and distinctive capabilities?

Furman Selz is focused on differentiating itself with regard to providing thoughtful, cutting-edge advice while at the same time delivering personal service. The firm maintains a familial heartbeat as it grows.

Furman Selz does not try to be all things to all people. We focus on selected industries including: Media & Communications, Health Care, Shipping, Automotive, Retailing & Consumer, Technology, Financial Services & Insurance, Utilities, and Special Situations. Our greatest strengths lie in our knowledge-based approach to our businesses derived from our origins in Research.

The Finance MBA's Job Description

Describe the career path and corresponding responsibilities for an MBA at your firm.

MBA career paths in Investment Banking, Fixed Income, and Research are open-ended based on the capabilities, diligence, willingness to accept responsibility, and accomplishment of the candidate. Mobility between departments does exist, but usually not until after the first two to three years of employment.

Discuss the lifestyle aspects of a career with your firm (i.e., average hours per week, amount of travel, flexibility to change offices, corporate culture, etc.).

Furman Selz prides itself in terms of employee satisfaction. Employees appreciate the work environment of the firm and feel aligned with the culture that has been created over the years.

The Recruiting Process

Describe your recruiting process and the criteria by which you select candidates. Is prior experience necessary?

Candidates are interviewed on campus; some are invited back to be interviewed by business line and senior management in New York. Intellect, academic achievement, work ethic, and the ability to interact with fellow employees are important. Prior experience is an advantage.

How many permanent associates and analysts do you hire in a typical year?

Approximately six associates are hired in a typical year.

General Motors Corporation
New York Treasurer's Office

GM Building
767 Fifth Avenue
New York, NY 10153
(212) 418-6193

MBA Recruiting Contact(s):
Dwaine Kimmet, HBS '95
Nick Hotchkin, HBS '93

Company Description

Describe your firm's business and the types of clients served by your finance group(s).

General Motors designs, manufactures, and sells automobiles, trucks, vans, locomotives, and other equipment and components related to the worldwide transportation industry. In addition, the corporation is involved in the design and manufacture of satellites, integrated circuits, electronic-optical sensors, guidance systems, and other defense electronics systems, as well as financial services and the application of a wide range of computer systems and software.

The global automobile industry is progressing into an era of unprecedented competition. At General Motors, we are approaching this challenge with a commitment to remaining the premier manufacturer of cars and trucks in North America and the rest of the world. As has been well documented in the press, this commitment has resulted in a period of incredible change, with the entire GM organization being scrutinized and restructured. This process is placing emphasis on the ability of GM's employees to manage its operations and finance effectively.

GM's New York Treasurer's Office plays a vital role in the decisions that affect both the current operations of the corporation and its future direction. The office is extensively responsible for a broad range of financial, strategic planning, and other business matters leading to the execution of transactions, including new business ventures, domestic and international subsidiary financings, investments, divestitures, capital planning, and foreign exchange trading. In addition to developing and executing action plans for top management, the Treasurer's Office is also responsible for presenting such action plans and other information to the Board of Directors and its Finance, Audit, Incentive and Compensation, and

Nominating Committees. As such, GM's New York Treasurer's Office distinguishes itself from other corporate treasury staffs by providing individuals with the opportunity to develop and practice corporate finance, consulting, and general management skills.

Furthermore, the appeal of the Treasurer's Office extends beyond that provided by traditional treasury functions. Specifically, GM's Treasurer's Office also functions as GM's in-house consulting firm. As such, the office's responsibilities include developing, assessing, negotiating, and implementing strategic business initiatives of the corporation. Reflecting the Treasurer's Office objectives of developing both the financial and general business acumen of its employees, many alumni have progressed to top financial and general management positions throughout the United States and virtually all of our international locations, including Europe, Asia, and South America.

The Finance MBA's Job Description

Describe the career path and corresponding responsibilities for an MBA at your firm.

A senior financial analyst in the office is exposed to a wide range of strategic and financial assignments that can be matched by very few other companies. For example, a typical business school graduate could immediately be engaged in any of several activities, including structuring an international subsidiary or joint venture, developing an entirely new form of equity or debt offering, managing GM's multibillion-dollar cash portfolio, or trading foreign currency on a global basis. Newly hired MBAs are provided with the opportunity to practice a wide range of corporate finance activities. In this regard, individuals in the Treasurer's Office are rotated from section to section in order to develop their breadth of expertise fully. Senior analysts would typically follow a rotational assignment system through several of nine office sections, which places emphasis on developing general managers proficient in many areas of finance. While the responsibilities of each section and position vary, analysts are expected to develop a broad knowledge of GM's operations, its products, and its markets on a worldwide basis. Key responsibilities within the sections include:

- Business Development and Analysis
  —Business associations and partnerships
  —Acquisition and divestiture analysis and execution

- Corporate Financing and Investment
  —Capital structure and analysis
  —Capital planning
  —Cash portfolio management
  —Capital markets

- Investor Relations and Competitive Analysis
  —Communication with Wall Street analysts
  —Competitive analysis and intelligence

- Overseas Finance
  —Overseas capital planning and control
  —All non-U.S. financings

- Overseas Financial Analysis and Special Projects
  —Analysis and structuring of overseas joint ventures, acquisitions, and divestitures
  —Analysis of overseas subsidiary printability and investment proposals

- Worldwide Banking and U.S. Cash Management
  —Banking and domestic cash resources management

- Foreign Exchange, Commodities Futures, and International Cash Management
  —Foreign exchange analysis and hedging
  —Metals futures trading
  —Export financing
  —Overseas subsidiaries cash management

- Executive Compensation
  —Parent company and subsidiary incentive compensation design and analysis

- Employee Benefit Plans Analysis
  —National negotiations with the United Auto Workers Union
  —Domestic and international benefit plan design and analysis
  —Salaried and hourly labor cost analysis

- Regional Treasury Center (satellite offices in Brussels, Belgium, Singapore)
  —Foreign exchange and interest rate exposure
  —Management of GM's European subsidiaries
  —Short-term funding requirements in Europe
  —Special project finance transactions

Outlined below are the job classifications within the New York Treasurer's Office and the average time it has historically taken qualified MBAs to attain these levels:

Job Classification	Average Time to Promotion
Senior Financial Analyst (entry-level position for MBA)	—
Manager (typically supervises 4 or 5 analysts)	2–3 years
Section Director (responsible for 1 or 2 managers and 7–9 analysts)	2 years
Assistant Treasurer	5 years

Describe the opportunities for professional mobility between the various departments in your firm.

In addition to promotions leading to a successful and rewarding experience at the Treasurer's Office in New York, numerous financial openings occur for Treasurer's Office employees at overseas and domestic subsidiaries and divisions (e.g., GM Hughes Electronics, NUMMI [GM's joint venture with Toyota in Fremont, CA], GMAC, Saturn, GM-Europe, EDS, and GM's North American Operations). Furthermore, many opportunities are available outside the financial side of the business, including general management, personnel, industrial relations, manufacturing, industry-government relations, and our worldwide trading corporation.

The Recruiting Process

Describe your recruiting process and the criteria by which you select candidates. Is prior experience necessary?

GM's Treasurer's Office is staffed with approximately 60 MBAs from the nation's top schools and from around the globe. We seek individuals with initiative and a willingness to assume a demanding work load in a challenging environment, as new analysts are expected to assume a significant amount of responsibility within a very short period of time. A typical senior financial analyst has a strong academic background, with particular emphasis on finance; a background in economics, accounting, engineering, or operations is also valuable. Attractive candidates demonstrate strong analytical and organizational abilities, as well as effective oral and written communication skills. Importantly, they also have a high level of interpersonal skills and an ability to function effectively as part of a team.

If you have a formal summer program, please describe it. Please be sure to indicate whether the summer program is in place for all offices or just some.

GM's Treasurer's Office has an excellent summer program that allows students between years of business school to learn about the New York office and gain valuable knowledge and skills in a particular section. Many of our recent summer analysts have elected to return to the Treasurer's Office upon graduating.

Goldman, Sachs & Co.

85 Broad Street
New York, NY 10004
(212) 902-1000

MBA Recruiting Contact(s):
David M. Darst, Vice President
Equities Division; for Equities Division and for Global
Operations and Technology Division

Chris C. Casciato, Vice President
Investment Banking Division

Jide J. Zeitlin, Vice President
Investment Banking Division; for Investment Banking
Division and Principal Investment Area

Frank J. Gaul, Vice President
Fixed Income Division; for Fixed Income Division

Brian J. Duffy, Vice President
J. Aron Currency and Commodities Division; for J. Aron
Currency and Commodities Division

Company Description

*Describe your firm's business and the types of clients served
by your finance group(s).*

Goldman, Sachs & Co. is a full-service international investment banking and securities firm headquartered in
New York City. Major offices in London and Tokyo serve
as European and Asia/Pacific Basin headquarters, respectively. Other offices are located throughout the
United States and in Frankfurt, Hong Kong, Montreal,
Paris, Singapore, Sydney, Toronto, and Zurich.

The firm is a leader in virtually every aspect of financing
and investing, serving corporations, institutions, governments, and individual clients. A recent survey of U.S.
corporate financial officers named Goldman, Sachs the
leading investment banking firm for overall service to large
public companies. Another survey of U.S. chief financial
officers and top institutional money managers names the
firm "best broker" for the second consecutive year.

Our leadership derives principally from the dedication,
talent, and professionalism of our people. We recruit and
train the very best graduates from leading colleges and
universities. These individuals become part of our noted

team effort, which provides the closely integrated financial skills and services necessary to help our clients meet
diverse goals and new challenges in global markets.

The following is a brief overview of the firm's organization and activities.

Investment Banking Division
The Investment Banking Division assists corporations, financial institutions, and governments in planning and executing financial strategies in the global capital markets.

Corporate Finance. Our Corporate Finance Department professionals concentrate the firm's resources on
identifying alternative sources of capital and on developing innovative techniques to match the interests of users
and providers of capital. Transactions, structured and
executed worldwide, include public debt and equity offerings and private placements of debt and equity. The
firm is a leading manager of public offerings in the United
States and abroad and a major factor in arranging private
financings. The firm is also active in corporate workouts
and restructurings.

Energy and Telecommunications Group. The Energy
and Telecommunications Group provides investment
banking services to Goldman, Sachs's clients in four principal industries: Oil and Gas, Pipelines, Utilities, and
Telecommunications.

Financial Institutions Group. Professionals in the Financial Institutions Group provide full-service investment banking services to many of the largest banks,
insurance companies, money managers, finance companies, and thrift institutions worldwide.

Structured Finance Group. The Structured Finance
Group is responsible for the conception, development,
promotion, and execution of a variety of types of financing transactions characterized by nonconventional features. These features include noncorporate legal structures, advantageous tax or accounting treatment,
nonconventional sources of capital, and contractual me-
chanics governing business input and output.

Mergers and Acquisitions. The Mergers and Acquisitions Department, consistently a leading advisor in major
merger transactions, assists corporations in achieving financial and strategic objectives through sales, acquisition, divestitures, leveraged buyouts, and recapitalizations, and defending against hostile takeovers.

Capital Markets. Professionals in our Capital Markets
Groups advise issuing clients on capital-raising strategies
and opportunities by communicating current fixed income
market and product information generated by our trading,
sales, and foreign exchange professionals worldwide.

Real Estate. The Real Estate Department serves the world's leading corporations, real estate developers, and institutions. The firm is dominant in arranging sales and financings of investment-grade office, retail, hotel, industrial, and multifamily properties. These transactions frequently involve foreign investors and lenders and include capital markets instruments such as securitized offerings, interest rate swaps, and credit enhancements.

Investment Banking Services. The Investment Banking Services Department is the marketing arm of the Investment Banking Division. Professionals are responsible for maintaining and strengthening client relationships and developing new relationships and business. In cooperation with each execution department, professionals create and implement marketing plans for specific products as well as strategies to enhance the firm's overall presence and reputation worldwide.

Principal Investment Area

Principal Investment professionals are responsible for the principal investing activities of the firm, including the firm-sponsored investment funds. All principal investments are made so as not to conflict with client objectives.

Fixed-Income Division

The Fixed-Income Division serves investing and issuing clients as a leader in marketing and trading fixed income securities and derivative products in all major financial markets. A majority of the division's professionals are involved in sales, trading, and research. The division also includes Municipal Finance and Asset-Backed Finance professionals.

Sales and Trading. Sales and Trading professionals work within groups that concentrate on such specific fixed-income products as government and agency securities, corporate securities, mortgage-backed securities, high-yield securities, municipal securities, futures and options, and preferred stock.

Sales professionals play a key role in the firm's capital markets transactions. They assist institutional investors in planning and implementing portfolio strategies. As a critical link between the firm's issuing and investing clients, they ensure the successful distribution of new issues and the firm's ability to underwrite the debt of corporations, governments, and other major borrowers.

Trading professionals make markets in major debt securities as well as in derivatives of those securities. They commit the firm's capital to ensure liquidity for investing clients. Traders are continually in touch with sales professionals, soliciting investor opinions and suggesting investment strategies. Traders also advise capital markets, investment banking, and syndicate professionals on the pricing, structuring, and timing of new issues, as well as on debt repurchase, synthetic securities, and asset swaps.

Fixed Income Research. The Fixed Income Research Department uses sophisticated analytical, mathematical, and computer capabilities to develop new ideas, products, and approaches for trading, hedging, and investment strategies as well as for asset-liability management. Professionals work in specialized sections covering debt options, trading systems, asset-liability management, risk management, sales support, financial modeling, hedging, portfolio optimization, new product development, and research.

Municipal Finance. Professionals in our Municipal Finance Department are responsible for developing new business opportunities, structuring and executing transactions, and providing ongoing financial advisory services for issuers of municipal bonds. Clients include states, state agencies, local governments, hospitals, health care systems, airports, public power authorities, colleges and universities, housing finance agencies, mass transit systems, and cultural institutions. The department originates and underwrites the full spectrum of tax-exempt and taxable municipal debt, ranging from tax-exempt commercial paper, variable-rate demand notes, and put bonds, to long-term, fixed-rate bonds.

Asset-Backed Finance. Our Asset-Backed Finance professionals—who are part of the Mortgage Securities Department—provide a full range of investment banking services to clients, including thrift institutions, mortgage bankers, federal agencies, home builders, commercial banks, and insurance, finance, and industrial companies.

Equities Division

Through its Equities Division, Goldman, Sachs underwrites, distributes, and trades equity securities and derivative products on a worldwide basis. Goldman, Sachs' position in the global equities marketplace results from its product innovation, distribution capability, and willingness to commit capital in response to clients' needs. The division has long-standing relationships with a wide range of institutional investors and wealthy family groups.

As a member of the New York, London, Frankfurt, and Tokyo stock exchanges, Goldman, Sachs is a trader and market maker in U.S., European, U.K., Japanese, and other global equities. Trading and execution activities are conducted as both agent and principal.

Institutional Investor Services. The Institutional Investor Services Department provides trading and research coverage, through product-focused specialists, to institutional clients, including public and private pension funds, insurance companies, mutual funds, hedge funds, banks, investment advisors, endowments, and foundations in the United States, Europe, and Asia.

Global Convertible Securities.   The Global Convertible Securities Department distributes, makes markets, and conducts arbitrage in U.S., yen-denominated, and Euro-convertible bonds and in a substantial portion of U.S.-convertible preferred stocks. Equity warrants specialists in New York, London, and Tokyo make markets and conduct arbitrage in U.S., Japanese, and European warrant issues.

Equity Derivatives.   The Equity Derivatives Department distributes and trades listed and unlisted options and futures on market indexes, industry groups, and individual companies. The department develops quantitative strategies to effect portfolio hedging and restructuring, asset allocation, equity index swaps, and the construction of synthetic instruments. These instruments enable sophisticated investors to undertake desired hedging strategies and establish or liquidate investment positions not otherwise available in the financial markets.

Equity Capital Markets.   The Equity Capital Markets Department advises corporate and governmental clients worldwide with regard to equity financing opportunities, privatization strategies, capital structure, and equity product design. Through the Equity Capital Markets Department, Goldman, Sachs manages international equity offerings, U.S. common stock offerings, and issues of ADRs by international companies.

Private Client Services.   The Private Client Services Department provides comprehensive equity, fixed income, and cash management services, as well as securities safekeeping, margin lending, portfolio reporting, and principal investment opportunities to wealthy family groups, medium-size institutions, corporations, and professional investors worldwide.

Investment Research.   The Investment Research Department consists of more than 80 analysts, located in New York, London, Frankfurt, and Tokyo, who provide quantitative and qualitative analyses of global economic, currency, and financial market trends; portfolio strategy; asset allocation recommendations; industry weighting; and investment options on 1300 companies in over 80 different industries in the United States, Japan, Europe, and elsewhere.

J. Aron Currency and Commodity Division
The J. Aron Currency and Commodity Division, with offices in New York, London, Tokyo, and Singapore, is a leading market maker in foreign exchange and commod-

ities worldwide, providing complete trading, hedging, and advisory services to corporations, institutions, and governments. The division's activities include:

> Foreign Exchange Trading Department
> Foreign Exchange Sales Department
> Oil and Natural Gas Trading Department
> Coffee Trading Department
> Grain Trading Department
> Metals Trading Department
> Currency and Commodity Investment Products
>   Department

Global Operations and Technology Division
Integral roles in firmwide activities are played by our information technologies, securities operations, controllers, credit, treasury, and personnel professionals.

Information Technologies.   Information Technologies serves the business, operations, and administrative areas of the firm by managing the delivery of high-quality computer systems.

Controllers.   The Controllers Department designs and monitors all internal financial functions. The department is responsible for internal financial analysis and consulting, external financial reporting, monitoring internal trading positions and regulatory compliance, and general accounting for the firm.

Credit.   The Credit Department approves and monitors the credit/exposure limits of many companies with which Goldman, Sachs does business. The department participates in the solicitation, structuring, and selling of commercial paper and conducts due diligence investigations.

Treasury.   Worldwide funding of the firm's operations is the responsibility of the Treasury Department. The firm is rated A1+, the highest ranking for commercial paper issuers assigned by Standard & Poor's.

Personnel.   Our Personnel professionals ensure that Goldman, Sachs maintains the highest standards in all human resources activities. Functional areas include benefits and compensation, employment and employee relations, training and professional development, personnel systems and administration, and international personnel operations.

Describe your ownership structure.

Founded in 1869, Goldman, Sachs is the only remaining private partnership among the major Wall Street organizations. Our partnership structure fosters a culture that is characterized by teamwork, aggressive pursuit of business opportunities, compensation that is commensurate with responsibility and performance, and sound financial management. We have historically been among the most profitable investment banking firms.

How does your approach to finance differ from that of other firms, and what do you consider to be your strengths and distinctive capabilities?

Commitment to client interests and teamwork are the most distinctive characteristics of our approach to investment banking. We emphasize relationships rather than the completion of individual transactions. Our success is directly related to our ability to provide our clients with exceptional service. Among our key strengths are the following:

> The skill, experience, and dedication of our people
> Leadership in financial markets worldwide
> Strong capital position
> Technological resources
> Reputation for excellence

Most important, we believe our ability to integrate all facets of the firm's areas of excellence through teamwork is unique in the industry.

The Finance MBA's Job Description

Describe the career path and corresponding responsibilities for an MBA at your firm.

The firm recruits MBAs for career positions in all divisions and operating entities. Initial training will depend on the new associate's background and functional area. Training emphasizes on-the-job learning, which is complemented by formal instruction. Professionals throughout the firm serve as instructors and mentors. During training, associates prepare for any registration exams that may be required for their specialization. They begin training in their functional areas after they complete those exams. Associates are encouraged to assume as much responsibility in their assignments as they can handle.

Associates play an integral role in planning, structuring, and executing transactions that range from a single private placement of equity or debt to a major portfolio restructuring or corporate reorganization. They work with partners, vice presidents, other associates, and analysts in an open atmosphere in which ideas are shared and creative thinking is encouraged. Because the firm has only three levels of professionals, new associates have significant contact with its senior members.

Describe the opportunities for professional mobility between the various departments in your firm.

As part of career development, we foster a working environment in which professionals are encouraged to explore their interests and develop their skills continuously. Believing that diversity of experience is beneficial not only to our professionals but also to the firm and its clients, we provide opportunities to work in other areas of the firm and to transfer to other departments, divisions, or offices.

We are diligent in evaluating professionals for career advancement and financial reward. Yearly reviews are made by teams of superiors and peers to ensure thoroughness and objectivity.

Discuss the lifestyle aspects of a career with your firm (i.e., average hours per week, amount of travel, flexibility to change offices, corporate culture, etc.).

A career at Goldman, Sachs is a challenging one that places significant demands on time and energy. Professionals are encouraged to make their lifestyle decisions within the context of doing the best job possible. The amount of travel varies greatly. In areas requiring the most travel, our professionals can average two or three days on the road each week.

As a result of our care in hiring, developing, challenging, and rewarding our people, the turnover rate for our professionals has consistently been one of the lowest in the industry.

The Recruiting Process

Describe your recruiting process and the criteria by which you select candidates. Is prior experience necessary?

In recruiting, we look for professionals who will flourish in a team-oriented environment. There is no single type of individual who fits in at Goldman, Sachs. We are an amalgam of people from around the world with different cultural and educational backgrounds and professional orientations. What we have in common are creativity, the confidence and willingness to take initiative and responsibility, an interest in being a part of a highly motivated group, and a desire to achieve beyond the norm.

Although each area of specialization requires certain qualities, most of our professionals demonstrate a keen interest in the financial markets; strong interpersonal, analytic, and communication skills; and an ability to respond creatively and quickly in a fast-paced, changing environment.

We believe that academic achievement is a good indication of potential, but it is not the most important criterion. Prior experience is usually not a major consideration for MBAs.

How many permanent associates and analysts do you hire in a typical year? How many summer interns do you expect to hire? If you have a formal summer program, please describe it. Please be sure to indicate whether the summer program is in place for all offices or just some.

We offer a two-year financial analyst program for college graduates. Each year, we hire a significant number of college graduates in the Investment Banking Division worldwide. In addition, there are select analyst positions elsewhere in the firm. As with MBAs, most of the training of college graduates is on the job. Many of our analysts earn an MBA and return to the firm as associates. The contact for the program is Andrea Baum, Investment Banking Division (212) 902-0003.

The firm actively recruits for its summer associate program. Our summer associates gain broad exposure to many areas of our business, and many return as full-time employees.

What international opportunities does your firm offer for U.S. citizens? For foreign nationals?

Investment banking has become an international business, and Goldman, Sachs is fully committed to the business on a worldwide basis. In addition to our headquarters in New York City, we have major offices in London and Tokyo, which serve as our European and Asian/Pacific Basin headquarters, respectively. We have other offices located throughout the United States, as well as Frankfurt, Hong Kong, Montreal, Paris, Singapore, Sydney, Toronto, and Zurich. Consequently, we offer many international opportunities for both U.S. citizens and foreign nationals.

Hewlett-Packard Company

3000 Hanover Street
Palo Alto, CA 94304

MBA Recruiting Contact(s):
Bill Mitchell
3000 Minuteman Road
Andover, MA 01810
(508) 659-2815

Company Description

Describe your firm's business and the types of clients served by your finance group(s).

Hewlett-Packard (HP) is a leading international manufacturer of computing and electronic measuring equipment for people in business, industry, science, engineering, health care, and education. The company's more than 12,000 products include computers and peripheral products, test and measuring instruments and computerized test systems, networking products, electronic components, hand-held calculators, medical electronic equipment, and instruments and systems for chemical analysis.

HP's basic business purpose is to help accelerate the advancement of knowledge and fundamentally improve the effectiveness of people and organizations worldwide.

Describe your ownership structure.

HP is a publicly owned company and is one of the 20 largest industrial corporations in America. HP stock is traded on the New York Stock Exchange.

How does your approach to finance differ from that of other firms, and what do you consider to be your strengths and distinctive capabilities?

HP's combination of strength and structure enables us to offer a broad spectrum of financial career opportunities and early responsibility.

HP's unique corporate culture, often referred to as the "HP Way," is a combination of organizational values, corporate objectives, and company practices. The company is built upon values such as honesty, teamwork, and respect that are reflected in everything we do.

One of our guiding objectives as a company is profit. The profit we generate from our operations is the ultimate source of the funds we need to prosper and grow. It is the one absolutely essential measure of our corporate performance over the long term. Without profit, the company is unable to grow or fulfill the rest of its objectives.

Our long-standing policy has been to reinvest most of our profits and to depend on this reinvestment, plus funds from employee stock purchases and other cash flow items, to finance our growth.

The day-to-day performance of each individual adds to—or subtracts from—our profit. Profit is seen as the responsibility of all HP employees.

Discuss changes in your firm's revenues (both domestic and international) and professional staff over the past year; over the past five years.

In fiscal year 1994, ending October 31, 1994, net revenues rose 23% to $25 billion, following a 23% increase in fiscal year 1993.

HP employs approximately 98,400 people.

The Finance MBA's Job Description

Describe the career path and corresponding responsibilities for an MBA at your firm.

Financial analyst positions are typically in HP product divisions, field sales organizations, or corporate functions. These initial experiences lead to careers in financial management or in other functional areas such as marketing and manufacturing.

In the divisions, financial analysts work closely with other functional areas. Tasks may include product/process cost analysis, financial planning and reporting, product pricing and profitability analysis, asset evaluation, and the design and implementation of financial models that will simulate division operations.

Financial analysts in the sales regions are responsible for financial planning and reporting, customer leasing arrangements, credit analysis and accounts receivable management, inventory analysis and control, and contracts and order administration.

In our corporate headquarters, responsibilities may include many of the activities described above plus cash, debt, and foreign exchange management; pensions and investment analysis; coordination of long-range plans; the development of corporate financial policy; external shareholder and Securities and Exchange Commission reporting; and internal audit tasks.

Describe the opportunities for professional mobility between the various departments in your firm.

The company is committed to giving people the flexibility to reach well-defined goals. HP believes that freedom encourages the creativity and initiative of every employee. Career paths are not defined formally at HP; rather, they are flexible by design. We strive to help our people succeed and move on to greater challenges and responsibilities. An extensive internal job posting system allows employees to change jobs within their site (both within their function and across functions) and to move to other sites.

Discuss the lifestyle aspects of a career with your firm (i.e., average hours per week, amount of travel, flexibility to change offices, corporate culture, etc.).

HP trusts individuals and believes that people are committed to doing a good job given the right environment. To create this environment, HP offers pay based on performance, pleasant and open work environments, flexible work hours, cash profit sharing, and recognition for achievement.

The Recruiting Process

Describe your recruiting process and the criteria by which you select candidates. Is prior experience necessary?

HP recruits highly motivated, successful MBAs with initiative and a strong desire to make a significant impact on our business. Prior experience is preferred although not mandatory. Candidates must have a thorough knowledge of financial and accounting principles and proficiency in PC-based analytical tools. We look for outstanding analytical and problem-solving ability, as well as flexibility and excellent communication skills.

How many permanent associates and analysts do you hire in a typical year? How many summer interns do you expect to hire? If you have a formal summer program, please describe it. Please be sure to indicate whether the summer program is in place for all offices or just some.

The number of openings varies from year to year, but we typically have several Fnance openings distributed among many of our operations.

HP's Student Employment and Educational Development (SEED) Program enables students who have completed their first year in business school to gain hands-on experience as contributing members of our Finance team.

What international opportunities does your firm offer for U.S. citizens? For foreign nationals?

Overseas employment opportunities are limited to foreign nationals.

IBM Corporation

IBM Staffing Services
3808 Six Forks Road
Raleigh, NC 27609
(800) 964-4473

Company Description

Describe your firm's business and the types of clients served by your finance group(s).

IBM is a unique organization—a major multinational corporation that takes pride in its small-team atmosphere.

Consider that the company stands at the leading edge of one of the world's most dynamic industries: information processing. Consider that it does business in over 130 countries.

Consider, also, that IBM is an organization known worldwide for its respect for the individual and its environment for personal and professional growth. Consider that it is a market-driven company dedicated to providing the best possible customer service and that it is committed to excellence in all activities. Consider that it is a dynamic organization constantly striving to be competitive, to be responsive, to push decision making down to manageable levels.

In fact, IBM is a number of things. It is products and services designed to help customers solve problems through the application of information solutions. It is mainframe, mid-range, and personal computer systems; software for systems, applications, communications, and application development; telecommunications products; office systems; and related supplies and services. All are products and services designed to help record, process, store, retrieve, and communicate information.

In addition, IBM is a technological leader—an innovator with over 32,000 patents worldwide and major contributions at all levels of information processing. The company invented FORTRAN, RAMAC, the floppy disk, the relational database concept, systems network architecture, RISC technology, and much more. It has continually increased the density of circuit packaging, recently producing the first 4-million-bit chip. IBM scientists have earned Nobel Prizes for advances in superconductivity and scanning tunneling microscopy. The company is exploring sub-half-micron lithography, optical storage, speech recognition, artificial intelligence—and a host of other technologies.

But IBM is also open communications channels and respect for privacy, career flexibility and promotion on merit, personal growth and recognition, shared employee/company responsibility, a balance of work and personal life, corporate citizenship, and a benefits program considered one of the finest in industry. In other words, IBM is a special place to work.

Within IBM, Finance is its own team, a function that cuts across organizational lines. A cadre of over 5,000 professionals in the United States, IBM Finance offers opportunities at U.S. plant, laboratory, marketing, and subsidiary locations, as well as at headquarters facilities. Joint ventures and business alliances are also mutually staffed with an IBM and partner financial team.

Working in IBM Finance, you will gain exposure to all aspects of the business. Financial decisions affect research, engineering, manufacturing, programming, marketing, administration, personnel, communications—all the basic functions of the company. As a member of an IBM financial team, you will be in frequent contact with senior management early in your career. From the start, you will also interact with your counterparts at other locations.

In the process, you will gain an understanding of the business and what makes it work. To build a career in IBM Finance, you need a perspective that cuts across functional lines. A pricing decision in Raleigh, NC, can affect accounting controls in Boca Raton, FL. Financial planning for the IBM Credit Corporation can affect the treasury function at corporate headquarters in Armonk, NY. Equity investments can have worldwide implications.

The Finance MBA's Job Description

Describe the career path and corresponding responsibilities for an MBA at your firm.

Career paths in IBM Finance are characterized by a variety of experience and responsibilities, with advancement on merit. The path you follow depends on your objectives and how well you do in the variety of job responsibilities you will be given. You can move ahead as fast as your capabilities permit.

You will most likely start in financial planning or accounting—with later assignments in these areas plus pricing, treasury, and controllership—and rotate assignments for balanced experience. You could start as a cost accounting analyst, become a planning manager, move on to be a product pricer in an international headquarters in Paris—all while moving up in your career. An assignment in the IBM Credit Corporation might be in the picture. Ideally, your performance will lead you to first-line management in an operation unit, then on toward executive positions in financial or general management or increased professional staff responsibility.

Throughout your career, training will be largely on the job, enriched by formal classroom work within and outside the company. In fact, your training and education will never stop.

Looking Ahead with Financial Planning

A major entry-level area is financial planning—the development of basic financial strategies by which IBM runs its business. Financial planning is to IBM management what flowcharting is to the programmer. It establishes short-range projections of income and expense—the operating plan—and long-range strategic planning for the business environment.

IBM financial planning starts with determination of the goals and objectives of the business deliberately set at challenging but realistically attainable levels. Basic inputs are the following: customer requirements, competitive analysis, industry opportunity, technology trends, and available resources (both dollars and people). From goals and objectives, financial planners develop strategies for the business. This demands analysis of the company's current position and the availability of alternate strategies for the future.

In this area, you will work hand-in-hand with the IBM engineering, manufacturing, marketing, and general management communities to understand requirements, analyze IBM's and competitors' strengths and weaknesses, and realistically assess opportunities. You will interact closely with product planners; forecasters; and development, marketing, and service organizations. You may develop business models with desired returns, do portfolio analysis, or make investment decisions.

Aside from overall short- and long-term evaluations, your work can extend to specific IBM lines of business. Here the focus is on discrete markets and products, including the impact of competition. Developing, implementing, and controlling IBM financial plans calls for rigorous objectivity. Every recommendation must be judged by one basic criterion: Is this a sound business decision for IBM?

Financial planning at IBM helps convert goals to reality. Your experience in this area can make a real difference. You will develop creative ability, business judgment, and strong communications skills.

Accounting: The Language of the Business

A function of the office of the controller, accounting also offers a range of opportunities. State-of-the-art tools and technologies are used to collect, record, and report the company's economic transactions; the accountant's skills are used to interpret past business performance and to present recommendations for management decisions. The function is highly communications-oriented, with data consolidated from many sources for analysis and reporting in commonly understood terms.

Accounting fills many roles at IBM, from measurements and planning to government reporting and preparation of financial statements. Schedules are sensitive and demanding, logistics complex. The work demands teamwork and communication. You must accurately record financial results, comply with government regulations, and report earnings in a variety of ways. You must also ensure consistent presentation of accounting data and compliance with generally accepted accounting principles.

Accounting plays a vital, creative role in the management decision-making process at IBM. In an accounting position, you not only affect all basic operational areas—engineering, programming, marketing, administration—but also play a key role with IBM Treasury, international operations, and internal business partnership arrangements.

IBM also offers internal education to help you prepare for and take the Certified Management Accountant (CMA) exams. IBM is a corporate leader in the number of CMA certificates in its financial ranks.

IBM Pricing: Much More Than Finance

The pricing of IBM products and services is one of the most important responsibilities of the business. It is much more than finance—it is business itself. To ensure an adequate profit and return on investment, the pricing function must manage a product or service throughout its life, from conception to withdrawal from the market.

In simple terms, the role of pricing is to select IBM offerings and their prices to maximize the corporation's profitability. The major challenge is to ensure recovery of all costs and expenses, direct or indirect, associated with the development, manufacture, marketing, and maintenance of IBM products and services. In addition, IBM hardware, software, and service offerings must be understood within the context of a global marketplace where product strategies vary from country to country.

In fact, the pricing area is instrumental in initial selection of IBM products to be developed. Pricing analysts work side by side with the product management and marketing teams to ensure that new product offerings will meet the needs of IBM customers. The pricing function takes a financial and general management role in the decision about a program's financial viability and match to IBM's strategic objectives.

Pricing has an impact on all stages of a product's life. In the introduction stage, price selection, and terms and conditions involve detailed analysis of several areas: business area opportunity, product function, strategy, positioning, price elasticity, supply constraints, cost trends in technologies, manufacturing process, research and development strengths, marketing support plans, and selection of cost-effective distribution channels. The product must be positioned with respect to competition, with respect to the needs of the customer, and within IBM's product line.

Once introduced, a product is open to competitive moves: new products, price cuts, discounting, creative marketing, and promotional tactics. Pricing's responsibility is to anticipate these actions and prepare appropriate responses. During the growth stage of the product life cycle, the generation of sales is paramount. This often means that competitive bid situations, existing prices, terms, conditions, and methodologies are constantly subject to review and fine tuning.

If you work in this area, you will draw on the full repertoire of financial skills acquired in business school. You will coordinate the efforts of many groups, including product managers, market requirements specialists, business planning managers, and product forecasters. It is a unique opportunity for cross-disciplinary exposure within IBM and excellent experience in the IBM Finance career.

Treasury: Providing Capital for the Business
The IBM Treasury function is responsible for managing the company's capital structure and securing funds needed to operate the business. This demands reliable forecasting of cash receipts and disbursements, up-to-the-minute knowledge of international money markets, selection of funding vehicles, and maintenance of relationships with investment banking and commercial banking institutions.

In effect, Treasury is a focal point for the evaluation of a broad range of complex financial alternatives. IBM is concerned with worldwide liquidity, asset safety, currency man-

agement, tax optimization and compliance, risk/insurance management, optimal capital structure, investor perceptions, portfolio returns, and cost of capital.

The worldwide nature of IBM's business also requires techniques to protect the company from fluctuation in the value of foreign currencies. The ultimate objective is to optimize the use of cash, to keep any excess funds appropriately invested until needed, and to ensure access to funds when needed at the most favorable terms possible.

Other activities within the Treasury organization include internal audit, retirement fund management, short-term investment supervision, intercompany relations, and IBM's corporate citizenship programs.

Opportunities in the IBM Credit Corporation
Opportunities are also available for recent graduates in the IBM Credit Corporation, a wholly owned corporate subsidiary. By helping customers acquire IBM products and services through competitive financing offerings, IBM Credit plays a pivotal role in providing complete customer solutions.

IBM Credit provides leases and other financing products, remarketing services, end-of-lease options, and—for IBM Business Partners—inventory financing programs. It also provides IBM employees with financial services such as a money market account and mutual funds.

IBM Credit contributes significantly to the corporation's competitiveness and to the growth and stability of IBM earnings.

Since IBM Credit's products are financing offerings, financial professionals are involved in every stage of product development and delivery. These stages include the following:

- Development of new financial offerings that respond to customer requirements and competitive opportunities

- Assessments of credit risk and recovery of investment in high-risk situations

- Pricing of specific customer proposals for financing, including unique terms and conditions and competitive tactics

- Borrowing of debt funds via commercial paper, medium-term notes, and bond issues; relationships with investment-banking advisors

- Managing capital structure, including asset and liability matching and relations with the principal rating agencies

- Planning, accounting, and modeling financial performance, including publication of annual reports and supporting external financial communications

The Recruiting Process

Describe your recruiting process and the criteria by which you select candidates. Is prior experience necessary?

Within this environment, IBM Finance needs talented people with MBA degrees. The qualities sought are leadership, intelligence and awareness, interpersonal skills, creativity and ingenuity, energy, business maturity and judgment, integrity, personal enthusiasm, a goal-setting outlook, a desire to compete among the best—and the ability to be yourself.

The International Finance Corporation

1818 H Street, NW
Room I-2193
Washington, DC 20433
(202) 473-7972

MBA Recruiting Contact(s):
Cornelis de Kievit, Manager
Recruitment

Total Number of Professionals (U.S. and worldwide):
1,200

Company Description

Describe your firm's business and the types of clients served by your finance group(s).

The International Finance Corporation (IFC) seeks to carry out its mandate—helping developing nations achieve sustained economic growth—by supporting private sector development. It proves this support through three types of operations.

Project Financing

The most traditional of IFC's operations, project financing, is also the largest. IFC commits over $1 billion in new project financing yearly. IFC finances the creation of new companies, as well as the expansion or modernization of established companies in virtually all sectors, from agribusiness to manufacturing to energy and mining. A significant number of projects backed by IFC, intended to help developing countries build up their financial sectors, involve the creation of institutions such as investment banks and venture capital, insurance, and leasing companies, as well as other specialized enterprises. IFC also provides lines of credit to financial intermediary institutions for onlending to enterprises too small to be the object of a direct investment by IFC. The Africa Enterprise Fund (AEF) directly finances small and midsize projects in sub-Saharan Africa.

The type of financial package provided by IFC is tailored to project requirements—IFC can provide loans, equity and quasi-equity, and guarantees, or a combination of these. Loans are offered at commercial rates with maturities and terms that vary with the needs of client companies. IFC finances only projects unable to obtain adequate funding from other sources and typically limits its loan or investment to 25% of total project costs, as it seeks not to replace private investment but to catalyze it. IFC does not accept government guarantees; it shares project risks with its investment partners. Before going ahead with a project, IFC undertakes a thorough technical, financial, and economic appraisal to verify that the project is viable and likely to benefit the economy of the host country.

Mobilization of Finance

IFC mobilizes funds from other investors and lenders in a variety of ways. It actively seeks partners for joint ventures and raises additional finance for the projects in which it has invested, either by encouraging other institutions to make loans or equity investments in parallel to its own or by arranging syndicated loans for groups of commercial banks.

IFC also raises capital for companies in developing countries in the international financial markets by underwriting security offerings and by promoting vehicles for foreign portfolio investment such as country funds. IFC's in-house financial engineering expertise is applied to designing innovative financial products such as swaps, options, and convertible instruments to mobilize needed risk capital.

Advisory Services and Technical Assistance

Advisory services and technical assistance are frequently provided in the context of IFC's project-related activities. In the course of conducting project appraisals, for instance, IFC may provide technical assistance to project sponsors. IFC may also help in finding foreign partners, structuring transactions, and facilitating negotiations between foreign and domestic financiers and governments.

IFC provides advisory services to both government and corporate clients independently of project finance. IFC's Capital Markets Department advises member governments on the establishment of fiscal, legal, and regulatory frameworks that support the development of a market-oriented financial sector. IFC's Corporate Finance Services Department provides advice, often on a fee-earning basis, to private companies with heavy debt-servicing burdens on balance sheet restructuring, as well as to state-owned companies undergoing privatization. The Foreign Investment Advisory Service, operated jointly by IFC and the Multilateral Investment Guarantee Agency (MIGA), another member of the World Bank Group, advises member governments on policies, regulations, and institutions that can help them attract more foreign direct investment to priority sectors.

The Africa and Caribbean Project Development Facilities (APDF and CPDF), established in collaboration with the United Nations Development Programme (UNDP) and other donor organizations, provide technical assistance to entrepreneurs in regions seeking to develop bankable projects and obtain financing. IFC recently established a similar facility for the South Pacific (SPPF).

The Finance MBA's Job Description

Describe the career path and corresponding responsibilities for an MBA at your firm.

As an IFC staff member, you will be part of a team of highly qualified and motivated professionals from around the world seeking creative—and profitable—solutions to complex business problems. You will face the challenges and earn the satisfactions of helping to further economic progress in the developing world through private sector development. And you will be working for a unique institution: IFC has a businesslike approach to development and believes that development and profitability go hand in hand.

Each staff member's performance is reviewed annually. Opportunities to maintain and expand individual skills are provided through an in-house training program particularly in technical subjects, finance, communications, and office technology.

IFC's more than 1200 staff members come from about 70 different countries, including over 50 developing countries.

Discuss the lifestyle aspects of a career with your firm (i.e., average hours per week, amount of travel, flexibility to change offices, corporate culture, etc.).

Staff normally join IFC on regular appointments with no time limit, although appointments for a fixed term can also be arranged. The majority of staff are based in Washington, DC. Operational staff are likely to spend about one-fourth of their time on overseas travel.

The Recruiting Process

Describe your recruiting process and the criteria by which you select candidates. Is prior experience necessary?

In addition to outstanding academic and professional qualifications, IFC's work requires creativity, flexibility, and imagination. Staff members are expected to take initiative and make sound independent judgments. Tact and sensitivity are critical, as staff will be working with private and public sector officials from many countries, often in very different cultural settings. Fluency and the ability to write cogently in English are required, and working knowledge of another language, particularly French, Spanish, Portuguese, Arabic, or Chinese, is an added advantage. Computer literacy is highly desirable.

IFC recruits professional staff on an international basis. The selection process is very competitive. Many of the professionals recruited by IFC are already in mid-career. However, IFC also recruits directly from leading business schools around the world to fill the growing number of openings for investment and financial officers. Recruitment teams visit a number of schools each year to conduct on-campus interviews. IFC is interested in interviewing MBA candidates in their last year of school who have at least a few years of experience relevant to IFC's needs and requirements.

J.P. Morgan & Co. Incorporated

60 Wall Street
New York, NY 10260
(212) 483-2323

MBA Recruiting Contact(s):
Andrea Beldecos, Vice President
Investment Banking Recruiting

Hiromi Kishi, Vice President
Markets Recruiting

Susan J. Baisley, Vice President
Private Client Services Recruiting

Company Description

Describe your firm's business and the types of clients served by your finance group(s).

J.P. Morgan provides sophisticated financial services to corporations, governments, financial institutions, private firms, not-for-profit institutions, and wealthy individuals throughout the world. Our activities include advising on corporate financial structure; arranging financing in capital and credit markets; underwriting, trading, and investing in an array of currencies and the full range of securities and derivative instruments; serving as investment advisor; and providing select trust, agency, and operational services.

J.P. Morgan advises its clients on the financial implications of corporate strategy and executes transactions when appropriate. These transactions include mergers, acquisitions, divestitures, other forms of corporate restructurings, and privatizations. The firm's global presence and experience are increasingly important to our advisory business as the focus shifts to cross-border transactions.

The firm is an expert on raising money for clients through the full range of instruments—equity and debt underwriting, loan syndications, private placements, and others—in all world markets. We advise clients on their optimal capital structure and implement that advice through transactions in local capital markets or through global offerings.

Morgan is active in the highly liquid debt and equity markets of the established markets, as well as in the markets of the emerging economies. We are a leader and innovator in the derivative business.

All of Morgan's business activities are supported by a strong research capability. In some cases, dedicated research units support specific business areas, such as Taxable Credit Research, Markets Research, and Equity Research, which provides sell-side research as part of our U.S. equity sales and distribution function.

Morgan works within the context of a few long-standing and fundamental strategic strengths. We always put our clients' interests first. We take advantage of our deeply rooted and long-standing global network in approaching the needs of our clients. A team approach gives our clients the benefit of the breadth of our capabilities. We operate always with the belief that our reputation for fair dealing is our greatest asset, and we are committed to maintaining the highest standard of conduct.

Investment Banking

A matrix of client and product specialists forms the core of J.P. Morgan's investment banking business. Client specialists are responsible for understanding a client's overall business and financial strategy, as well as for developing an understanding of Morgan's full range of products and services. Product specialists develop expertise in a specific financial area. Investment banking professionals counsel clients on and execute the full range of restructuring transactions, including mergers, acquisition, divestitures, recapitalizations, and privatizations. As the leading international firm doing business in Latin America, Morgan provides advisory services to local governments and businesses. Morgan is extending its expertise to emerging markets elsewhere in the world, including Eastern Europe and the Asia Pacific region. J.P. Morgan offers a full range of financing options to its clients, including public and privately placed debt and equity securities, syndicated loans, and other credit products in all major world financial markets.

Markets

J.P. Morgan's markets businesses engage in sales and distribution, market making, proprietary risk taking, and investment on a global basis. Morgan has built a well-managed global network of trading locations, supported by decentralized research and a solid infrastructure of communications. The firm makes markets in 21 locations worldwide and takes positions in debt and equity securities, foreign currencies, derivative instruments, government bonds, and developing-country debt. Morgan traders manage risk, liquidity, and interest rate exposure. Morgan has become a strong market leader in the global derivatives business, including swaps, forwards, options and their derivatives, and equity and commodity derivatives, which we use to help clients manage risk as well as for our own account. The firm has focused on building a global sales capability. Sales professionals cover a portfolio of clients based on product/instrument or geography. Research plays a critical role in our markets-related activities, and our research professionals work closely with our traders, sales force, and clients.

Private Client Services
In our private client division, J.P. Morgan assists wealthy individuals make investment selections from among the increasingly complicated and often conflicting choices available in the market. Client managers work with clients to help them optimize their wealth by working through three closely related sets of issues. One is investment strategy: mapping out an overall allocation of assets and recommending specific investment vehicles geared to a client's appetite for risk and desire for involvement in day-to-day portfolio management decisions. Client managers also help clients unlock the full value of their assets by exchanging them for more liquid alternatives or by placing them in tax-advantaged structures that facilitate the transfer of wealth to philanthropic organizations and heirs. With wealth invested and structured, we provide vehicles that give clients control over the management of liquid assets to meet current needs. Morgan is a leader in this business, offering a full range of investment-related services, including portfolio management, securities brokerage, mutual funds, direct investments, fiduciary services, and liquidity management.

The Finance MBA's Job Description

Describe the career path and corresponding responsibilities for an MBA at your firm.

Business units within Investment Banking, Markets, and Private Client Services employ MBAs. Morgan professionals usually have the opportunity to work in various areas of the firm during the course of their career. This helps them better understand the needs of Morgan's clients and enables them to maximize the firm's abilities to meet these needs.

The first assignment for MBAs hired for Investment Banking is in Investment Banking Services (IBS), a group of professionals who work with client and product teams in the marketing, structuring, and execution of financing and advisory assignments. New associates will be assigned on a rotation to a specific business area. The IBS assignment is followed by an assignment to one of a number of areas such as clients, mergers and acquisitions, and debt or equity capital markets. An MBA associate's career will continue to evolve as the individual develops a broad and solid base of knowledge and experience. The

direction of the evolution will be the result of several factors, including an individual's skills and interests as well as the needs of the firm. Some individuals may have the opportunity to experience an assignment in one of our international offices.

MBAs hired for Markets will begin their careers in the positions for which they were hired in one of our Markets areas. Careers in Markets are flexible, and, after gaining some hands-on experience, an individual may have the opportunity to transfer his or her skills to a new market or product.

Private Client Services hires MBAs for positions in domestic and international client management and in security sales. Client managers are the primary business developers and are responsible for the overall client investment relationship with the firm. Security sales people work with clients to provide markets research and advice and to execute their brokerage needs. Individuals hired by our Private Client Services group attend our six-month training program and, upon completion, begin working with clients immediately.

The Recruiting Process

Describe your recruiting process and the criteria by which you select candidates. Is prior experience necessary?

Morgan seeks outstanding, creative, analytical, and committed individuals who work well with others and who are willing to assume responsibility. The firm offers hard-working individuals the opportunity to make a significant contribution quickly. Morgan operates with a team approach, which promotes an open discussion of ideas and enables its professionals to learn about parts of Morgan's business outside their own. Members of the firm stress dealing honorably and responsibly with others to maintain the firm's high-quality work environment and high standard of integrity.

J.P. Morgan's Investment Banking, Markets, and Private Client Services groups conduct on-campus interviews for full-time and summer positions. Prior experience in the financial services industry is not required or expected for employment. Foreign language skills are considered an asset but are not a requirement.

How many permanent associates and analysts do you hire in a typical year? How many summer interns do you expect to hire? If you have a formal summer program, please describe it. Please be sure to indicate whether the summer program is in place for all offices or just some.

Summer Intern Program

J.P. Morgan's extensive program for MBA students during the summer between their first and second years of business school provides a broad exposure to the firm and its businesses. Summer associates are hired for a general area, based on interests, skills, and past experience, as well as the needs of the firm. Summer associates have the opportunity to learn about other areas through presentations by Morgan managers and are briefed by senior managers on the firm's business strategy and management philosophy. We also encourage summer associates to take the time to meet with officers throughout the firm to identify areas for further exploration. Candidates for the summer associate program should have a serious interest in finance and the financial markets. Most positions are in New York, though opportunities to work abroad may exist for students with the right to work in other jurisdictions. Positions last 10 to 12 weeks and are scheduled between mid-May and mid-September.

What international opportunities does your firm offer for U.S. citizens? For foreign nationals?

J.P. Morgan recruits MBAs primarily for positions in New York. The firm also hires MBA students with the right to work overseas for positions in Morgan's offices in Asia, Europe, and Latin America.

James D. Wolfensohn Incorporated

599 Lexington Avenue
New York, NY 10022
(212) 909-8100
Fax: (212) 909-8161

MBA Recruiting Contact(s):
Rhonda Johnson, Recruiting Administrator

Company Description

Describe your firm's business and the types of clients served by your finance group(s).

James D. Wolfensohn Incorporated (Wolfensohn) provides personalized financial advisory and investment banking services on a global basis to international industrial corporations and financial institutions in the following areas:

- Mergers, acquisitions, divestitures, and strategic alliances;

- Corporate share value and asset optimization; and

- Corporation reorganizations, workouts and bankruptcy.

Wolfensohn ranks among the top investment banks as measured by the value of the transactions in which it has acted as financial advisor to its clients. These transactions have included several highly visible, important transactions such as the acquisition of Capital Cities/ABC by The Walt Disney Company; the sale of U.S. Shoe Corporation to Luxottica; the sale of Labatt to Interbrew; the buyback of Seagram's stake in Du Pont; the acquisition of Midland Bank by the Hongkong and Shanghai Bank; the purchase by NCNB, now NationsBank, of C&S Sovran and MNC Financial Inc.; the purchase of the Boston Globe by The New York Times Company; the merger of Cyprus Minerals and Amax Inc.; and significant corporate spin-offs by American Express, Baxter International, Marriott Corporation, and Amax Inc. In addition, the firm has been involved in the financial restructuring of Olympia & York and the GPA Group plc.

Wolfensohn provides its services in the context of broad, long-term relationships with its clients. Wolfensohn believes that it can be much more effective on behalf of its clients when it works on a long-term strategic basis rather than on a transaction-by-transaction basis. The firm often participates in the development of its clients' finan-cial strategy, providing transaction-related advisory services in the context of these strategic objectives.

Wolfensohn acts exclusively as a strategic and financial advisor. The firm does not underwrite securities, issue debt, take equity stakes, or engage in activities that could lead to a conflict with its clients' best interests. This approach ensures a level of objectivity and confidentiality unsurpassed on Wall Street.

Wolfensohn was founded in 1981 by James D. Wolfensohn, who served as the firm's president and chief executive officer until his appointment as president of the World Bank in June 1995. Wolfensohn employs today over 50 bankers (12 partners and approximately 20 associates and 20 analysts) with varied backgrounds in corporate finance, mergers, acquisitions, reorganizations and restructurings. Paul A. Volcker, who joined the firm as its chairman in 1988 when he retired as chairman of the Federal Reserve Board, is now chief executive officer of Wolfensohn.

The Latin American and Iberian Group
In January 1994, Wolfensohn launched an effort to focus on mergers, acquisitions and financial advisory opportunities in Latin America and Spain. The firm now has nine professionals dedicated to developing the effort. Wolfensohn recently represented Cemex, S.A. in its acquisition of a controlling interest in Vencemos, S.A.C.A., and represented John Labatt Ltd. in its acquisition of a 22% stake in FEMSA Cerveza. The Latin American group delivers the full range of Wolfensohn's services and resources to some of the region's largest multinational industrial groups.

International Joint Ventures
Several joint ventures abroad, coupled with an international network of senior relationships and execution capabilities in New York, allow Wolfensohn to provide its clients with in-depth global and local expertise.

Fuji-Wolfensohn International
Fuji-Wolfensohn International advises retainer clients on strategic and transaction matters with a focus exclusively on Japan-U.S. transactions. Fuji-Wolfensohn International enjoys calling upon the full range of expertise provided by both Wolfensohn and Fuji Bank.

J Rothschild, Wolfensohn & Co.
In March of 1992, Wolfensohn formed J Rothschild, Wolfensohn & Co. in London, a joint venture with St. James's Place Capital, the investment holding company for the J Rothschild group. The largest shareholder of St. James's Place Capital is Lord Rothschild, one of the world's eminent financiers. J Rothschild, Wolfensohn & Co. provides corporate advisory and investment banking services throughout Europe.

Russian-American Investment Bank

J Rothschild, Wolfensohn & Co. is a partner, along with American International Group (AIG), Chemical Bank, Smith Barney, and various Russian investors, in a new investment bank in the Russian Federation. The bank's mission is to assist local enterprises in restructuring Russian industry.

Describe your ownership structure.

Wolfensohn has opted to remain private and small in order to work only with those clients who share its business philosophy, interests, and vision. Its private status permits Wolfensohn to forego transactions that are not in the client's best interest, as the firm's judgment is not influenced by public reporting pressures.

How does your approach to finance differ from that of other firms, and what do you consider to be your strengths and distinctive capabilities?

To accomplish its mission, Wolfensohn's advisory practice was oriented such that the client would always come first:

- **Congruent client/advisor interest:** Wolfensohn does not provide capital or compete with its clients for principal investments, thus ensuring that its clients' interests and the firm's interests are always one and the same.

- **Advisory excellence:** Wolfensohn secures a small number of high-quality professionals to provide experienced advice based on an analytical approach, taking into account long-term strategic and operating considerations, and not exclusively near-term market trends.

- **Personalized approach:** Wolfensohn provides consistent senior-level participation to all clients, regardless of size, throughout a project and not merely in the selling/closing stages. Wolfensohn believes in long-term partner/client teamwork and the same rigorous attention to every client.

- **Long-term relationship culture:** Wolfensohn devotes the time and analysis necessary to get to know its clients as well as they know themselves, so that its contributions can truly generate value and minimize risk. Being consistently alert to competitive, regulatory, and market conditions allows Wolfensohn to anticipate risk and uncover value-enhancing opportunities.

The Finance MBA's Job Description

Describe the career path and corresponding responsibilities for an MBA at your firm.

Given Wolfensohn's size and structure, associates can assume significant levels of responsibility early in their careers. During the first years, an associate works as a member of several client teams engaged in specific transactions or analyses. Each client team typically consists of the partner responsible for the client, a senior associate (typically with over five years of experience), an associate (typically with one to five years of experience) and an analyst. As associates gain experience, they take on greater responsibilities within the team, as well as additional client responsibilities. Wolfensohn's philosophy is to develop its bankers as generalists. Associates are therefore given the opportunity to work on assignments across a range of clients and industries in order to gain experience on the strategic and financial issues facing corporations.

Successful associates at Wolfensohn possess a balance of sound analytical abilities and the potential to develop strong client and transaction skills. Due to the size and culture of Wolfensohn, its bankers work closely with each other. It is therefore critical for new associates to enjoy working in an extremely interactive and tightly-knit environment.

Wolfensohn's basic approach is on-the-job training for associates. However, new associates are also provided with a two-week orientation and training program upon their joining the firm.

The Recruiting Process

Describe your recruiting process and the criteria by which you select candidates. Is prior experience necessary?

Wolfensohn's philosophy is to concentrate hiring at the entry level, seeking each year to attract a small number of MBA candidates with the highest academic standing and greatest potential to become outstanding professionals. New associates come from a variety of education, cultural, and geographic backgrounds. However, given Wolfensohn's focus on investment banking and advisory services, most entering associates typically have some previous experience in corporate finance or M&A.

How many permanent associates and analysts do you hire in a typical year? How many summer interns do you expect to hire? If you have a formal summer program, please describe it. Please be sure to indicate whether the summer program is in place for all offices or just some.

Wolfensohn's advisory business has grown at a significant rate over the past several years, and the firm has actively recruited three to five new associates.

Wolfensohn plans to hire three to five summer associates each year and considers the summer program a critical component of its full-time recruiting process.

Lehman Brothers

Three World Financial Center
New York, NY 10285
(212) 526-2000

MBA Recruiting Contact(s):
Rita Haring
Investment Banking
(212) 526-4162

Sarah Seaman
Sales, Trading & Research
(212) 526-4895

Company Description

Describe your firm's business and the types of clients served by your finance group(s).

Lehman Brothers' is one of Wall Street's premier investment banks, serving the needs of corporations, institutions, governments, and high-net-worth individuals in the United States and throughout the rest of the world. Lehman Brothers' business lines include investment, fixed income, equities, commodities and foreign exchange (as well as derivatives of these products), and private client services.

Lehman Brothers has major operating centers in New York, London, and Tokyo, and over 35 additional offices worldwide.

Describe your ownership structure.

Lehman Brothers has been a publicly traded company since May 31, 1994, when it was spun off from American Express. As of the end of 1994, 10% of Lehman Brothers common stock was employee owned.

How does your approach to finance differ from that of other firms, and what do you consider to be your strengths and distinctive capabilities?

Lehman Brothers' goal is to build upon the firm's 145-year history of success and to be a leader in all the markets and businesses in which it participates. We will achieve this goal by having the right people in our organization and by adhering to clearly defined objectives and our stated values.

These values are grouped around four major themes:

1. acting as one firm,

2. characterized by teamwork,

3. with effective and flexible leadership and management,

4. making the firm a world class organization known for its global presence, profitability, client service, integrity, and superior people.

Lehman Brothers' approach is to work in concert with clients, integrating our efforts with theirs to provide superior service across the investment banking and capital markets businesses. The firm has a long, well-earned reputation for serving its clients and for the professionalism and creativity of its employees. We are continually striving to improve our ability to work as a team, to heighten awareness of client needs, and to deliver still higher levels of service excellence.

Building relationships with clients is the foundation of Lehman Brothers' business philosophy. Toward this end, the firm organizes investment bankers by industry group to enable them to develop expertise in a specific industry, and thus understand and anticipate client's needs.

The contributions of our people are critical. We maintain a professional atmosphere that fosters cooperation rather than competition without stifling individuality. We place a strong emphasis on teamwork and on leveraging one another's skills, while encouraging each individual's unique creativity and entrepreneurial spirit.

Discuss changes in your firm's revenues (both domestic and international) and professional staff over the past year; over the past five years.

Lehman Brothers' net revenues for the eleven month reporting period ended November 30, 1994, totaled $2.7 billion. Net operating income, excluding special charges related to severance, expenses for the spin-off from American Express, and a change in accounting principle, was $156 million. Net income after these charges totaled $113 million.

Despite the challenging market environment in 1994, Lehman Brothers strengthened its franchise and market position. This is evident in the various industry rankings achieved during the year:

- Lehman Brothers was the number two ranked underwriter for lead-managed debt and equity offerings in the United States and the number three ranked lead manager for offerings worldwide.[1]

- Lehman Brothers lead managed $84.1 billion of fixed income securities globally in 1994, ranking third among underwriters.[1]

- Lehman Brothers lead-managed $5.8 billion of common stock and convertible securities worldwide in 1994, ranking fifth among underwriters.[1]

---

1. Source: Securities Data Company.

- In 1994, Lehman Brothers acted as advisor on 115 completed mergers and acquisition transactions, ranking fourth by number of transactions and sixth by dollar volume among investment banks. Thirty-five of these transactions were cross-border.

- Lehman Brothers is a leader in origination, distribution, and trading of municipal securities. In 1994, the firm lead-managed $17.8 billion in long- and short-term municipal securities, ranking third among competitors with an 8.8% market share.

- Lehman Brothers continued to grow some of its high margin businesses such as derivatives, assisting approximately 1,300 clients and customers worldwide in over 7,500 fixed income derivatives transactions in 1994.

- Lehman Brothers was awarded 21 positions on *Institutional Investor*'s 1994 All-America Research Team, ranking first for the third year in a row.

Over the past years Lehman Brothers has pursued a strategy of growing revenues and profitability outside the United States. Under this strategy, net revenues derived from international sources increased in 1994 to more than $1.1 billion, accounting for 42% of total net revenues. During 1994, the firm significantly strengthened its position in its targeted European and Asian markets. Lehman Brothers became a reporting dealer, or CVT, in France and a primary dealer in Italy. The firm opened new offices in Beijing and Tel Aviv, expanded the scope of its operations in Singapore, and received regulatory approvals or banking licenses to expand its operations in various international locations.

The Finance MBA's Job Description

Describe the career path and corresponding responsibilities for an MBA at your firm.

Lehman Brothers prides itself on the variety of backgrounds and range of achievements represented by its professionals. Before joining the firm, many Lehman Brothers professionals had careers in areas such as law, medicine, public service, and private industry, as well as in finance. This diversity instills creativity in and provides depth to the firm.

Lehman Brothers is committed to developing well-rounded professionals and encourages associates to take on as much responsibility as they can handle. Each associate is given the opportunity to build a broad base of

skills, and the firm constantly monitors each associate's development, working with him or her to help achieve specific career goals.

All Investment Banking, and Sales, Trading & Research associates begin their career at Lehman Brothers participating in a "One Firm" training program that introduces you to Lehman Brothers, its clients, products and services. Classroom training during the first two months enables you to hone your skills in finance and accounting and to develop the analytical tools they will use throughout their careers. Specific training is also provided in fixed income, equity, foreign exchange, commodities and derivative products. In addition, you will share in team-building activities and social events. This strategy helps build internal networks and working relationships among professionals throughout the organization.

Following the training program, Investment Banking associates rotate through various industry coverage and product specialty groups. During the rotation, you will gain exposure to several groups within Investment Banking and are able to apply the analytical tools developed during the training program. The rotation is followed by a six-month assignment in a specific group. The associates may then choose to continue with the same group or move into another area. International associates benefit from the same training and rotation as U.S. associates. At the end of this 18-month period in Lehman Brothers' New York headquarters, the international associates begin their permanent assignments in Lehman Brothers' international offices.

Associates for Sales, Trading & Research move from the training program into a two-month generalist rotation. There you will be exposed to a variety of product areas before joining a specific business. High Net Worth Sales associates also benefit from the generalist rotation, prior to joining Private Client Services. International Sales, Trading & Research associates also begin their careers in Lehman Brothers' New York headquarters. Following classroom training, associates complete a rotation through various product areas. This rotation may take place in New York, the international offices, or both, and provides associates with an overview of the product areas.

After completing the training program, Public Finance associates serve as generalists during their entire first year, working with a variety of municipal clients. Associates then join either a specialty group, such as Housing, Education, or Health Care, or a regional group covering a geographically defined area of the United States.

The Recruiting Process

Describe your recruiting process and the criteria by which you select candidates. Is prior experience necessary?

In our recruiting efforts we look for individuals who possess a keen intellect, a powerful desire to succeed, and the resourcefulness to produce results. Because of the emphasis on teamwork, we also want people who can cooperate and leverage one another's skills while encouraging each individual's unique creativity and entrepreneurial spirit.

How many summer interns do you expect to hire? If you have a formal summer program, please describe it. Please be sure to indicate whether the summer program is in place for all offices or just some.

Lehman Brothers' Summer Associate Program provides students at the midpoint of their graduate school educa-tion an opportunity to evaluate the working environment and career opportunities at the firm.

Investment Banking and Public Finance summer associates work as full members of client teams on a variety of transactions. They also enjoy extensive contact with Lehman Brothers professionals at all levels through discussion groups, seminars, and informal social functions.

Sales and Trading summer associates are assigned to a 10-week placement in an individual business unit, although they spend one day of each week in different product areas, covering a variety of businesses over the course of the summer. In addition, they attend lectures by senior professionals and participate in weekly market update sessions.

Merrill Lynch & Co., Inc.

World Financial Center
250 Vesey Street
New York, NY 10281-1331
(212) 449-8790

MBA Recruiting Contact(s):
Roslyn N. Dickerson, Vice President & Manager
Corporate & Institutional Client Group Recruiting

Company Description

Describe your firm's business and the types of clients served.

Merrill Lynch is a global investment banking firm, headquartered in New York with a presence in 35 countries worldwide. It is the leading underwriting and brokerage firm in the United States.

Merrill Lynch acts as principal, agent, underwriter, market maker, broker, and financial advisor to its clients. The firm is fundamentally client driven, bringing together issuers and investors.

Our institutional businesses—Investment Banking, Institutional Investment Management Services, Institutional Client, Debt Markets, Capital Markets, Municipal Markets, and Equity Markets—offer an expansive range of services to 6,000 corporate, institutional, and governmental clients worldwide. These groups are based in New York with major offices in London, Tokyo, and Hong Kong and representation in other major financial centers. Our individual investor business—Private Client—provides investment, banking, credit, money management, and insurance products and services to 7 million individuals and small businesses worldwide. These groups are headquartered in Princeton, NJ.

In a little over a decade, the firm has built a premier institutional franchise with clients on a worldwide basis. Since 1988, Merrill Lynch has been the leading global underwriter of debt and equity securities. Two major trends are creating new opportunities for the firm globally: the spread of capitalism and an increasing variety of financing alternatives. In Latin America, Eastern Europe, and Asia-Pacific, we expect growth to outpace that of more developed regions.

Describe your ownership structure.

Merrill Lynch & Co. is a publicly owned corporation, trading on the principal stock exchanges in New York, London, Toronto, Paris, and Tokyo. Stockholders' equity at December 25, 1994, totaled $5.8 billion, with 181 million shares outstanding.

Merrill Lynch was the first member firm of the New York Stock Exchange to go public in June 1971, and a month later it became the first member firm whose own stock was traded on the Big Board. Previously it had been a partnership.

How does your approach to finance differ from that of other firms, and what do you consider to be your strengths and distinctive capabilities?

The strength of our organization is based on leadership in both the institutional and retail sectors. Merrill Lynch's ability to capitalize on the synergy that exists between these sectors—specifically, a strong distribution function complementing an origination and trading capability—distinguishes its strategy from that of its competitors. With the largest distribution capabilities on Wall Street and an integrated global network, the firm has the unique ability to place deals and facilitate transactions worldwide.

Discuss changes in your firm's revenues (both domestic and international) and professional staff over the past five years.

1994 was the second most profitable year in Merrill Lynch history. Net earnings to common shareholders were $1.02 billion, our second consecutive year of billion-dollar profits. Shareholders' equity rose to $5.8 billion. The firm's return on average common equity was 18.6%. The firm employs 43,800 people worldwide.

The Finance MBA's Job Description

Describe the career path and corresponding responsibilities for an MBA at your firm.

Merrill Lynch invests substantial resources in identifying and recruiting superior candidates. In the graduating class of 1995, the firm hired 129 MBAs: 61 in Investment Banking, 35 in Debt Markets, 19 in Institutional Client, 6 in Equity Markets, 5 in Municipal Markets, and 3 in Securities Research.

The following businesses recruit the most MBAs:

- Investment Banking is responsible for corporate and institutional client relationships worldwide. Through the delivery of advisory services and financial products, the division focuses on the needs of issuer clients.

Included in this division are mergers and acquisitions, leveraged buyout fund management, real estate, project financing, relationship management, and several specialty functions.

- Debt Markets offers issuing and investing clients a complete array of debt financing alternatives in short-, medium-, and long-term debt products. The division is integrated vertically to include origination, trading, fixed income, marketing, research, and new product development. Major product areas are money markets, global debt financing, mortgage capital, financial futures and options, U.S. governments and agencies, foreign exchange, and municipal markets.

- Equity Markets is structured to provide institutional investor clients with origination, trading, syndication, and wholesale services worldwide. The division also works with investment banking in serving corporate and government issuers.

- Municipal Markets encompasses all activities related to the origination, pricing, sales, and trading of tax-exempt debt instruments. These include fixed rate bonds and notes, commercial paper and other variable rate products, interest rate swaps, hedges, and embedded derivative products.

- Capital Markets has primary responsibilities in product origination in coordination with Investment Banking; and product innovation and marketing in coordination with Debt and Equity Markets as well as Institutional Client.

- Institutional Client includes a network of teams specializing in selling or trading a specific fixed income or equity product. This business unit serves institutional accounts worldwide.

Career paths and corresponding responsibilities vary depending on the business division. An MBA joining Investment Banking, for example, typically enters as an associate, responsible for the details of executing transactions and preparing proposals. After approximately four years, associates are eligible for promotion to vice president. Vice presidents manage the execution of transactions and identify new opportunities with clients. About three years later, vice presidents become eligible for promotion to director, or the more senior title of managing director. Directors and managing directors are responsible for maintenance of client relationships and identification of new business opportunities.

New associates generally join the firm in early August and complete a five-week firmwide development program. Besides serving as an orientation to Merrill Lynch, the program builds strong ties among the participants.

The academic component includes team assignments, case studies, simulations, and hands-on interaction with trading games.

Describe the opportunities for professional mobility between the various departments in your firm.

New associates work in a specific department, though they have much contact throughout the firm. As their interests change and as our businesses evolve, new opportunities are often available firmwide.

Discuss the lifestyle aspects of a career with your firm (i.e., average hours per week, amount of travel, flexibility to change offices, corporate culture, etc.).

Lifestyles vary depending on which business unit an MBA joins. Requirements for each division are typical for the financial services industry.

The Recruiting Process

Describe your recruiting process and the criteria by which you select candidates. Is prior experience necessary?

Merrill Lynch participates in on-campus presentations and events and on-campus interviews. Successful candidates are called back for final interviews in New York.

We seek individuals with a record of achievement and excellence. Successful candidates have strong analytical skills and an understanding of strategic issues. They communicate effectively, think creatively, work well with others, and act decisively. Academic performance and prior work experience are also important criteria, though prior work in the industry is not necessary.

How many permanent associates and analysts do you hire in a typical year? How many summer interns do you expect to hire? If you have a formal summer program, please describe it. Please be sure to indicate whether the summer program is in place for all offices or just some.

Hiring is based on the needs of each business division, and recruiting goals are set early in the fall for the coming recruiting season. In 1995, we hired 129 MBAs.

Most business divisions of the firm participate in the summer associate program. Summer associates have significant responsibilities and are involved with a variety of transactions. Scheduled activities and seminars with senior management offer summer associates frequent exposure and the opportunity to expand their knowledge of the firm. In 1995, 122 summer associates were hired across the firm.

Montgomery Securities

600 Montgomery Street
San Francisco, CA 94111
(415) 627-2000

MBA Recruiting Contact(s):
Sharon Henning, Vice President
(415) 627-2793

Company Description

Describe your firm's business and the types of clients served by your finance group(s).

Montgomery Securities is a San Francisco–based investment bank with a national and international presence. Privately held, Montgomery Securities is the nation's premier equity-focused broker/dealer specializing in emerging-growth companies. In 1992, the firm managed over $9 billion in public and private offerings and merger and acquisition transactions and traded over 1.6 billion shares on the listed and over-the-counter markets, ranking sixteenth. Montgomery's investment banking activities are conducted through four departments: Corporate Finance, which includes underwritings, mergers and acquisitions, and private placements; Research; Sales; and Trading. In addition, Montgomery's investment management business, with assets of over $3 billion, manages a family of mutual funds and handles the money management needs of corporations and high-net-worth individuals. In 1993, the firm established a fixed income effort, which will focus on private placement and public debt financings for its growing client base.

The activities of each of the firm's departments are closely coordinated and are focused on four industries: technology, consumer, health care, and financial services. Montgomery's investment banking clients consist of emerging- and established-growth companies located throughout the United States. The firm's institutional brokerage clients include over 1,100 institutions worldwide. A description of the firm's departments follows.

Corporate Finance
The Corporate Finance Department initiates, develops, and maintains relationships with the premier emerging-growth companies in each of the industry groups Montgomery focuses on. Corporate finance professionals have extensive experience in analyzing and identifying a company's financing requirements and in executing transactions, including public and private equity offerings, merg-

ers and acquisitions, and public and private debt. The department is staffed with over 60 professionals whose skills combine specific industry experience and investment banking expertise. The department is organized along industry lines to take advantage of the firm's research and trading strengths in technology, consumer services, health care, and financial services.

Research Department
The foundation for Montgomery's success in serving both its corporate finance clients and its institutional brokerage customers is its strong Research Department. The department is staffed with over 40 senior analysts and analyst associates whose skills combine industry-specific focus and expertise covering large and small capitalization companies. Montgomery covers 350 companies, including 190 noninvestment banking clients. The department is organized along industry groups—technology, consumer services, health care, and financial services—and its primary goal is superior performance for Montgomery clients.

Sales Department
Montgomery Securities' effectiveness as an underwriter owes much to the strength and reputation of its Institutional Sales Department. This reputation has been built over two decades through relationships with clients that are based on trust, knowledge of the markets, past money-making performance, and superior service. Montgomery's institutional sales force covers more than 1,100 domestic and international institutions.

In 1992, the Private Client Department of Montgomery Securities was established in keeping with the corporate philosophy of providing focused attention to an exclusive universe of clients. Just as our firm has focused on the largest and most influential financial institutions and the most substantial and fastest growing corporations, Montgomery Securities has now built a private investor business based on exclusively servicing the investment needs of wealthy individuals and their families.

Trading Department
The Trading Department, one of the largest outside New York, complements and enhances the Corporate Finance, Research, and Sales Departments. Montgomery is a major market maker in common stocks traded in the over-the-counter market. In addition, Montgomery is very active in the trading of blocks of common stock of companies listed on the New York Stock Exchange and other national securities exchanges. Our trading focus is in the stocks of companies that are actively covered by the

78

Research Department. These activities provide the after-market trading support that is essential in ensuring a successful public offering and maintaining an efficient market for a company's stock.

Fixed Income Department

As the firm's client base continued to expand and its clients continued to grow, Montgomery made a strategic decision to enter the fixed income market in 1993. It is the intention of the firm to develop highly competitive private and public debt financing capabilities. The group is initially focusing on public and private new issues.

Describe your ownership structure.

Montgomery Securities is a privately held general partnership.

How does your approach to finance differ from that of other firms, and what do you consider to be your strengths and distinctive capabilities?

Montgomery Securities differentiates itself through an integrated, focused approach that offers selected investment banking services to emerging- and established-growth companies. The firm's investment banking relationships, quality research, and trading capabilities, coupled with an industry-focused orientation, allow Montgomery professionals to become experts in specific sectors. The close communication among the firm's corporate finance personnel, research analysts, and sales force gives Montgomery a unique ability to communicate a client company's story to institutional investors effectively and to distribute that company's securities efficiently. This is made possible by Montgomery's small size and single location, together with the firm's acknowledged expertise in the companies and industries it follows. Montgomery's after-market support for its corporate finance clients, including ongoing research coverage, institutional road shows, investment conferences, corporate finance advice, and trading of the clients' stock, is superior and again reflects Montgomery's focused approach, close communications, and industry expertise. This focused market strategy differentiates Montgomery from the larger New York–based investment banks and is the primary reason for Montgomery's tremendous growth and profitability in its 24-year history.

The Finance MBA's Job Description

Describe the career path and corresponding responsibilities for an MBA at your firm.

In the Corporate Finance Department, an MBA begins her or his career as a generalist associate before specializing in one of Montgomery's four business sectors. Montgomery's client teams are traditionally lean, so an associate is ensured significant client contact and responsibility from the beginning. An associate's responsibilities focus primarily on analyzing, structuring, and executing transactions, as well as assisting in new business development. The levels above associate are (in order) vice president, principal, and managing director (partner). Advancement and success are contingent on personal performance. As an individual advances, that individual's responsibilities for clients and new business development increase.

Upon the completion of a comprehensive training program in the Private Client Department, associates help facilitate long-term investment relationships with wealthy individuals and family groups. Interacting closely with the research and trading departments, associates will provide a portfolio approach for private clients' investment needs. Associates will be trained as product generalists, knowledgeable in all markets and supported by a network of specialists in each. The Associate Program offers individuals a unique entrepreneurial experience with compensation tied directly to one's efforts.

In the Research Department, entry-level associates are assigned to work directly with research analysts and may come in on many different levels, depending on prior knowledge and experience. Working with the analyst, the associate develops her or his expertise researching industries and analyzing companies, with the goal of being promoted to an analyst with a specific industry and company focus.

Entry-level MBAs joining the Trading Department begin their career at Montgomery as junior traders with the goal of being promoted to a senior trader with their own group of stocks.

Discuss the lifestyle aspects of a career with your firm (i.e., average hours per week, amount of travel, flexibility to change offices, corporate culture, etc.).

A career in investment banking at Montgomery is exciting and rewarding and requires a significant commitment of time and energy. The hours can be long and the travel extensive. Montgomery is, however, located in San Francisco, and this location reflects a commitment to a lifestyle outside the office. The hours worked and the extent of travel vary depending on an individual's workload.

The Recruiting Process

Describe your recruiting process and the criteria by which you select candidates. Is prior experience necessary?

Because of its size and corporate philosophy, Montgomery offers an unstructured investment banking environment. Montgomery is seeking bright, hard-working, personable candidates who are self-motivated. Strong analytical and communication skills, as well as creativity and initiative, are important. Prior investment banking experience is definitely helpful but not always necessary. Advancement and success are contingent upon personal performance.

How many permanent associates and analysts do you hire in a typical year? How many summer interns do you expect to hire? If you have a formal summer program, please describe it. Please be sure to indicate whether the summer program is in place for all offices or just some.

The firm expects to hire 15–20 entry-level MBAs. Montgomery does not offer a summer program for MBAs.

Morgan Stanley Group Inc.

1251 Avenue of the Americas
New York, NY 10020
(212) 703-4000

(Note: In late 1995, the Firm will relocate its corporate headquarters and many of its operations to 1585 Broadway, New York, NY 10036-8239.)

MBA Recruiting Contact(s):
Marilyn Booker, Vice President
Firmwide Coordination

Erik Olsen, Associate
Corporate Treasury

Pam Carlton, Principal
Equity Research

Katherine Blackmon, Recruiting Manager
Equity Sales And Trading

Megan Pelino, Recruiting Manager
Fixed Income Sales and Trading and Research
/Public Finance/Foreign Exchange/Commodities

Pat Palumbo, Recruiting Manager
Investment Banking

Angela McNelis, Recruiting Manager
Private Client Services

Locations of Offices:
34 offices in 18 different countries
13 in the United States

Total Number of Professionals (U.S. and worldwide):
9,454 worldwide

Company Description

Describe your firm's business and the types of clients served by your finance group(s).

Morgan Stanley Group Inc. is a global firm providing a wide range of financial services to corporations, governments, financial institutions, and individual investors. Our businesses include securities underwriting, distribution, and trading; merger, acquisition, restructuring, real estate, project finance, and other corporate finance advisory activities; merchant banking and other principal investment activities; brokerage and research services; asset management; trading foreign exchange, commodities,

and structured financial products on a broad range of asset categories; and global custody, securities clearance services, and securities lending.

Morgan Stanley's finance groups provide the following services to our clients:

Corporate Treasury
Corporate Treasury manages the firm's financial resources on a global basis, coordinating its activities among offices in New York, London, Tokyo, and Hong Kong. Corporate Treasury associates are initially placed in one of eight areas: Bank and Creditor Relations, Capital Planning, Cash Management, Finance and Asset Liability Management, Foreign Exchange Exposure Management, Investor Relations, Risk and Insurance Management, or Short-Term Funding. Initial assignments are followed by one- to two-year rotations through areas of the department and might include the opportunity to work in another office. Associates work directly with senior management on high-profile assignments and gain invaluable experience in all areas of finance, from strategic finance to trading analytics. Associates work with people in all areas of the firm, enjoying the dynamic environment and applying the firm's resources for its own benefit.

Equity Research
Equity Research provides timely, high-quality, in-depth analysis to enhance the performance of Morgan Stanley's clients' global portfolios. Using economic, market, industry, and company studies, equity research analysts, economists, and strategists strive to anticipate developments that will affect security values worldwide. New research analysts are assigned to a specific industry at the very outset. Our program is designed to develop proficiency in one to two years, with the ultimate goal of our analysts becoming recognized as experts in their respective industries. Equity Research professionals analyze company financial data, industry trends and macroeconomics factors; forecast earnings and stock prices; write research reports and updates on companies and industries, and make independent buy and sell recommendations. Research analysts work closely with equity salespeople and traders, investment banking professionals, clients, and institutional investors.

Equity Sales and Trading
The Equity Division provides Morgan Stanley clients with global distribution capabilities, liquidity, and a high level of trading expertise in all major world markets. It also offers sophisticated analytics and ready access to a broad range of equity products and issues. Associates in Equity Sales and Trading are involved in the worldwide

selling and trading of equity and equity derivative securities. After a three-month training program conducted in New York, associates immediately go to work on their assigned desk covering either the traditional stock business, equity derivatives, or convertible securities. New associates are assigned their own accounts and act as backup to some of our major accounts; they also have the opportunity to work with many different investors, products, and areas of the firm.

The Equity Division consists of three major areas:

Core Equity. Core Equity consists of the traditional stock business and encompasses the sales and trading of equity securities around the world. Customers include banks, insurance companies, private pension funds, mutual funds, investment advisors, endowments, foundations, and hedge funds. There are two main sources of revenue: sales of primary and secondary offerings and trading commissions (which customers pay in return for liquidity, the firm's trading expertise, and access to equity research).

Convertible Securities. Convertible Securities plays a leading role in both the primary and secondary markets in global convertible securities, one of the earliest forms of equity derivative instruments. Through its operations in New York, London, Tokyo, and Hong Kong, Morgan Stanley is able to exercise its expertise in domestic and global markets.

Equity Derivatives. Equity Derivatives executes stock index futures and options and individual stock options on a global basis. In addition, it executes customer trading programs for institutions wishing to liquidate, invest, or restructure large equity portfolios. The group offers a range of services in synthetic equity products, including executions of long-dated options, index-linked bonds, and equity swaps. The global equity derivatives sales force advises institutional clients on the use of listed equity derivatives, portfolio trading strategies, and synthetic equity products to meet their unique risk profiles. Our equity derivative sales and trading activities have increased substantially in recent years and will continue to expand to meet the changing needs of our client base. The group now reaches all major international listed markets, while also supporting the latest techniques in structured financial engineering.

Fixed Income Sales, Trading and Research

Morgan Stanley's Fixed Income Division offers clients a wide range of products and services, including government securities, capital markets products (corporate debt, preferred stock, and money markets), high-yield securities, mortgage- and asset-backed securities, derivative products, tax-exempt securities, and fixed income research. The division's sales and distribution teams are organized geographically and supported by product specialists. Using a broad and growing range of financial products, fixed income associates working in sales assist institutional investors plan and implement portfolio strategies. Associates working as traders commit the firm's capital to ensure liquidity for our clients. Research associates provide fixed income strategy and corporate credit research, and develop quantitative models for analytical support.

The Fixed Income Division consists of seven principal global product areas:

Government Bonds. Trades, makes markets, and has specialists in many of the world's government securities. Morgan Stanley is one of a select group of primary dealers in U.S. and French government debt and participates in underwriting syndicates for domestic bond issues in Germany, Italy, and Japan. The financing desk finances the firm's inventory of government securities and money market and mortgage- and asset-backed securities, through repurchase and reverse repurchase agreements.

Capital Markets Products. Products include intermediate- and long-term corporate debt, medium-term notes, commercial paper, floating-rate notes, certificates of deposit, and preferred stock for industrial corporations, utilities, banks, thrifts, and finance companies. Makes markets in securities to provide liquidity for institutional investors; provides investment strategies for institutional investors; advises Morgan Stanley's capital markets services group on pricing and timing of new issues; develops portfolio swapping strategies for customers and assists corporations in repurchasing debt.

High Yield/Lesser Developed Country (LDC) Securities. Focuses on noninvestment grade and LDC debt securities; objectives similar to the capital markets product group. Distributes, trades, and has specialists in straight and zero-coupon high-yield bonds. Expert in placing and making markets in complex high-yield securities issued for start-up ventures in emerging markets.

Tax Exempt Securities. Sells and trades new and secondary issues of tax-exempt securities issued by U.S. cities, state, and other public authorities. Tax exempt area also includes public finance, which originates and structures negotiated new issues, syndicate, which is responsible for setting the prices and yields on competitive and negotiated new issues and research.

Mortgage- and Asset-Backed Securities. Originates, structures, and trades mortgage- and asset-backed securities, which are collateralized by residential first mortgages, commercial mortgages, aircraft leases, and such consumer receivables as auto loans, credit card balances, and home equity loans.

Derivative Products. Integrates the origination and trading of structured products, currency and interest rate swaps, and synthetic securities. In January 1994, the group launched Morgan Stanley Derivative Products Inc. (MSDP), which is triple-A rated by Moody's Investors Service and Standard & Poor's Corporation. MSDP gives the firm access to the credit-sensitive sector of the derivatives market at a time when the credit ratings of derivatives providers are coming under increasingly close scrutiny.

Fixed Income Research. Provides global research and analytical support for traders, salespeople, and customers. There are four major areas: Credit Research (industry and company credit prospects), Modeling (quantitative models such as optimization and trading strategies), Mortgage-Backed (analytical support for the mortgage-backed securities salespeople and traders), and Portfolio Strategy (fundamental trends).

Investment Banking

Morgan Stanley's Investment Banking Division utilizes both traditional and innovative financing techniques to help corporations and governments around the world make and execute decisions regarding their capital. New associates begin in Investment Banking as generalists, gaining broad exposure to a variety of the division's products, services, and clients. Associates work on a mix of assignments ranging from transaction execution to business development initiatives. Associates have the opportunity to work directly with the senior-level financial and strategic decision-makers of some of the world's largest corporations, as well as with smaller, emerging growth clients. After a one- or two-year generalist experience, associates begin to specialize in either an industry, product area or geographic region.

The Investment Banking Division consists of four closely related business units: Corporate Finance; Mergers, Acquisitions and Restructuring; Morgan Stanley Realty; and Capital Market Services.

Corporate Finance. Corporate Finance is responsible for initiating, developing and maintaining the firm's investment banking relationships with clients worldwide; for providing financial advice; and, in partnership with other specialized areas of the firm, for executing specific client transactions. The Corporate Finance Department is organized into teams of regional and industry specialists. The regional coverage groups provide a strong Morgan Stanley presence in the United States, Canada, Western and Eastern Europe, Latin America, the Middle East, the Far East, and Australia. The industry groups provide special expertise in the following sectors: commercial banking, financial entrepreneurs, food and consumer products, health care, insurance, media, natural resources, public utilities, retail, technology, telecommunications, and transportation. We also advise government and private sector clients on the privatization of state-owned enterprises.

Mergers, Acquisitions and Restructuring (MARD). MARD is a confederation of those groups having responsibility for executing most investment banking transactions for our clients. MARD consists of Mergers and Acquisitions, Financing Services, Private Investment, and Project Finance. All junior associates joining the firm begin their careers in the generalist group within MARD.

Mergers and Acquisitions (M&A). M&A provides corporate and financial clients with financial advisory services in situations involving mergers, acquisitions, defenses, proxy contests, divestitures, spin-offs, joint ventures, and restructuring. Many of our M&A assignments involve complex, competitive situations that require a high degree of creativity, analytical skill, and judgment. M&A professionals must be proficient in a wide range of technical skills (e.g., legal, tax, and accounting) and understand an extensive number of strategic alternatives in the context of any particular transaction.

Financing Services (FSG). FSG is responsible for the execution of all equity offerings (initial public offerings, reverse leveraged buyout and recapitalizations, convertible securities, derivative securities, common stock, and warrants), complex debt issuances, and other capital markets–related business. Amongst other things, FSG professionals have responsibility for the business investigation and due diligence process, registration statement and prospectus drafting, documentation, development of the road show presentation and schedule, and negotiation of the terms under which the firm will underwrite a company's securities.

Private Investment. The Private Investment Group manages an investment partnership, Princes Gate Investors, L.P. This partnership was established in 1992 to invest globally in special situations that help to facilitate the strategic or financial objectives of companies and to date has invested $207 million. The purpose of the partnership is to seek out investment opportunities generally in the form of minority equity positions of short- to medium-term duration.

Project Finance. Based in London, this group works in close coordination with other areas of the firm, such as Corporate Finance and Capital Markets, to structure discrete financing for major capital projects around the world.

Morgan Stanley Realty (MSR). MSR is responsible for providing real estate services for Morgan Stanley's corporate clients and for major owners and developers of real estate. As a principal, MSR invests in real estate through the Morgan Stanley Real Estate Fund, L.P. (MSREF I) and The Morgan Stanley Real Estate Fund II, L.P. (MSREF II), which together have more than $2 billion of equity capital. Both MSREF I and MSREF II are focused on high-yield real estate investments that utilize MSR's creativity in structuring acquisitions and selecting venture partners. MSR has established a joint venture with Morgan Stanley's Fixed Income Division called Real Estate Capital Markets (REDCM). REDCM's activities encompass both new issues, origination and distribution, as well as trading commercial whole loans and collateralized mortgage-backed securities.

Capital Market Services. Capital Market Services, which is responsible for structuring, pricing, and managing public offerings and private placements of debt and equity securities, provides a link between Investment Banking and Equity and Fixed Income Divisions of the firm. This area is composed of Debt Capital Markets and Equity Capital Markets.

Debt Capital Markets (DCM). DCM is responsible for the solicitation and execution of Morgan Stanley's primary debt and related products business. The group consists of Syndicate, Continuously Offered Products, Market Coverage, High Yield, Private Placements, and Preferred Stock. Together these groups provide a sophisticated global capital markets service, including product development, marketing, and execution from Morgan Stanley offices in New York, London, Tokyo, Frankfurt, and Zurich.

Equity Capital Markets (ECM). ECM has global product responsibility for corporate equity-related transactions, including common stock, initial public offerings, subsidiary initial public offerings, convertibles, warrants, and share repurchases in the domestic and global markets. The specific functions of the group include product management, syndicate, business development, product development, and strategic advice.

Private Client Services
Private Client Services (PCS) provides world-class brokerage and investment advisory services to high-net-worth individuals and smaller institutional investors.

PCS offers its clients the same services the firm provides to large banks, pension funds, governments, and multinational corporations. After a six-month training program, new investment representatives begin to develop their own brokerage and asset management businesses with the support of the firm's sales, trading, research, and advisory resources. Investment representatives develop and manage relationships with clients, review their portfolios, identify opportunities, and evaluate and execute investment strategies. Investment representatives sell and manage products in every asset class including global equities, fixed income securities, currencies, and commodities.

Public Finance
Public Finance provides investment banking and financial advisory services to U.S. public sector entities. All associates hired in Public Finance spend up to two years working on a variety of transactions with team leaders in the different geographical and industry coverage groups. A mix of assignments, ranging from business solicitations to performing extensive quantitative analyses, and rotations in quantitative new product areas provide a fundamental training and experience base. Associates are generally assigned to a specific coverage group by the close of their second year. It is our philosophy with regard to the Public Finance business that it must be managed on a long-term basis; therefore, we must emphasize the importance of training and career development of our junior professionals. Thus, associates are provided the opportunity to develop broad-based execution skills. At the same time, through specific client coverage assignments, associates have the opportunity to establish and cultivate working relationships with our clients.

The Public Finance group consists of three geographic coverage groups (Northeast/Midwest, Southeast/Southwest, and West), six industry groups (Education, Health Care, Project Finance/Corporate-Related, Structured Finance, including student loans and housing, Transportation and Utilities) and one specialty group (Capital Markets/Derivative Products).

Describe your ownership structure.

The common stock of Morgan Stanley Group Inc. is listed on the New York Stock Exchange and several other U.S. stock exchanges. Employees and directors of the company own approximately 40% of the common stock.

The Finance MBA's Job Description

Describe the career path and corresponding responsibilities for an MBA at your firm.

Regardless of the business area in which one works, most Morgan Stanley careers share similar characteristics. New hires spend their initial years learning about our technology, products, services, and clients. Thereafter, they take on more operational responsibility and coach the junior people who are entering the business. We encourage professionals to start developing new business opportunities and client relationships, whether those clients are external or internal, as soon as their abilities permit.

The firm is committed to the recruitment of MBAs and to creating an environment for individuals to achieve professional and personal growth in the context of diverse career challenges and opportunities. When it makes sense, we encourage specialization—but we do not mandate it. We have a tradition of developing our people and matching our best people with our best opportunities, relying on the transferability of skills among businesses.

The Recruiting Process

Describe your recruiting process and the criteria by which you select candidates. Is prior experience necessary?

Each year the firm seeks to recruit and hire a diverse group of highly motivated, intelligent MBAs to join us in a number of business areas. Prior experience in the investment banking industry is not a prerequisite. We typically conduct a traditional recruiting process including campus presentations and interviews followed by final round in-office interviews for selected students.

How many permanent associates and analysts do you hire in a typical year? How many summer interns do you expect to hire? If you have a formal summer program, please describe it. Please be sure to indicate whether the summer program is in place for all offices or just some.

In addition to full-time hires, many areas of the firm seek to hire summer interns. Full-time position initial placement and summer internships are generally available in New York, London, Tokyo, and Hong Kong, although availability varies by business area. International opportunities exist both initially and later in one's career based on the firm's needs and individual qualifications.

The firm works through the school's placement office and interested students should look for our advertisements and announcements both there and in the campus newspaper.

Morgan Stanley is an Equal Opportunity Employer

NationsBank

100 N. Tryon Street
NC1007-21-10
Charlotte, NC 28255

MBA Recruiting Contact(s):
Courtenay Buchan, Assistant Vice President
(704) 386-1159

Stanley Merriwether, College Recruiter
(704) 386-4258

Locations of Offices:
Offices are throughout the United States as well as in Frankfurt, London, Hong Kong, Singapore, and Mexico City.

Total Number of Professionals (U.S. and worldwide):
Approximately 60,000

Company Description

Describe your firm's business and the types of clients served by your finance group(s).

NationsBank Corporation is one of the largest financial services companies in the United States, well-known for its capital strength, market position, and bias for doing business in all sectors of the communities and markets it serves.

The company is organized by three major business groups:

- **Global Finance Businesses**—A diverse organization that provides a broad range of financial services to large domestic and international corporations and institutions.

- **General Bank**—The NationsBank retail banking network that spans the Southeast, Southwest, and Mid-Atlantic states.

- **Financial Services**—A growing unit, with specialized services in corporate finance, commercial real estate, project finance and capital assets, as well as business inventory financing and consumer credit for customers who traditionally do not use banks.

From its historical roots as a Southern bank dating back to the early 1800s, the company has grown into what has been called an emerging model for financial services in the twenty-first century. Today, NationsBank serves clients throughout the United States and international markets with a broad spectrum of financial products.

Such an evolution would not have been possible without an executive commitment to grow NationsBank Global Finance into a leading provider of credit, investment banking, capital markets, and specialized financial services to corporate clients in America and around the world.

Having brought the capabilities of Wall Street to its investment, international, and corporate banking businesses—as well as in global trading and distribution—NationsBank remains committed to the culture and heritage that is uniquely its own.

NationsBank Global Finance Businesses
NationsBank meets the needs of the domestic and international corporate marketplace through its Global Finance Businesses. The company has a long and distinguished track record in corporate banking, built on one of the largest client bases of any American financial institution.

Recent years have been pivotal at NationsBank. Investment banking, capital raising, and risk management capabilities have been dramatically expanded and strengthened. In short, NationsBank set a goal to move beyond its traditional, regional focus and into direct competition with Wall Street firms. That goal has now been achieved.

Global Finance
Businesses are comprised of three groups:

Corporate Finance Group

- Corporate Finance (including specialty industry groups)

- Industry Analysis

- Leveraged Finance (non-investment grade debt)

- Advisory Services/Mergers and Acquisitions

- Loan Syndications

- Treasury Management

Specialized Finance Group

- Real Estate Finance (real estate lending and finance)

- Asset-backed Finance (leasing, specialized lending)

- Capital Investments (providing and managing risk capital)

- International (corporate finance, trade banking, structured/project finance)

Capital Markets Group

- NationsBank — CRT

- Research

- Trading and Distribution

The Finance MBA's Job Description

Describe the career path and corresponding responsibilities for an MBA at your firm.

Global Finance Associate

Global Finance professionals at NationsBank provide a full array of sophisticated products and services to the largest American and international corporations and institutions. Success depends on their ability to proactively identify current and future client needs—and then make sure those needs are met.

As opportunities are targeted, the NationsBank Client Management Process is implemented. Senior relationship managers and associates from product specialties are assembled into client teams. The client team has a wide range of responsibilities—from providing advisory expertise and implementation to extending credit. As client needs change, so may the composition of a particular team. But one thing is constant: the commitment to meet and then exceed client expectations.

Classroom training, which is held in Charlotte, consists of three modules. Modules cover financial analysis, accounting, legal issues and documentation, corporate finance, derivatives, financial advisory, and capital markets. Module I is three months long and Modules II and III last for three weeks each and are interspersed between rotations. Rotations could be in any one of these offices: Atlanta, Bethesda, Charlotte, Chicago, Dallas, Denver, Los Angeles, Miami, New York, Richmond, or Tampa. Origination and product rotations could be Advisory Services and Mergers and Acquisitions, Syndications and Leveraged Finance, Debt Finance, Research, and Securities Sales and Trading.

Capital Markets Associate

Capital Markets represents the underwriting, distribution, and trading arm of Global Finance. Its two primary divisions are NationsBanc Capital Markets, Inc. (NCMI) and NationsBanc-CRT.

NCMI houses the institutional securities dealing activities and is a registered broker/dealer and a primary dealer of U.S. government and government agency securities. NationsBanc-CRT brings the risk management expertise of one of the world's largest derivative products market making and trading firms to its clients.

The Capital Markets Group has sales and/or trading offices in Atlanta, Austin, Baltimore, Bethesda, Charlotte, Chicago, Dallas, Houston, New York, Pittsburgh, Richmond, Stanford, Tampa, Washington, D.C., Frankfurt, London, Paris, Singapore, Tokyo, and Osaka.

Working closely with Corporate Finance senior relationship managers and Specialized Finance team members, Capital Markets associates are responsible for the underwriting, trading, and distribution of a broad selection of fixed income securities, foreign exchange products, options and derivative products.

Training begins with orientation to NationsBank Global Finance and a comprehensive three-to five-month rotation through the Charlotte sales and trading office, including derivatives, debt finance, and research.

The Recruiting Process

Describe your recruiting process and the criteria by which you select candidates. Is prior experience necessary?

These positions are for the MBA interested in corporate finance, specialized financing, advisory services, and capital markets. At least two years of related work experience and an MBA qualifies applicants for these programs. Strong analytical, communications, and teamwork skills are necessary along with a willingness to relocate.

How many permanent associates and analysts do you hire in a typical year? How many summer interns do you expect to hire? If you have a formal summer program, please describe it. Please be sure to indicate whether the summer program is in place for all offices or just some.

Graduating MBAs and summer associates between their first and second year of business school are hired by Global Finance. Approximately 40–50 permanent associates are hired each year. Our Summer Associate Program enables candidates to spend 10–12 weeks under the leadership and guidance of senior staff. Our goal is to create a mutually beneficial partnership that will result in placement after graduation.

NationsBank is an Equal Opportunity Employer.

Nesbitt Burns Inc.

1 First Canadian Place
4th Floor
P.O. Box 150
Toronto, Ontario
M5X 1H3 Canada
(416) 359-4000

MBA Recruiting Contact(s):
Jeff Watchorn
Boris Novansky

Company Description

Describe your firm's business and the types of clients served by your finance group(s).

The creation of Nesbitt Burns on September 1, 1994, was a strategic merger of two respected and successful investment dealers. The decision to combine the two firms was motivated by a shared vision and desire: to emerge first as Canada's preeminent investment bank and then, through growth and acquisition in the United States, to become the first full-service North American investment bank headquartered in Canada.

Nesbitt Burns is a powerhouse that offers a depth and breadth of services not previously available from a Canadian firm. Nesbitt Burns is the largest, most comprehensive investment bank in Canada:

- With a capital base of approximately $500 million and a total of 3,500 employees, Nesbitt Burns is significantly larger than any of its Canadian competitors.

- Nesbitt Burns has an Investment Banking team that is the largest and most experienced of any firm operating in Canada and of any Canadian firm in the United States. We are a leader in both financing and advisory services. Our Merger and Acquisition team leads the industry in terms of experience and the number, value, and diversity of transactions completed.

- Our Institutional Equity sales and trading team is the top trader and distributor of Canadian equities throughout the world.

- Nesbitt Burns' Fixed Income group is the largest among Canadian investment dealers. Over half of our resources are dedicated outside Canada, allowing us to provide the most comprehensive service to our clients worldwide.

- Private clients are serviced by approximately 1,200 qualified investment advisors from 110 branches in over 40 communities—the largest retail sales force in Canada.

- Nesbitt Burns has the preeminent Research group in Canada with the most top three ranked analysts in economics, fundamental equity research, technical analysis, quantitative analysis, and fixed income analytics.

- With 11 offices outside Canada and more than 275 international employees, Nesbitt Burns is at the forefront of bringing Canadian securities to international investors and international securities to Canadians.

Describe your ownership structure.

Nesbitt Burns is a part of the Bank of Montreal financial group and operates autonomously to offer securities-related services on its behalf. Our partnership with the bank reinforces our capital base, increases our distribution capabilities, and greatly enhances our ability to compete effectively in global capital markets.

How does your approach to finance differ from that of other firms, and what do you consider to be your strengths and distinctive capabilities?

We believe that what differentiates Nesbitt Burns from other investment dealers is our dedication to being the best in addition to the biggest. This focus on uncompromising quality and integrity is incorporated in all aspects of the way we do business. It underpins the success we have had in identifying financings opportunities and designing new products, the preeminence we have achieved as a major market maker in Canadian corporate and government securities, and the stature we have attained as a world-ranked mergers and acquisitions financial advisor. Our work throughout has been supported by our top-ranked economics and investment research team.

Nesbitt Burns' Investment Banking group consists of over 100 professionals in Canada based in Toronto, Montreal, Calgary, and Vancouver and more than 30 professionals located in offices in New York, Chicago, and London. The Investment Banking Department provides a broad range of services, including corporate finance, mergers, acquisitions and divestitures, restructuring, consulting, and advisory services to corporations, governments, and other organizations. We achieve success for our clients by having a thorough understanding of client needs combined with a sensitivity and swift response to market opportunities. For Nesbitt Burns, a corporate-client relationship is a long-term partnership. Conscious of our continuing obligation to provide financial service, a team of highly skilled individuals is assembled to ensure full client coverage. Our team approach to assignments serves as a catalyst to combine experience and knowledge with innovation and creativity.

Investment Banking includes industry specialists who focus on the real estate, mining, financial services, forest products, communications, utilities, oil and gas, and consumer products industries. Industry specialists work closely with product specialists. The approach of our Investment Banking group is to combine an in-depth knowledge of our clients' needs and goals with creative thought, a thorough understanding of the capital markets, and integrity.

The Finance MBA's Job Description

Describe the career path and corresponding responsibilities for an MBA at your firm.

Career opportunities are available in all areas of the firm, including Investment Banking and Fixed Income and Equity Sales and Trading.

Nesbitt Burns encourages Investment Banking associates to generalize during their first two years in order to develop a broad range of investment banking skills. Associates work with senior members of the department on a variety of corporate financing and M&A-related projects, including prospectus or offering memorandum work, analysis of a corporation's financing needs, drafting corporate presentations, assisting on valuations and fairness opinions, managing solicitations, and assisting in the marketing of new issues, both private and public. As an associate gains more experience and product knowledge, he or she may decide to specialize in a particular industry or product group.

A career in Fixed Income or Institutional Equity begins directly on the sales and trading floor. Working alongside an experienced professional, the trainee will master an understanding of market behavior and will develop marketing skills and strategies for arbitrage, market making, and taking positions as both principal and agent.

Nesbitt Burns offers a dynamic, challenging work environment with tremendous career opportunities. Nesbitt Burns stresses a team-oriented approach to assignments and encourages an environment open to providing innovative solutions for clients.

Discuss the lifestyle aspects of a career with your firm (i.e., average hours per week, amount of travel, flexibility to change offices, corporate culture, etc.).

The time commitment required to provide the quality of work required in the competitive investment banking environment is considerable, particularly for new recruits.

The Recruiting Process

Describe your recruiting process and the criteria by which you select candidates. Is prior experience necessary?

We look for highly motivated individuals with strong analytical skills, sound judgment, and a high level of integrity. Academic achievement is important. Prior related work experience is an asset.

How many permanent associates and analysts do you hire in a typical year? How many summer interns do you expect to hire? If you have a formal summer program, please describe it. Please be sure to indicate whether the summer program is in place for all offices or just some.

In a typical year, Nesbitt Burns hires three or four associates, four or five analysts, and others as required. In the past, we have also hired summer associates and analysts.

Nomura Securities International, Inc.

2 World Financial Center
Building B
New York, NY 10281

MBA Recruiting Contact(s):
Human Resources Department

Company Description

Describe your firm's business and the types of clients served by your finance group(s).

Nomura Securities International, Inc. (NSI) is a wholly owned subsidiary of the Nomura Securities Co., Ltd. (Nomura), the world's largest securities firm. With shareholder equity exceeding $14 billion and total assets of more than $23.2 billion, Nomura is the most profitable financial institution in the world.

A medium-size investment banking company, NSI employs more than 800 people in the United States. NSI has evolved from a company handling primarily Japanese-related securities into a full-fledged member of the American financial community and also is a member of the major securities and commodities exchanges, as well as a primary dealer in U.S. Treasury securities. U.S. operations, which began in 1927, have expanded to include two branch offices in Chicago and one in Los Angeles. Today, NSI offers a wide range of products and services: sales, trading, investment banking, mutual funds, and portfolio and asset management.

NSI is continually in a state of evolution as the firm works to develop new businesses, such as the high-yield and Latin American departments. Two years ago, 80% of NSI's investment banking revenues were due to Japanese-related business (country funds distributed in Japan, Tokyo Stock Exchange listing fees, etc.). This past year over 40% of revenues were from non-Japan-related business (Compania Cervecerias Unidas S.A., Chic by H.I.S., and JAFCO II). Our investment banking group was active with numerous initial public offerings and private placements and created innovative financing structures such as ROSA II and Ivory.

In addition to its financial strength and the breadth of its capabilities, Nomura is internationally renowned for its innovation in finance:

- Nomura introduced and popularized the Gensaki, a Japanese bond sale and repurchase agreement that has developed into an important short-term investment instrument.

- Nomura pioneered the expansion of the Japanese financial community by introducing foreign companies to the country's rapidly growing capital markets. The firm designs and implements investor relations programs for client companies and arranges the listing of their shares on the Tokyo Stock Exchange. In the past, Nomura has listed Anheuser-Busch, AT&T, General Electric, Kraft, and J.P. Morgan, among others.

- With the increase in global investing, more and more institutional and individual investors rely on Nomura's international research, sales, and trading capabilities. Nomura's leadership position in the Japanese market as a broker/dealer and market maker provides an unparalleled resource for investors.

- Working to meet clients' needs, Nomura has established relationships with financial institutions to help ensure the development of innovative products in the areas of leveraged leasing, project financing, real estate investing within the United States, and mergers and acquisitions.

- NSI's Equity Derivatives group is constantly at the top of the New York Stock Exchange chart of 15 most active firms in program trading volume.

The growing importance of investment management has led NSI to form additional companies to provide service to clients. Nomura Corporate Research and Asset Management (NCRAM) is a money management firm with a worldwide client base specializing in high-yield bond investments. Combining the credit expertise of NCRAM with Nomura's tremendous capital base and global distribution capability has helped the firm to achieve a preeminent position in asset management. Expertise in corporate credit also provides the foundation for our aggressive worldwide expansion into proprietary trading, structured finance, and other related merchant and investment banking activities.

With our mortgage-backed securities business continuing to grow, Nomura created a subsidiary, Nomura Asset Capital Corporation (NACC), to conduct our real estate and nonagency trading and financing. NACC, though initially focusing on commercial mortgages, will transact in the commercial and residential loan markets, as well as the asset-backed securities market.

Emphasizing an empirical, problem-solving approach to its studies, Nomura Research Institutes conducts fundamental research on a wide range of socioeconomic and socioscientific issues, as well as on matters of long-term relevance to the securities industry.

The Finance MBA's Job Description

Describe the career path and corresponding responsibilities for an MBA at your firm.

Full-time associates receive global finance training in such areas as investment banking and sales and trading through our associates program. As a sales and trading associate, individuals undergo a six-month training program during which they rotate through various sales and trading areas and participate in intensive product training seminars. In investment banking, associates are expected to become a contributing member of the department immediately. Most of the training is conducted on the job by teaming senior executives in the department with the associates. Since the firm encourages initiative, the degree of responsibility of an associate's assignment is determined to a large extent by an individual's desire and ability to learn and contribute.

The Recruiting Process

Describe your recruiting process and the criteria by which you select candidates. Is prior experience necessary?

NSI seeks people with strong academic records and excellent analytical and communication skills. Demonstration of leadership, high levels of self-motivation, initiative, and commitment, and the ability to work effectively with others in an intense and demanding environment are crucial.

How many permanent associates and analysts do you hire in a typical year? How many summer interns do you expect to hire? If you have a formal summer program, please describe it. Please be sure to indicate whether the summer program is in place for all offices or just some.

NSI's summer associate program provides a select group of students with an intense, hands-on view of the securities industry, as well as the extensive global operations at Nomura. After choosing to work in one of the following areas—investment banking, derivative products or fixed income, or equity sales and trading—the summer associate is quickly integrated into the department's daily operations. In sales and trading, there is a rotation through the different sales and trading areas. Investment banking and derivative products tend to be more project oriented. Additionally, through a series of weekly seminars with senior managers, the MBAs have the opportunity to be exposed to the many facets of our business.

What international opportunities does your firm offer for U.S. citizens? For foreign nationals?

NSI does not recruit for the other overseas offices. Individuals interested in working internationally should contact NSI for additional information.

Piper Jaffray Inc.

222 South Ninth Street
Minneapolis, MN 55402
(612) 342-6000

MBA Recruiting Contact(s):
Lurah Bean

Company Description

Describe your firm's business and the types of clients served by your finance group(s).

Piper Jaffray Inc., a full-service investment banking firm headquartered in Minneapolis, is one of the leading investment banks based outside New York City. Established in 1895, it has over 2,400 employees. Piper Jaffray services consist of Equity and Fixed Income Capital Markets, Asset Management with over $10 billion under management, and Retail Distribution, with 875 brokers located in 68 offices across the western United States.

Piper Jaffray's capital markets activities encompass corporate finance, equity research, public finance, debt and equity trading, and equity and fixed income sales. The Corporate Finance Department consists of 35 professionals who are divided along industry or functional specialties. The Research Department has 25 professionals who, with their Corporate Finance peers, lead industry teams. Piper Jaffray has five industry teams—Healthcare, Financial Services, Technology, Consumer, and Food and Agribusiness—as well as functional specialists performing private placements, mergers and acquisitions, venture capital, and valuations. The majority of these services originate from the company's Minneapolis headquarters.

Describe your ownership structure.

Piper Jaffray's stock is listed on the New York Stock Exchange. Approximately 42% of the company's common shares are owned by its employee stock ownership trust. Another 18% is held by employees directly.

How does your approach to finance differ from that of other firms, and what do you consider to be your strengths and distinctive capabilities?

The ownership structure of Piper Jaffray is a distinctive strength. Because much of Piper Jaffray's equity is broadly owned by its employees, there is a strong sense of loyalty to the company and commitment to its professionalism and profitability. Consistent with its focus on servicing the financial needs of emerging-growth companies, Piper Jaffray is also able to commit its own capital to new ventures. It has made a number of venture capital investments in recent years and intends to increase investment in this area in the future.

Piper Jaffray places strong emphasis on the importance of long-term investment banking relationships. The company devotes substantial resources to trading, research coverage, and corporate finance expertise to provide its investment banking clients with the highest levels of service. Piper Jaffray also has one of the industry's lowest turnover rates, which is important to maintaining long-term banking commitments.

The Finance MBA's Job Description

Describe the career path and corresponding responsibilities for an MBA at your firm.

Piper Jaffray emphasizes hiring good people and giving them as much freedom and responsibility as is possible, consistent with general corporate objectives, to determine their own focus and goals. The good people rise to the top on their own initiative, and they remain with Piper Jaffray, in many instances because no other organization can offer them as much latitude to exercise their initiative. This unstructured atmosphere and emphasis on the individual, coupled with our employee ownership structure, have made it possible for entrepreneurial people to satisfy many of their goals within the corporate structure. For example, the Corporate Finance Department has built a partnership mechanism whereby its people, along with other members of management, can build capital by participating in some of the investment opportunities developed in the department.

New associates are hired as generalists and given substantial latitude to develop industry expertise and functional specialties that are compatible with their particular interests and capabilities. Associates are immediately assigned to a wide variety of projects and given as much responsibility as their experience and capabilities permit. A senior officer in the department supervises all client relationships and engagements. Associates generally choose a particular industry or functional specialty area after a couple of years at Piper Jaffray.

The Recruiting Process

Describe your recruiting process and the criteria by which you select candidates. Is prior experience necessary?

The most successful people in Corporate Finance have come to Piper Jaffray with some significant financially related working experience. This experience has enabled them to contribute effectively to the department at an early stage in their development. Members of the group also must have the confidence, maturity, and personal attributes necessary to develop successful client relationships. In most instances, the current professionals in the department are people who have spent time in financial centers such as New York, or would have done so, but preferred the working environment and growth opportunities that a smaller organization can offer and the lifestyle available in the Twin Cities or Seattle area.

How many permanent associates and analysts do you hire in a typical year? How many summer interns do you expect to hire? If you have a formal summer program, please describe it. Please be sure to indicate whether the summer program is in place for all offices or just some.

New associates are hired primarily into the Corporate Finance Department. Because of the department's size, it is not possible to offer a formal training program. Piper Jaffray typically hires two to five MBA graduates each year.

Piper Jaffray has no organized summer program.

Raymond James & Associates, Inc.

800 Carillon Parkway
St. Petersburg, FL 33716
(813) 573-3800

MBA Recruiting Contact(s):
Gary A. Downing, Managing Director
Corporate Finance

Robert F. Shuck, Vice Chairman
Raymond James Financial

Company Description

Describe your firm's business and the types of clients served by your finance group(s).

Raymond James & Associates is a leading securities firm that offers comprehensive financial services to individuals, corporations, municipalities, and institutions. Since our founding in 1962, Raymond James has grown dramatically by providing these services to our clients and customers with a superior level of execution and integrity. Today, Raymond James is the largest investment banking and brokerage firm headquartered in the Southeast and maintains one of the largest retail brokerage networks in the United States.

Raymond James & Associates provides investment banking services to emerging-growth and established companies throughout the country and in Europe. Both private and public companies are clients. The primary emphasis is on companies within a limited number of industries where sufficient industry knowledge has been developed to deliver an extremely high level of value-added service. Florida and southeastern companies are also well represented on our client list due to geographic location. Investment banking services include public underwritings; private placements; merger, acquisition, and divestiture representation; and various advisory services.

Describe your ownership structure.

Raymond James Financial, the parent company of Raymond James & Associates, is a public corporation and its shares are traded on the New York Stock Exchange.

How does your approach to finance differ from that of other firms, and what do you consider to be your strengths and distinctive capabilities?

Raymond James has developed a reputation for providing capital and advice to emerging-growth and medium-size companies in a limited number of industries. Members of the Investment Banking Department work closely with our highly acclaimed Research Department to develop an in-depth understanding of our clients and their businesses. This allows a high level of value-added services to be provided to the client.

Discuss changes in your firm's revenues (both domestic and international) and professional staff over the past year; over the past five years.

Raymond James is one of the leading growth companies in the country with a compound growth rate in revenues and earnings in excess of 25% per year during the past 15 years. In our most recently completed fiscal year, revenues exceeded $360 million, and profits exceeded $40 million. All major areas of the firm have grown dramatically in the past five years, including expansion of our institutional sales effort to six offices in Europe. The Investment Banking Department has grown from 5 to 15 professionals in the past five years. The number of transactions completed and revenues generated by the Investment Banking Department has also increased dramatically over the past five years.

The Finance MBA's Job Description

Describe the career path and corresponding responsibilities for an MBA at your firm.

Raymond James hires MBAs for a variety of positions within the firm. The most common position is as an associate within the Investment Banking Department. As an associate, the recently hired MBA will receive broad exposure to a variety of transactions within a specific industry group. Increased responsibility and client contact occur quickly, assuming the associate performs well and displays the necessary skills. MBAs can also be hired into Public Finance, Research, Sales and Trading, and Administrative positions.

Describe the opportunities for professional mobility between the various departments in your firm.

There are numerous examples of MBAs moving from one department to another within the firm as their interests change. Our philosophy is to hire people who are highly qualified and choose to live in Florida for the lifestyle alternative. Thus, we are flexible in meeting their needs over time in recognition of their contributions to the success of the firm.

Discuss the lifestyle aspects of a career with your firm (i.e., average hours per week, amount of travel, flexibility to change offices, corporate culture, etc.).

Raymond James offers an attractive alternative to the lifestyle offered by the major firms in New York. A typical workweek is 60–70 hours, and travel ranges from 40% to 50%. The real benefit is returning to the warm climate of Florida, where many leisure activities can be pursued year-round. The corporate culture at Raymond James can best be described as "work hard, play hard."

The Recruiting Process

Describe your recruiting process and the criteria by which you select candidates. Is prior experience necessary?

Raymond James seeks individuals with a track record of superior achievement who wish to work in an entrepreneurial environment in the Southeast. All aspects of a candidate's background are considered and measured against a high set of standards. Personality fit is also an important factor. Prior experience is not required.

RBC Dominion Securities Inc.

P.O. Box 21
Commerce Court South
Toronto, Ontario
M5L 1A7
Canada
(416) 864-4000
Fax: (416) 864-4143

MBA Recruiting Contact(s):
Douglas A. Guzman, Vice President

Company Description

Describe your firm's business and the types of clients served by your finance group(s).

RBC Dominion Securities is a fully integrated Canadian investment bank that enjoys a leading position in all segments of the securities business in Canada. Its principal investment banking activities are general corporate and government finance, mergers and acquisitions, corporate restructuring, real estate, fixed income and equity sales and trading, international financing, commercial paper, and foreign exchange. The firm has an extensive retail sales network of approximately 1,000 registered representatives located in over 70 cities across Canada. RBC Dominion Securities also has a strong international presence, with offices in New York, Boston, London, Paris, Lausanne, Hong Kong, and Tokyo.

RBC Dominion Securities has grown through a series of mergers over the past two decades to become one of the largest, most profitable investment banks in Canada. The firm's investment banking clients include most of Canada's largest and fastest-growing companies, as well as 10 Canadian provinces, the federal government, and numerous government agencies. Over the past several years, RBC Dominion Securities has lead-managed over 25% of all public Canadian corporate debt and equity offerings in Canada. The firm has demonstrated a consistent ability to meet the changing needs of its many clients while maintaining a superior rate of return on its own capital, a performance that is of interest to potential employees, as 25% of the firm is owned by professional-level employees. RBC Dominion Securities has been able to take advantage of its strong capital base and exceptional distribution capability to compete effectively and profitably.

The firm's corporate strategy is to be the leading investment bank to Canadian clients in both domestic and international markets and to be the leading invest-ment bank to foreign clients in the Canadian market. The firm achieves this goal through its ability to view client interests as paramount and to deliver superior services that integrate the various areas of strength throughout the firm. This integrated, client-oriented approach has distinguished RBC Dominion Securities in terms of both its reputation and its performance over the past several years.

Describe your ownership structure.

As a consequence of financial services deregulation in Canada, the firm sold a 75% equity interest to the Royal Bank of Canada, Canada's largest commercial bank, in March 1988. The transaction provided the firm with access to the Royal's formidable international network, as well as the financial backing of a major international financial institution. The remaining 25% of RBC Dominion Securities' shares are owned by employees and traded at book value. Associates in investment banking are typically first offered an opportunity to purchase shares in the firm within the first several years of their careers.

Unlike some other commercial bank–investment bank relationships in Canada, RBC Dominion Securities has maintained complete independence of operations. No Royal Bank executives have taken positions at RBC Dominion Securities, and the bank fills only 2 of 15 positions on the firm's board of directors. Career opportunities and compensation structures for professional staff have and will remain unchanged.

The Finance MBA's Job Description

Describe the career path and corresponding responsibilities for an MBA at your firm.

The firm employs approximately 90 investment banking professionals located in Toronto, Montreal, Calgary, Vancouver, Regina, and New York, as well as in London and other overseas offices. RBC Dominion Securities devotes a great deal of time and consideration to its search for associates. The firm's intention is to hire outstanding graduates who will continue with the firm throughout their careers. It has among the lowest turnover rates in the industry.

Associates who join the investment banking group at RBC Dominion Securities generally do not specialize in any one particular industry or product group. The firm prefers to develop well-rounded professionals who have participated in a wide variety of transactions, whether debt or equity, domestic or international, private or public. Associates are nevertheless encouraged to develop expertise in areas that interest them, and the firm makes every effort to satisfy a professional's ambitions in a particular specialty area. The firm is large enough to be able to offer both a generalist approach to the business and the opportunity to specialize in specific areas of interest but small enough to take a flexible approach in the career development of high-performing employees.

Other aspects of RBC Dominion Securities would be of interest to potential associates, including the firm's reputation for excellence, innovation, and high ethical standards. Moreover, there are comparatively few associates, which results in new professionals being given substantial responsibilities early in their careers. RBC Dominion Securities' position in the domestic underwriting league table affords new associates the deal flow necessary to develop well-rounded professionals skills.

Discuss the lifestyle aspects of a career with your firm (i.e., average hours per week, amount of travel, flexibility to change offices, corporate culture, etc.).

An open and collegial atmosphere prevails throughout the firm. There is a genuine concern on the part of senior management that young professionals develop a number of outside interests and have the ability to devote a significant portion of time to their families. While the highest value is placed on productive output by professionals, the firm does not encourage long hours when they are unnecessary.

The Recruiting Process

Describe your recruiting process and the criteria by which you select candidates. Is prior experience necessary?

RBC Dominion Securities is highly selective in its hiring program. The firm has made a consistent commitment over the years to hire from the top business schools in both North America and Europe. A number of criteria are applied, including academic excellence, energetic presentation, evidence of strong outside interests, and overall fit with the firm. Grades by themselves are not given undue consideration. No prior investment banking experience is necessary, and the firm encourages applicants from a wide variety of academic disciplines and work experience. Successful candidates are typically persistent self-starters with a keen interest in financial markets and a good sense of humor.

How many permanent associates and analysts do you hire in a typical year? How many summer interns do you expect to hire? If you have a formal summer program, please describe it. Please be sure to indicate whether the summer program is in place for all offices or just some.

Each year three to five full-time associates and a smaller number of summer associates are hired into investment banking. There is no formal training program. Associates are immediately assigned to client transaction teams to learn on the job.

The Robinson-Humphrey Company, Inc.

Atlanta Financial Center
3333 Peachtree Road, NE
Atlanta, GA 30326
(404) 266-6000

MBA Recruiting Contact(s):
Halsey Wise, Associate
(404) 266-6915

Company Description

Describe your firm's business and the types of clients served by your finance group(s).

The Corporate Finance Department at Robinson-Humphrey consists of 38 professionals. The entire department is located in Robinson-Humphrey's headquarters in Atlanta. Essentially, everyone in the Corporate Finance Department is regarded as a generalist in terms of type of project. Teams of professionals focus on certain industries (e.g., technology, health care, retailing, financial institutions), but a flexible approach to industry coverage is maintained at the junior level. Robinson-Humphrey attempts to position itself as a complete investment banker to its clients. Robinson-Humphrey's primary corporate finance clientele is middle-market, emerging-growth companies.

Describe your ownership structure.

The Robinson-Humphrey Company, Inc. was purchased by American Express in 1982 and operated as a wholly owned subsidiary of Shearson Lehman Brothers, Inc. As part of Primerica's acquisition of Shearson in 1993, Robinson-Humphrey operates today as a subsidiary of Smith Barney Inc.

How does your approach to finance differ from that of other firms, and what do you consider to be your strengths and distinctive capabilities?

Robinson-Humphrey positions itself as a full- service investment bank to emerging-growth and middle-market companies. Because of its outstanding retail distribution system (55 branches across 10 states), as well as its ability to tap the worldwide resources of Smith Barney, Robinson-Humphrey has capabilities unique among regional investment banking firms. The Corporate Finance

Department has grown from approximately 20 people to 38 people over the past five years. Robinson-Humphrey is the largest corporate finance and investment banking operation in the Southeast, an area realizing tremendous gains in economic growth and in the origination of capital.

Discuss changes in your firm's revenues (both domestic and international) and professional staff over the past year; over the past five years.

Robinson-Humphrey, like most other investment banking firms, has benefited over the past year from the surge in public underwriting activity. Robinson-Humphrey has been a particularly active underwriter of new equity issues, both initial public offerings and issues for companies whose stocks are already publicly traded. The Corporate Finance Department, however, still maintains a balance between public underwriting and other activities, such as mergers and acquisitions and private capital raising. Over the past five years, merger and acquisition work has comprised from 20% to 80% of the department's business.

This past year the department's professional staff has grown to 38 professionals. Three bankers were hired laterally, and two new associates joined the firm during the summer of 1995. These additions continue the growth that the department has experienced during the past five years.

The Finance MBA's Job Description

Describe the career path and corresponding responsibilities for an MBA at your firm.

An associate works as a key member of transaction teams typically comprising two to three professionals. The associate's primary responsibilities consist of transaction execution duties, including financial analysis and project management. The associate also works with senior professionals to develop new business by meeting with and making presentations to prospective clients. An associate's degree of responsibility depends on the type and scope of a project and on his or her particular capabilities.

Describe the opportunities for professional mobility between the various departments in your firm.

There is very little mobility between the various departments within Robinson-Humphrey.

Discuss the lifestyle aspects of a career with your firm (i.e., average hours per week, amount of travel, flexibility to change offices, corporate culture, etc.).

People who work at Robinson-Humphrey generally seem to enjoy the lifestyle offered by a career with the firm and fostered by its location in the Southeast. In addition, the relatively small size of the department and of the firm by Wall Street standards tends to encourage close relationships among co-workers. While investment banking inevitably demands a significant time commitment, one's average hours worked and travel schedule will vary depending on market conditions and the number and types of projects on which one is working.

The Recruiting Process

Describe your recruiting process and the criteria by which you select candidates. Is prior experience necessary?

The company hires graduating MBAs to entry-level positions every year, depending on market conditions. Our annual recruiting effort usually begins in the fall, when we solicit cover letters and résumés from interested, qualified candidates. In the past we have not scheduled on-campus recruiting visits, and we do not anticipate a change in that policy. Typically, an entering MBA will have some experience in investment banking or a closely related financial services business. All factors such as grades, prior experience, and personal attributes are taken into consideration in the decision process. However, final recruiting decisions are based on interviews with several people in the department who make judgments concerning a candidate's ability to make a meaningful contribution to the department.

How many permanent associates and analysts do you hire in a typical year? How many summer interns do you expect to hire? If you have a formal summer program, please describe it. Please be sure to indicate whether the summer program is in place for all offices or just some.

Hiring decisions are based solely on current and perceived market conditions and an assessment of the department's overall needs. The department has hired from one to three associates each of the past four years. Most likely, we will hire at least one entry-level MBA in the upcoming year.

The firm does not have a summer program and does not interview for summer associates or analysts.

Rothschild Canada Limited

1 First Canadian Place
Suite 3800
P.O. Box 77
Toronto, Ontario
M5X 1B1
Canada
(416) 369-9600

MBA Recruiting Contact(s):
Stephen L. Shapiro, Vice President

Company Description

Describe your firm's business and the types of clients served by your finance group(s).

Rothschild Canada provides independent investment banking, corporate finance, and financial advisory services to selected Canadian and international clients in Canada and offers the global capability and expertise of the Rothschild Group around the world. Our range of experiences to date includes advising on acquisitions, mergers, divestitures, reorganizations, financings, spin-offs, privatizations, and restructurings. In addition, Rothschild Canada is involved in valuing and selling, both nationally and globally, private and public companies as a whole, operating units of large companies, and, in some cases, specific assets.

Rothschild Canada works with the other offices in the Rothschild Group to identify target companies for acquisition or investment purposes for current and prospective clients. There is a steady flow of ideas between Rothschild's offices with respect to opportunities in the mergers and acquisitions market in Canada and internationally.

As part of our long-term relationships with our clients, we advise them on their ongoing corporate and financial strategies and corporate finance activities and on the implementation of their strategic plans.

Rothschild Canada is not associated with commercial banks, financial institutions, or industrial groups in Canada, nor does it engage in public underwriting, market trading, arbitrage, or principal investing. Rothschild Canada is able to provide unbiased judgments free from potential conflicts of interest.

Describe your ownership structure.

Rothschild Canada Limited is the Canadian member of one of the world's leading independent merchant banking organizations, the Rothschild Group. The main operating company of the Rothschild Group in the United Kingdom is N M Rothschild & Sons Limited, the merchant bank that has been based at New Court in the City of London for nearly 200 years. The Rothschild Group has expanded globally to meet the increasingly diverse needs of its clients and now has offices in 20 countries worldwide. The Canadian office was opened in 1990 and has grown each year.

How does your approach to finance differ from that of other firms, and what do you consider to be your strengths and distinctive capabilities?

Rothschild Canada's independence and professional client-related approach to its focused business of providing advisory services differentiates it from its competitors in Canada.

The Finance MBA's Job Description

Describe the career path and corresponding responsibilities for an MBA at your firm.

A new member of the investment banking team has the opportunity to gain experience quickly in a vast number of transactions. Our experience to date has covered all major industries in Canada and a wide range of various types of transactions. Our professionals do not specialize in industrial sectors or products, although the majority of our professionals have brought years of experience to Rothschild Canada in all aspects of industry. All professionals begin as generalists, gathering as wide a portfolio of experiences as possible. As the firm grows, professionals naturally develop areas of particular expertise upon which the Canadian office, as well as our international group, will draw in dealing with various clients' needs.

Describe the opportunities for professional mobility between the various departments in your firm.

There are opportunities to meet and work with professionals from Rothschild's other offices, or the Rothschild Group, as well as opportunities to consider extended assignments in other offices.

Discuss the lifestyle aspects of a career with your firm (i.e., average hours per week, amount of travel, flexibility to change offices, corporate culture, etc.).

While the lifestyle of an investment banker is renowned for its hard work and long hours, Rothschild Canada maintains a friendly and cooperative atmosphere. Within a very short period, every new associate will have worked with all members of the office. The professionals are relatively young, and this allows for common interests and non-work-related activities.

The Recruiting Process

Describe your recruiting process and the criteria by which you select candidates. Is prior experience necessary?

The recruiting process at Rothschild Canada has identified certain characteristics that we feel are crucial to having a successful and long-term career in investment banking. While strong academic performance is not in itself a requirement, it does tend to indicate the dedication and commitment that recruits have made in their past endeavors. Experience in the industry or in related fields will also act as guidance in identifying those recruits who have decided to make investment banking their career choice. A third requirement, of course, is that recruits be familiar and knowledgeable of the Canadian business environment and be able to work in Canada.

Salomon Brothers Inc

Seven World Trade Center
New York, NY 10048
(212) 783-7000

MBA Recruiting Contact(s):
Maureen Horan, Recruiting Manager
Investment Banking Recruiting
(212) 783-5924

Susan H. Glendon, Vice President
Sales and Trading Recruiting
(212) 783-6197

Company Description

Describe your firm's business and the types of clients served by your finance group(s).

Salomon Brothers is a full-service financial institution engaged in investment banking, market making and trading of financial instruments, fixed income and equity market research, and institutional money management. Salomon's services and activities include advisory services provided for mergers and acquisitions and financial restructurings; capital-raising activities, including the underwriting and distribution of debt, equity, and derivative securities; trading and arbitrage strategies using debt, equity, and derivative instruments; entering into contractual commitments, such as forward securities and currency agreements, interest rate swap, cap, and floor agreements; options, warrants, and derivative products; fixed income and equity market research; institutional money management services; precious metals trading; and mortgage banking. Salomon Brothers conducts its business globally, with offices in Australia, Canada, France, Germany, Hong Kong, Japan, South Korea, Spain, Switzerland, Taiwan, Thailand, the United Kingdom, and the United States. Its customer base consists primarily of large- and medium-size corporations, governments, and financial institutions. Financial services are also provided to individuals on a limited basis.

Investment Banking
Salomon Brothers' investment banking activities consist principally of raising capital and providing strategic advisory services. Capital-raising activities include underwriting and distributing debt and equity securities and involve the development, underwriting, and distribution of derivative products. These products include warrants linked to a variety of instruments, such as debt securities, equity securities, baskets of equity securities, indexes based upon stock markets throughout the world, and commodities such as gold and oil. Strategic advisory services are provided in connection with mergers and acquisitions, leveraged buyouts, financial restructurings, and privatizations.

Sales and Trading
Salomon Brothers is a major dealer in government securities in New York, Tokyo, London, and Frankfurt and is a member of major international securities, financial futures, and options exchanges. It has extensive distribution capabilities and one of the largest capital bases in the U.S. securities industry. Salomon Brothers is a major underwriter of securities for governments and high-grade primary issuers and is capable of executing trading strategies on behalf of its customers and for its own account requiring significant commitments of capital.

Salomon's trading expertise, which dates back more than 80 years, together with the ability to execute a high volume of transactions with counterparties, enables it to provide liquidity to investors across a broad range of markets and financial instruments. Salomon Brothers' ability to execute arbitrage strategies is enhanced not only by its established presence in international capital markets but also by its utilization of information technology, quantitative methods, and risk management tools; its research capabilities; and its leadership position in the development and use of financial derivative products.

Describe your ownership structure.

Salomon Brothers Inc is the investment banking/brokerage subsidiary of Salomon Inc, a New York Stock Exchange–listed firm. A substantial portion of Salomon Inc.'s equity is owned by its employees and Berkshire Hathaway, Inc. In 1990, Salomon Inc implemented the Equity Partnership Plan for Key Employees (EPP), designed to provide participants, including newly hired MBAs, with a continuing long-term investment in common stock of Salomon Inc. Through the EPP and other programs designed to increase employee ownership, Salomon Inc expects that within the next few years, its employees will own 30% of the firm's common stock.

How does your approach to finance differ from that of other firms, and what do you consider to be your strengths and distinctive capabilities?

Several areas of competence distinguish the businesses of Salomon Inc: our ability and willingness to commit capital for our clients and for ourselves; our superior risk management and financial engineering capabilities; our geographic breadth, with strong customer and proprietary businesses on four continents; our first-class financial advisory and analytical skills and databases; and the character of our professionals.

Discuss changes in your firm's revenues (both domestic and international) and professional staff over the past year; over the past five years.

The financial services industry is characterized by change. Increasingly, the businesses of Salomon Brothers are becoming global. A number of products, markets, and clients that contribute significantly to the revenue and profitability of Salomon Brothers today were nonexistent five years ago. The establishment of a Tokyo office, where Salomon Brothers has become the leading non-Japanese competitor in terms of both revenue and profitability, and the development of its derivative product businesses are illustrative of such markets and products. A hallmark of Salomon Brothers has been its willingness to commit capital, both financial and human, to the development of promising emerging businesses such as these.

As of July 30, 1995, Salomon Brothers employed approximately 6,500 employees worldwide, approximately the same number employed as of December 31, 1986.

The Finance MBA's Job Description

Describe the career path and corresponding responsibilities for an MBA at your firm. Describe the opportunities for professional mobility between the various departments in your firm.

New associates, as well as senior investment bankers, have identified career mobility, cohesiveness, early professional responsibility, and comprehensive training as salient considerations in their decision to join Salomon Brothers.

Flexibility and Options

Flexibility is the hallmark of a professional career at Salomon Brothers. In Investment Banking, several options are available. In contrast with a number of other major investment banks, Salomon does not compel a candidate to choose a specific functional specialty in order to get an offer.

Associates who join Investment Banking enter the generalist associate program, where they have the opportunity to work with many product and coverage areas to develop a broad banking competence. During their first year at the firm, generalists typically spend approximately 25% of their time on financings, 30% on mergers and acquisitions assignments, 25% on financial advisory and restructuring work, and 20% on business development.

After their first one to two years in Investment Banking, associates usually select an initial specialization that best fits their interest and background. Areas of specialization include the following:

Capital Market Services (synthesizes the efforts of Corporate Finance, Sales, and Trading in new product development and public debt offerings)
Mergers and Acquisitions
Leveraged Finance
Specialty Industries (i.e., media, telecommunications and technology, forest products/paper, retailing, transportation, utilities, and regional industrial and high-yield coverage in the eastern United States)
Specialty Finance Products (high yield, private placements, project finance, and leasing)
International (coverage of foreign and international corporations and governments: London, Tokyo, Frankfurt, Sydney, New York)
Financial Institutions (insurance coverage, depository institutions, diversified financials, government finance, insurance, and real estate)

Similarly, Salomon takes the generalist approach in hiring for sales and trading. All interns are recruited for the training program and then choose their areas of specialty after exposure to all facets of sales and trading through our intensive training and rotation process. These areas of specialization include the following:

Corporate Bonds
Derivative Securities
Emerging Markets
Finance
Foreign Exchange
Government Bonds
High Yield
Mortgage Bonds
Syndicate
Equity Derivatives
Equity Convertibles
Equity Sales Trading
Equity Syndicates
Equity Block Trading
Equity Over the Counter

A career at Salomon Brothers is dynamic. Many of today's most important product lines and services either did not exist or were relatively small portions of our business a few years ago. Many of our people are now working in product areas that did not exist at the time they joined the firm. We are confident that Salomon's flexibility will enable the organization to continue to capitalize on emerging market opportunities and challenges.

Integration and Teamwork

The integration of the firm's investment banking, research, sales, and trading capabilities is responsible for Salomon's performance. Our achievements reflect the combined expertise of many areas within Finance, as well as contributions from other departments and our international network.

Teamwork is ingrained in Salomon Brothers' professionals. Investment Banking professionals work closely with members of the Sales, Trading, and Syndicate Departments on the trading floor, as well as with Research. For example, while working on an initial public offering, an associate will interact extensively with Syndicate, Equity Sales, and Stock Research.

Salomon's performance-based compensation policy underscores the fact that teamwork and cooperation are the basis of our business success. Unlike many of its competitors, Salomon Brothers does not pay commissions to sales and trading professionals. Instead, a broad group of senior managers carefully assesses each person's contributions to the firm's overall performance.

Responsibility and Participation

Although the number of professionals has grown to meet new market opportunities, Salomon remains committed to a leanly staffed organization. The firm emphasizes small working groups that give new associates room in which to operate and develop.

A first-year Finance associate works closely with a managing director and a vice president on each of his or her important assignments. Rapid client responsibility is encouraged. We are anxious to bring new Associates into client contact at the earliest possible stage so that they will cultivate the relationships that are critical to the firm's long-term success.

In Sales and Trading, a first-year associate's exposure to managing directors and vice presidents is also immediate. Sales units and trading desks are run by managing directors who spend most of their time on the sales or trading desk. Furthermore, sales units and trading desks are broken down into small subunits run by experienced vice presidents who act as mentors to train the young associates. Salespeople are given account assignments soon after their placement on a desk, and traders receive

risk-taking responsibilities at a very rapid pace. Hands-on training and significant early responsibility are hallmarks of the Salomon sales and trading program.

The Recruiting Process

Describe your recruiting process and the criteria by which you select candidates. Is prior experience necessary?

Salomon's character is reflected in the diversity, talents, and various backgrounds of its new associates. Salomon recruits associates who have displayed exceptional talent at whatever they have set their minds to. Rather than seeking a particular résumé, experience, or personality, we look for individuals with a proven record of achievement, entrepreneurial initiative, outstanding integrity, and continuing desire to work hard and excel. Salomon's 1995 class includes representatives from a large number of business, law, and other graduate schools, of which a significant proportion were international.

Professional development has always been a top priority of the firm. New members of all departments—from Investment Banking and Research to Sales and Trading—complete the firm's training program, widely considered the broadest in scope and most challenging of its kind on Wall Street. The program has three basic components:

1. Two months of classroom training, which is conducted at the firm's New York headquarters for all new associates in Investment Banking and Sales and Trading worldwide. Senior managers provide instruction on all firm capabilities and organizations. Trainees are expected to complete assignments and rotate responsibilities for monitoring and summarizing market activities to the class each morning.

2. Rotation among sales and trading desks in key product areas to work alongside senior managers.

3. Preparation for the Registered Representative examination given by the National Association of Securities Dealers and the New York Stock Exchange.

Training modules continue for three weeks in Investment Banking and eight weeks in Sales and Trading.

Salomon Brothers' compensation policy reflects the firm's belief in a team approach to business. Bonuses and salaries are based on each professional's overall contribution to the firm's performance, which includes such factors as creativity and imagination, management potential, and the ability to train others within the firm.

How many permanent associates and analysts do you hire in a typical year? How many summer interns do you expect to hire? If you have a formal summer program, please describe it. Please be sure to indicate whether the summer program is in place for all offices or just some.

In 1995 our Investment Banking Department plans to hire approximately 18–20 summer and 20–25 full-time associates. In addition, our Sales and Trading Department estimates that it will hire 10–15 summer and 10–15 full-time MBA candidates.

The Salomon summer program is designed to identify candidates for full-time positions. More than 75% of Salomon summer associates have received offers, filling approximately half of our full-time hiring needs.

The Investment Banking summer program provides a realistic introduction to the firm and work experience comparable to that of a full-time associate. Summer professionals function as full-time associates and become integral team members working on financings, mergers and acquisitions, and new business presentations.

The Sales and Trading summer program is a flexible, unstructured program that allows associates to rotate to different areas of the firm in both equities and fixed income. Presentations and product-specific classes are an integral part of the program, giving the associate an introduction to a full range of security products, as well as a realistic experience in Sales and Trading.

What international opportunities does your firm offer for U.S. citizens? For foreign nationals?

Salomon Brothers' Investment Banking operations in Asia include offices in Bangkok, Melbourne, Seoul, Singapore, Sydney, Taipei, and Tokyo and affiliations in Bombay and Kuala Lumpur. In addition, there are professionals based in our New York office who are dedicated to servicing the requirements of our Asian clients in the United States. This network enables Salomon to maintain regular contact with governments and major industrial and financial institutions throughout the region. These offices are staffed with Investment Banking professionals with both regional and product expertise, including capital markets, mergers and acquisitions, project and lease finance, and real estate.

Europe is a key component of Salomon Brothers' global investment banking network. Salomon Brothers' activities in Europe are headquartered in London, and Salomon Brothers is also supported by offices in Berlin, Frankfurt, Madrid, Milan, Paris, and Zurich. In Europe, Salomon Brothers provides a full range of investment banking services to corporations and to sovereign and supranational organizations. The Investment Banking group in London is staffed primarily by European nationals and includes individuals from over a dozen countries. Salomon Brothers' continuing commitment to Europe reflects the importance of the European economies on the world stage and the vital role Europe plays in the international financial markets.

For further information, contact Tracy Parnell, Salomon Brothers International Limited, Victoria Plaza, 111 Buckingham Palace Road, London SW1W 0SB England.

Schroder Wertheim & Co. Incorporated

787 Seventh Avenue
New York, NY 10019
(212) 492-6000

MBA Recruiting Contact(s):
Andrew J. Frankle, Vice President
Corporate Finance
(212) 492-6478
Fax: (212) 492-7031

Locations of Offices:
Schroders worldwide: offices in 40 cities in 30 countries, headquartered in London. Schroder Wertheim headquartered in New York, with other offices in Los Angeles, Chicago, Boston, Philadelphia, London, Paris, Geneva, and Amsterdam.

Total Number of Professionals (U.S. and worldwide):
4,300 worldwide, 1,100 in the United States

Company Description:

Describe your firm's business and the types of clients served by your finance group(s).

Schroder Wertheim & Co. Incorporated is part of Schroders, an international investment banking group with extensive operations in the three major financial centers of the world: North America, Europe, and the Asia Pacific region. Schroder Wertheim, founded as Wertheim & Co. in 1927, is a full-service major bracket investment banking firm, based in New York. The firm is actively involved in all aspects of investment banking, including corporate finance, mergers and acquisitions advisory, sales and trading, arbitrage, securities research, and asset management.

The Group employs approximately 300 investment banking professionals worldwide, with approximately 90 bankers based in North America. The Schroder Wertheim Corporate Finance Department is actively involved in all major areas of investment banking. Specific areas of expertise include mergers and acquisitions, both domestic and cross-border, public offerings of debt and equity securities, private placements of debt and equity securities, financial restructurings, and general financial advisory services. The firm is active in the public and private capital markets and Schroders has consistently ranked in the top 10 M&A advisors worldwide. Schroders

provides investment banking services to companies in all industries. Schroder Wertheim has teams of corporate finance and research professionals with particular expertise in the chemical, energy, financial services, health care, industrial manufacturing, lodging and gaming, media, restaurant, and transportation industries.

The partnership with Schroders has served as the foundation for Schroder Wertheim to participate in the growing international financing and mergers and acquisitions markets. Schroders is and historically has been one of the preeminent merchant banks in Europe and the Far East, with 4,300 employees in offices in 40 cities in 30 countries worldwide, including London, Paris, Milan, Amsterdam, Frankfurt, Warsaw, Tokyo, Singapore, Hong Kong, Shanghai, and Sydney.

Describe your ownership structure.

Schroder Wertheim & Co. Incorporated is a wholly owned subsidiary of Schroders plc, the leading global investment bank based in London. Schroders is publicly traded on the London Stock Exchange and has an equity market capitalization of approximately $4 billion.

How does your approach to finance differ from that of other firms, and what do you consider to be your distinctive strengths and capabilities?

The business of Schroder Wertheim is creating value for clients. The firm conducts its business in a personalized manner, building long-term client relationships founded on value creation over time. The Corporate Finance Department focuses its efforts on its particular areas of expertise, which are institutionalized in a number of industry groups. Senior professionals are very actively involved in serving clients, ensuring the highest level of client service. The firm has a strong research tradition and is often among the top rated research organizations relative to its size. The industry group organization promotes strong cooperation and coordination between research and corporate finance.

Mergers and acquisitions has traditionally been a strength of the firm and Schroders traditionally ranks among the most prominent firms in transactions worldwide. With respect to capital raising, the firm is a major bracket underwriter of public equity and debt, with particular strength in institutional sales and trading. The firm brings this same level of expertise to the private financing markets.

Discuss changes in your firm's revenues (both domestic and international) and professional staff over the past year; the past five years.

The firm has grown steadily over the past ten years and has not been subject to the volatility and erratic expansion and contraction that have typified many other investment banks. Because of Schroder Wertheim's orientation to long-term relationships and a relatively lower level of proprietary trading (and therefore lower level of exposure to the volatility of the financial markets), revenues and profitability have tended to be relatively stable compared to many of our competitors.

The Finance MBA's Job Description

Describe the career path and corresponding responsibilities for an MBA at your firm.

Schroder Wertheim offers its associates the opportunities inherent in a growing international investment banking firm with the atmosphere of a traditional Wall Street partnership.

Though the career path is similar to that of most investment banks, the role of an associate in Schroder Wertheim's Corporate Finance Department differs significantly from the role of an associate in a bulge bracket investment bank. In their early years, associates are encouraged to obtain as broad experience as possible, before developing a specific industry or product specialization. Schroder Wertheim endeavors to ensure that all incoming associates obtain experience in all major areas of investment banking: general financial advisory, mergers and acquisitions, public and private placements of securities, and financial restructurings. Incoming associates are also encouraged to become involved with clients in a diverse group of industries.

Because of the size and open structure of our department, associates are encouraged to learn as much as possible and develop responsibility early. Rarely is a transaction or client serviced by more than three professionals or more than one associate.

Describe the opportunities for professional mobility with the various departments in your firm.

The best opportunities for mobility are among the numerous Schroders corporate finance offices around the world. Within the limits of the requirements of the business and availability of positions, international movement is encouraged as a way of enhancing an individual's career development.

Discuss the lifestyle aspects of a career with your firm.

The firm supports a collegial, supportive culture in a professional environment. Professionals work as part of relationship or transaction teams (which may vary project to project) and successful investment bankers should have both strong individual and team skills. Hours and travel are typical for an investment bank and vary according to the demands of particular clients and projects. Travel tends to be one or two days at a time, as opposed to extended stays away from home.

The Recruiting Process

Describe your recruiting process and the criterion by which you select candidates. Is prior experience necessary?

Schroder Wertheim interviews at the top MBA programs to find the select group of associates it hires each year. Schroder Wertheim seeks highly motivated individuals with a record of business and academic achievement. Schroder Wertheim maintains a collegial atmosphere which supports initiative at all levels and Schroder Wertheim seeks individuals who will succeed in this environment. Prior experience in finance or financial analysis is considered helpful, but not required.

How many permanent associates and analysts do you hire in a typical year? How many summer interns do you expect to hire? If you have a formal summer program, please describe it. Please be sure to indicate whether the summer program is in place for all offices or just some.

Schroder Wertheim's Corporate Finance Department expects to hire approximately 10 associates and 10 analysts this year, primarily for the New York office, with the possibility of additional hiring for the Los Angeles office. These levels are equal to 1995 hiring. Schroders does additional hiring for its other offices around the world. Interested persons should apply directly to the applicable office.

Schroder Wertheim has a 10-week Summer Associate Program within the Corporate Finance Department. Summer associates function as full members of the department and contribute to several transaction teams as part of a program designed to introduce the summer associate to as broad a client and transaction base as possible. The program gives students an opportunity to learn or expand their experience in the various areas of investment banking.

We expect to hire three summer associates for the New York office for the summer of 1996.

What international opportunities does the firm offer U.S. citizens? Foreign nationals?

Our employees have the opportunity to seek positions in Schroder offices around the world. Within the limits of the requirements of the business and availability of positions, international movement is encouraged as a way of enhancing an individual's career development. Foreign nationals are encouraged to apply to particular foreign offices directly, if interested.

Simmons & Company International

700 Louisiana
Suite 5000
Houston, TX 77002
(713) 236-9999

MBA Recruiting Contact(s):
Matthew R. Simmons, President

Andrew L. Waite, Associate

Company Description

Describe your firm's business and the types of clients served by your finance group(s).

Simmons & Company International is a privately owned full service investment banking firm based in Houston. The firm was founded in 1974 by Matthew R. Simmons, an HBS graduate from the Class of 1967. Simmons & Company provides corporate finance advisory services, equity research coverage, and institutional sales and trading activities. All of Simmons' activities are focused on companies participating in the international oil and gas service and equipment industry ("oil service industry"). Simmons & Company is one of a limited number of investment banking firms not based in New York City.

The firm's corporate finance activities include mergers and acquisitions advisory services, private placements of debt and equity, financial restructuring advisory work, and a variety of consulting assignments. Simmons & Company has implemented more than 300 transactions having an aggregate value of over $12 billion. The firm's institutional securities business was established in 1992. Simmons & Company underwrites and co-manages public debt and equity offerings, provides equity research and institutional sales activities, and makes markets in selected over-the-counter stocks. Since that time, Simmons & Company has acted as a co-manager for approximately $2 billion of public securities offerings.

Simmons & Company conducts its business worldwide. Approximately 25% of the firm's clients are Texas based, 50% are in other parts of the United States, and 25% are international.

Since its founding, Simmons & Company has maintained four overriding corporate goals that define the firm's culture:

1. Specialization. We provide financial services exclusively to the oil service industry.

2. Quality. We aim to deliver the absolutely highest-quality "product" to our clients.

3. Size. We want to remain a relatively small, highly specialized group of professionals.

4. Culture. We offer a stimulating work environment for our professional staff and those who work with us.

How does your approach to finance differ from that of other firms, and what do you consider to be your strengths and distinctive capabilities?

The key difference and competitive advantage of Simmons & Company is our exclusive focus on the international oil service industry.

This industry is incredibly diverse, large, and vital to the international economy. It includes any firm that supplies any product or service involved in the exploration, production, transportation, or processing of hydrocarbons. The industry comprises thousands of companies with aggregate estimated annual revenues of $150 billion.

Simmons & Company is considered the preeminent financial advisor to the oil service industry. The firm's specialization and unique knowledge base provide a distinctive competitive advantage over the firm's major competitors, the large Wall Street investment banking firms. Our market share for transactions in the oil service industry that are handled by investment banking firms is more than three times any other investment banking firm in the world.

Several other aspects of our business are different from many of our competitors. First, we operate strictly on a team basis, and in any given year, all associates have the opportunity to participate as a team member with virtually all other professionals in the firm. Second, we maintain strict control over the number and types of projects we undertake and believe that our close rate on committed projects is as high as any other firm in our business. Finally, the depth of our analysis exceeds most of our competition.

Discuss changes in your firm's revenues (both domestic and international) and professional staff over the past year; over the past five years.

The oil service industry has proved to be one of the most volatile parts of the world economy. The past decade has included a boom and then a depression of a magnitude unprecedented in any other industry in any historical period. This unparalleled volatility has created tremendous opportunities for Simmons & Company. Over the past five years, the firm has approximately doubled its professional staff and revenue base, and growth is expected to continue. However, the firm intends to remain relatively small and specialized. Simmons & Company's professional staff now includes five partners, three vice presidents, and a group of 12 associates and analysts, plus a support staff of approximately 20.

In late 1992 Simmons & Company established the Institutional Securities division. The focus of this new division is to capitalize on the firm's unique expertise in the oil service industry by providing research on the approximately 90 publicly traded oil service companies and on industry trends to the institutional investor community. Simmons has expanded its services to include participation in public offerings of oil service equities as both an underwriter and co-manager. We established a clearing relationship with Morgan Stanley & Company Inc. and have expanded into market making in over-the-counter stocks. The Institutional Securities division remains completely focused on the oil service industry.

The Finance MBA's Job Description

Describe the career path and corresponding responsibilities for an MBA at your firm.

The primary objective for an incoming associate is to gain the experience, judgment, and maturity to assume a leadership role in managing our projects and to market the firm's services effectively. As an associate, an MBA can expect to progress through assignments of increasing responsibility toward partnership and ultimate ownership in the firm.

An MBA can expect to have immediate and substantial client contact, including written and oral presentations. Simmons & Company emphasizes analysis, so an associate should anticipate considerable quantitative work. All projects are organized on a team basis, with one or more associates and analysts supporting a managing director who serves as project manager. In a typical year, an as-

sociate would work on between 10 and 20 projects and work with virtually all the other professionals of the firm as a member of different project teams.

Discuss the lifestyle aspects of a career with your firm (i.e., average hours per week, amount of travel, flexibility to change offices, corporate culture, etc.).

One of Simmons & Company's enduring corporate goals is to offer a stimulating work environment for our professional staff and those who work with us. The work environment is fast-paced and engrossing, and domestic and international travel is involved; however, work hours and travel requirements do not preclude members of the firm from developing outside interests. Many of our associates and analysts are married and a number have small children.

The Recruiting Process

Describe your recruiting process and the criteria by which you select candidates. Is prior experience necessary?

Simmons & Company seeks MBAs with two or more years of professional business experience, strong analytical ability, intellectual curiosity, a desire to work with people, a desire to keep on a fast learning curve, a sense of humor, and, most important, a commitment to excellence. The most important criterion for success is the "chemistry" with other members of the firm.

Our professionals come from remarkably diverse backgrounds. No prior exposure to the oil service industry is either required or necessary.

How many permanent associates and analysts do you hire in a typical year? How many summer interns do you expect to hire? If you have a formal summer program, please describe it. Please be sure to indicate whether the summer program is in place for all offices or just some.

Because Simmons & Company is, and plans to remain, a relatively small firm, recruiting for associates is limited. Four associates have joined the firm from HBS in the past three years. Simmons & Company has no formal summer program for MBAs.

Smith Barney Inc.

388 Greenwich Street
New York, NY 10013
(212) 816-6000

MBA Recruiting Contact(s):
Chip Rae, Senior Vice President
Investment Banking Recruiting
(212) 816-1764
Fax: (212) 816-2839

Judy Meyers, Director Capital Markets Recruiting
(212) 723-4987
Fax: (212) 723-8763

Company Description

Describe your firm's business and the types of clients served by your finance group(s).

Smith Barney is a global securities firm that provides brokerage, investment banking, and asset management services to corporations, governments, and individuals. Our firm includes nearly 28,000 people in more than 500 locations worldwide. Smith Barney has offices throughout the United States, as well as in Amsterdam, Bahrain, Geneva, Hong Kong, London, Paris, Tokyo, Toronto, and Zurich. Strategic alliances with international organizations and our ownership of Atlanta-based Robinson-Humphrey, the nation's leading regional investment bank, expand Smith Barney's capabilities beyond our geographic locations.

We are active in all major sectors of finance and the second largest brokerage firm in the United States. Our core services include sales, research, and trading for individuals and institutions; underwriting, advisory, and specialty financing for corporations and government entities; mutual fund services; and futures and asset management. Smith Barney now manages over $75 billion in assets and oversees client accounts totaling more than $320 billion.

Describe your ownership structure.

Smith Barney's corporate foundations are strong. It is a wholly owned subsidiary of The Travelers Group with more than $115 billion in assets and $10 billion in equity capital. Travelers provides a full range of investment, insurance, and consumer finance services to individual, institutional, and government clients around the world.

How does your approach to finance differ from that of other firms, and what do you consider to be your strengths and distinctive capabilities?

In many ways, Smith Barney is a young company with old roots. We are well established in key markets, yet still in the process of building a unique franchise for the future. Our working environment is entrepreneurial. Individual effort is encouraged and recognized. Initiative is prized. The combination of our investment banking and trading capabilities with the power of our distribution network creates a broad and diversified revenue stream ensuring greater stability.

Our greatest strength is the ability of each business unit to work in close cooperation with the others. We have begun to create a culture that is unique on Wall Street, in which true integration and cooperation exists among investment banking, capital markets, research, asset management, and brokerage. It is a way of doing business that focuses the full force of our resources on the needs of every client, regardless of whether they are municipal governments, global corporations, large institutions, or enterprising individuals.

Discuss changes in your firm's revenues (both domestic and international) and professional staff over the past year; over the past five years.

The securities industry experienced a widespread slowdown in activity, revenues, and profitability in 1994 compared to 1993. While Smith Barney was affected by this industry wide slowdown, the inclusion of Shearson for the full year in 1994 versus five months in 1993 resulted in substantial increases in revenues from commissions, principal trading, asset management fees, and net interest income. Investment banking revenues rose slightly over 1993, in the face of a weak environment for stock and bond issuances and lower new issue volume in the securities markets. Net revenues, net of interest expense, totaled $4.8 million in 1994 versus $3.1 million in 1993.

Smith Barney's return on equity declined from 26.7% for 1993, excluding the $65 million merger-related provisions, to 16.4% for 1994, excluding the $21 million gain on HG Asia, on a higher equity base, and is still among the highest of its industry peer group.

Since mid-1993 the Investment Banking Department has nearly doubled in terms of the number of professionals and now numbers about 400 worldwide. The increase is partly attributable to a targeted hiring program of experienced bankers, as well as an aggressive analyst and associate recruiting strategy.

110

Smith Barney has grown dramatically—and is substantially a different firm from five years ago. Any comparison would not be meaningful.

The Finance MBA's Job Description

Describe the career path and corresponding responsibilities for an MBA at your firm.

Smith Barney's long-term success depends on the quality of the individuals hired over time. In 1994-95 the firm hired 19 associates in Investment Banking, 23 in Capital Markets, and one in Public Finance. The summer associate class included 16 in Investment Banking, nine in Capital Markets, one in Public Finance, and one in Research.

- Investment Banking associates initially receive offers to join the group, with assignments to specific departments determined after acceptance of our offer. Each associate is given the opportunity to meet a wide variety of departments prior to making a decision.

Associates in Smith Barney's Investment Banking Group are quickly expected to become active contributors to the firm's overall investment banking effort. The organization of the group is structured to offer rapid advancement and outstanding financial rewards to successful associates. Associates work directly with senior members of the Investment Banking Group as well as representatives of other divisions within the firm on a wide variety of transactions and financial projects. Transactions include domestic and international public offerings and private acquisitions, financial consulting projects, tender offers, and mergers and acquisitions. Financial consulting projects range from assisting corporate clients in formulating capitalization and dividend policies to evaluating acquisition or divestiture strategies. In addition, associates participate in the firm's ongoing business development activities.

All new associates start their careers with five weeks of intensive classroom training beginning in August. The program focuses on a firmwide orientation, accounting principles, investment banking products, financial statement analysis, financial modeling, taxation, and valuation. Projects and case studies are also assigned giving new associates hands-on experience as well as the opportunity to work in teams. Our program also allows associates to take the General Securities (Series 7) Exam and the Uniform Securities Agent State Law (Series 63) Exam. The training is conducted by Smith Barney professionals, business school professors, and industry experts.

- Capital Markets covers the sales and trading of all debt and equity products globally. All new associates participate in a six-month comprehensive training program beginning in early August.

During the first three months, seminars on selling skills, fixed income math, negotiation skills, macroeconomics, research, portfolio analysis, and product knowledge are taught by Smith Barney professionals, business school professors, and industry experts. Series 7 training is also provided.

Associates spend the next three months rotating through various desks, gaining exposure to corporate bond trading, mortgage-backed trading, government trading, fixed income sales, high yield trading and sales, municipal trading and sales, derivatives, emerging markets, equity trading and sales, securities lending, and risk arbitrage.

During the final phase of the program, associates are given the opportunity to do internships at three different desks, each lasting two weeks. These internships provide the desks as well as the associates the opportunity to assess whether there is a fit for final placement.

- Public Finance has long been a leader in the organization and distribution of tax-exempt municipal securities. An associate in the Public Finance Group is an important member of a client's financing team. Responsibilities include the structuring of a wide variety of complex transactions, providing marketing support for bond offerings, the coordination and review of legal documents for transactions, and interaction with clients as well as other parties to the transaction.

Associates actively participate in maintaining client relationships and developing new business opportunities by preparing financing analyses and presenting financial proposals to existing and prospective clients.

Associates work and learn as generalists and are assigned to various project teams at any given time, leading to long hours and frequent deadline pressures. After one or two years as generalists, associates have the opportunity to specialize in one of our various industry specialty groups as electric utilities, health care, transportation, derivative products, airports, or project finance.

Associates go through a two-month comprehensive training program conducted by Smith Barney professionals, business school professors, and industry experts. Extensive training is given in credit analysis for all major industry areas, financial analysis, financial modeling, and tax and legal issues. Projects and case studies including actual transactions are also assigned to give new associates a hands-on experience as well as the opportunity to work in teams.

Career paths and corresponding responsibilities vary depending on the business division. An MBA joining Investment Banking, for example, typically enters as an associate, responsible for the details of executing transactions and preparing proposals. After approximately four years, associates are eligible for promotion to vice president. Vice presidents manage the execution of transactions and identify new opportunities with clients.

About three years later, vice presidents become eligible for promotion to director, or to the more senior title of managing director. Directors and managing directors are responsible for ongoing client relationships and identification of new business opportunities.

Describe the opportunities for professional mobility between the various departments in your firm.

First year associates join their department at the conclusion of the training program. Their success is often based on their ability to leverage the firm's resources and to develop contacts across the firm. As an individual's interests change, and as our businesses develop and evolve, new opportunities are often available firmwide.

The Recruiting Process

Describe your recruiting process and the criteria by which you select candidates. Is prior experience necessary?

Smith Barney participates in a wide range of campus recruiting events and on-campus interviews. Successful candidates are invited to New York for a final Super Saturday or equivalent round. The firm respects school policies in its recruiting practices.

We seek individuals with a record of achievement. Successful candidates display:

- Demonstrated leadership skills

- Relevant business experience

- Demonstrated work ethic

- Quantitative skills

- Client relationship ability

- Academic excellence

- Maturity and focus

Teachers Insurance and Annuity Association-College Retirement Equities Fund (TIAA-CREF)

730 Third Avenue
New York, NY 10017
(800) 842-2733

MBA Recruiting Contact(s):
Robert A. Moll, Human Resources Officer
Robert J. Burke, Staffing Specialist

Company Description

Describe your firm's business and the types of clients served by your finance group(s).

As the world's largest pension fund, with over $150 billion in assets under management, TIAA-CREF professionals skillfully invest in virtually every economic sector. TIAA assets are broadly diversified among private placements, publicly traded bonds, commercial mortgages, and real estate. CREF, the companion corporation, is a registered investment company.

Quality and yield are the bedrock of our investment activities. In fact, TIAA is a top performer in the insurance industry, and its strong balance sheets earn the highest possible ratings from Moody's, Standard & Poor's, Duff & Phelps, and A.M. Best.

TIAA-CREF originated a pension system of portable benefits in 1918 to help ensure the financial security of people employed in education and research. Today, over 1.7 million professors, research scientists, and other educators turn to TIAA-CREF for expert benefits counseling, affordable insurance protection, and retirement income that cannot be outlived.

Stable cash flows, innovative strategies, and years of experience make TIAA a leader in direct placement loans to private and public companies, as well as in publicly traded bonds. TIAA also invests in highly structured deals, including private securitized financings, hybrid credit/real estate deals, project financings, and secondary private placements.

The Finance MBA's Job Description

Describe the career path and corresponding responsibilities for an MBA at your firm.

Our steady stream of investment activity is ideal for MBAs who want to put their talent to work immediately, with financings in a broad range of industries. Individual responsibilities are balanced with teamwork at every level, enabling associates to gain broad industry knowledge and market experience.

Specifically, private placement associates monitor portfolios with investments in about 25 companies, valued at about a half-billion dollars. Associates analyze industry trends, make on-site evaluations of potential investments, negotiate new deals, and present recommendations to senior management.

Public market associates evaluate market trends, research bond offerings, develop trading strategies, and present recommendations to senior managers responsible for multibillion-dollar portfolios.

The Recruiting Process

Describe your recruiting process and the criteria by which you select candidates. Is prior experience necessary?

TIAA Investments seeks talented MBAs majoring in finance to join our Securities Division. Superior communications skills and prior credit training and analysis experience at a major financial institution are strongly preferred. Along with quality investing, we emphasize teamwork and a balanced work and personal lifestyle.

A successful screening interview will be followed by an opportunity to meet with Securities officers and associates at our New York City headquarters.

We believe cultural and ethnic diversity is the lifeblood of a successful corporation, and this is reflected in our hiring record, our tradition of promoting from within, and our career development activities.

Toronto Dominion Bank

31 West 52nd Street
New York, NY 10019-6101
(212) 468-0633

MBA Recruiting Contact(s):
Reginald A. McQuay, Manager
Human Resources

Company Description

Describe your firm's business and the types of clients served by your finance group(s).

Toronto Dominion Bank is a widely held, public corporation whose shares are listed on the Toronto, Montreal, Vancouver, Alberta, Winnipeg, International (London), and Tokyo Stock Exchanges. Total assets, as of April 30, 1995, were Cdn. $103.7 billion. TD is the fifth largest Canadian bank in terms of total assets and on the basis of common shareholders' equity.

Formally titled the Toronto-Dominion Bank, but usually referred to as TD Bank or simply TD, the bank was formed in 1955 through the merger of the Bank of Toronto (founded 1855) and the Dominion Bank (established 1869).

In Canada, TD serves individuals, businesses, financial institutions, and governments through a network of over 900 branches from coast to coast. With the acquisition of Central Guaranty Trust, the bank now offers complete trust and fiduciary services in both the personal and business fields.

TD's corporate business is focused primarily on North America. In the United States and internationally, TD offers a broad range of credit, financial, and advisory services to businesses, multinational corporations, governments, and correspondent banks through a network of offices in New York, Chicago, and Houston; London, Tokyo, Hong Kong, Singapore, and Taipei; and its Australian subsidiary in Melbourne.

A major strength of TD is its financial position. TD maintains the position of one of the best-capitalized banks in the world, with one of the highest credit ratings of all major North American banks. Financial strength is a major advantage in tough times; customers may be drawn to a bank offering financial stability that also has the capital to invest in service, to pursue new strategies, and to take advantage of opportunities that arise.

Another strength is that TD, unlike its major competitors, has built, rather than bought, its own securities operation and offers integrated corporate and investment banking services. This provides the bank with an edge in its ability to react innovatively to shifting customer needs and changing economic times.

TD has a relatively flat, flexible organizational structure, which enables it to respond quickly and mobilize to meet new challenges, and it has been an innovative leader in many areas. Its discount brokerage is a prime example. Green Line Investor Services Inc. is now Canada's top discount broker and challenges all other brokerage houses for the top spot in absolute number of trading orders on the Toronto Stock Exchange.

In recent years there has been a significant shift away from interest income to fee income, and with its many noninterest products and services, TD has largely offset the decline in credit. The growth of such TD services as private placements, fixed income issues, and financial advisory services have played a major role in this change, as have other relationship building services such as payroll and cash management, of which there are many options available, enabling TD to service the largest to the smallest customers efficiently and profitably.

The Finance MBA's Job Description

Describe the career path and corresponding responsibilities for an MBA at your firm.

The Associate Development Program, a structured rotational program, gives a broad understanding of our business strategy, organization, and values; fundamental product knowledge and skills; and the professional contacts and visibility that help integrate an individual into the firm. Following formal orientation, MBAs rotate through Corporate Banking, Toronto Dominion Securities, Inc., Sales & Trading, and Special Industries (Communications Finance, Forest Products Finance, Health Care Finance, and Utilities Finance). After the program, associates typically work in a group charged with researching, structuring, and negotiating transactions. Most individuals will experience several groups during their career with the bank.

The Recruiting Process

Describe your recruiting process and the criteria by which you select candidates. Is prior experience necessary?

To excel as an associate at Toronto Dominion, one must be resourceful, flexible, and exhibit the desire and ability to work independently. While senior colleagues provide career direction, your path toward promotion and advancement is your own.

United Airlines

P.O. Box 66100
Chicago, IL 60666
(708) 952-4000

MBA Recruiting Contact(s):
Jim Rynott
College Relations

Company Description

Describe your firm's business and the types of clients served by your finance group(s).

United Airlines is one of the largest international airlines in the world, with annual revenues in excess of $12 billion, more than 76,000 employees and a fleet of over 500 aircraft.

Headquartered in Chicago, United Airlines flies to 112 domestic and 40 international airports serving 32 countries on five continents. Our United Express partners fly to more than 180 destinations. Domestically, we maintain key hubs in Washington, D.C., Chicago, Denver, and San Francisco.

Independent industry sources rank United Airlines as one of the U.S. "big three" in terms of size and other operating criteria. Much of the airline's recent focus has been expansion into the European Community, South America, and Latin America and continued strengthening of our extensive route structure in the Pacific Basin. In June 1995 we introduced the B777 aircraft into our fleet of modern, spacious, quiet, and fuel-efficient aircraft.

Describe your ownership structure.

United Airlines is 55% employee owned with public shares being traded on the New York Stock Exchange, Midwest Stock Exchange, and the Pacific Stock Exchange under the symbol UAL. A copy of UAL Corporation's annual report to the Securities and Exchange Commission on form 10-K may be obtained from Investor Relations, UAL Corporation, (708) 952-7501.

The Finance MBA's Job Description

Describe the career path and corresponding responsibilities for an MBA at your firm.

MBA professionals who join United are initially assigned to positions in the Finance, Marketing, or Operations areas, providing a range of exposure to management issues. The continued emphasis is to utilize analytical tools to improve our competitiveness in both operations and financial markets. Our company has highly leveraged assets, thus, the goal is to maintain a balance sheet that gives management the freedom to pursue market opportunities competitively.

The Recruiting Process

Describe your recruiting process and the criteria by which you select candidates. Is prior experience necessary?

United Airlines seeks highly motivated individuals who have the ability to work in a team environment across functional organizations. Most MBAs enjoy our fast-paced, project-oriented environment. The majority have two to three years of work experience prior to attending graduate school. Progression is staff analyst, senior staff analyst, manager, and director and is based on a merit performance system.

Wasserstein Perella & Co. Inc.

31 West 52d Street
New York, NY 10019
(212) 969-2700

MBA Recruiting Contact(s):
Frances A. Lyman, Recruiting Manager

Company Description

Describe your firm's business and the types of clients served by your finance group(s).

Wasserstein Perella Group, Inc. is a leading international investment banking firm active in three related lines of business: (1) advising a global base of clients on matters of corporate strategy, mergers, acquisitions, divestitures and restructurings, and corporate finance; (2) specialized sales, trading, and research of debt and equity securities; and (3) management of investment funds and products that seek superior risk-adjusted returns for investors.

Our firm is dedicated to providing superior client service and building long-term relationships. In pursuit of these goals, Wasserstein Perella has established an international presence through a network of offices in New York, London, Paris, Frankfurt, Tokyo, Chicago, Los Angeles, and Dallas. Our strategic alliance with The Nomura Securities Co., Ltd., the world's largest securities firm, which was formed in 1988, shortly after the firm's founding, gives Wasserstein Perella an unparalleled presence in and access to Japan and the Asian markets. Since its inception, Wasserstein Perella's professional staff has grown to number approximately 200 worldwide.

Wasserstein Perella has participated in many of the largest and most significant mergers and acquisitions in recent history and in some of the most innovative financings. The firm is equally proud of the many small divestitures and other transactions it has managed on behalf of its long-term clients and the numerous occasions when clients have been advised to forego transactions as a result of market or strategic factors. The firm has developed a strong high-yield origination effort targeting financial entrepreneurs and growth companies, and has served as a sounding board for larger clients with respect to various financing alternatives.

Wasserstein Perella's specialized sales, trading, and research activities are carried out through its wholly owned subsidiary, Wasserstein Perella Securities, Inc. ("WPS").

Within WPS, the Grantchester Securities Division is one of the leading dealers of high-yield debt securities. Grantchester traded more than $43 billion of high-yield securities over the last three years and has transacted business with 200 different institutions having varied investment profiles. The WPS Equity Division is a highly focused team that concentrates on the sales, trading, and research of selected equity securities. WPS's Emerging Markets Division provides investor and corporate finance services in the Latin American, Eastern European, African, and Asian markets.

Wasserstein Perella continues to build its asset management capabilities. The firm's focus is on equity and fixed income money management of U.S. securities, selected international products, and an array of higher return, higher risk private investment funds. The cornerstone of this effort to date is the firm's merchant banking fund.

Describe your ownership structure.

Wasserstein Perella is a privately owned corporation. Twenty percent of its equity is held by Nomura Securities, Ltd.

How does your approach to finance differ from that of other firms, and what do you consider to be your strengths and distinctive capabilities?

Wasserstein Perella offers custom-tailored mergers and acquisitions (M&A) and corporate finance solutions to meet clients' unique needs. The firm is known for its ability to solve complex financial and strategic problems. We are also viewed as an objective sounding board for financing decisions, and we are not prejudiced by a need to underwrite securities to cover the overhead of a large underwriting operation.

Discuss changes in your firm's revenues (both domestic and international) and professional staff over the past year; over the past five years.

We have had a gradual diversification of revenues away from domestic M&A toward high-yield and equity sales, trading and research, international M&A, privatizations, and asset management.

The Finance MBA's Job Description

Describe the career path and corresponding responsibilities for an MBA at your firm.

Financial associates at Wasserstein Perella & Co., Inc. are responsible for all aspects of analysis relating to mergers, acquisitions, restructuring, divestitures, and leveraged buyouts. After a relatively short "training" period, associates are expected to be proficient with the fundamental analytical principals of mergers and acquisitions and general corporate finance. Associates will participate in structuring and negotiating M&A transactions and financings and will gain increasing experience and responsibility as they develop expertise in these areas. In addition, associates will play a significant role in the firm's "new business" efforts and ongoing client relationships.

Associates are given responsibilities that are typically one year ahead of those at other investment banks. The typical time period between associate and vice president is three and a half years.

Describe the opportunities for professional mobility between the various departments in your firm.

Wasserstein Perella provides tremendous flexibility between departments and geographic locations.

Discuss the lifestyle aspects of a career with your firm (i.e., average hours per week, amount of travel, flexibility to change offices, corporate culture, etc.).

Lifestyle/culture is characterized as fun and entrepreneurial yet intense. Average hours per week are 60–70. Travel depends on the nature of projects. Associates usually travel 15–25% of their time.

The Recruiting Process

Describe your recruiting process and the criteria by which you select candidates. Is prior experience necessary?

We usually conduct two-on-one on-campus interviews, followed by one or two visits to our New York office. Decisions are usually made quickly. We look for smart, energetic self-starters. Grades and previous experience are important factors.

How many permanent associates and analysts do you hire in a typical year? How many summer interns do you expect to hire? If you have a formal summer program, please describe it. Please be sure to indicate whether the summer program is in place for all offices or just some.

Wasserstein Perella typically hires four to five associates domestically and one to two internationally. We also hire two to three summer associates.

Wessels, Arnold & Henderson

901 Marquette Ave.
Minneapolis, MN 55402
(612) 373-6100
(800) 955-0920

MBA Recruiting Contact(s):
Jeremy Hedberg
Mike Ogborne

Location of Office:
Minneapolis, MN

No. of Professionals:
Approximately 50–55

Company Description

Describe your firm's business and the types of clients served by your finance group(s).

Wessels, Arnold & Henderson is a rapidly growing institutional investment banking firm based in Minneapolis that focuses on providing high-quality research, sales and trading, and investment banking services to growth companies in the technology, health care, and consumer sectors. Since its inception as a partnership in 1986, Wessels, Arnold & Henderson has focused on selectively building our firm through the hiring of highly motivated professionals. Our strength is our focus on very specific industry sectors and our commitment to building long-term relationships with our clients in order to provide them with the absolute highest level of service.

Wessels, Arnold & Henderson's Corporate Finance staff focuses on the management of public and private equity offerings, merger and acquisition advisory services, fairness opinions, and other financial services to companies in our selected industry sectors. Some of our recent clients include ArcSys, Inc., Ascend Communications, Inc., Chipcom Corporation, Damark International, Inc., Ap-

ple South, Inc., and Parametric Technology Corporation. Corporate Finance associates work directly with senior investment bankers on these assignments.

The Finance MBA's Job Description

Describe the career path and corresponding responsibilities for an MBA at your firm.

Wessels, Arnold & Henderson seeks to hire MBAs that possess solid academic credentials, are highly competitive, are self-motivated, and have demonstrated the ability to work as part of a team. In return for displaying these attributes, will be rewarded with a highly challenging, well-compensated career in a competitive work environment. A typical career path varies depending on the business division. An MBA in corporate finance would typically enter our firm at the associate level and be responsible for the details of executing a transaction. When an associate displays an aptitude for identifying new business opportunities and maintaining client relationships, he or she would be eligible to become a managing director.

At the hub of our company is our Research Department, whose focus and ideas drive the Trading and Corporate Finance Departments. Our research effort is aimed at providing value to our institutional customers by providing a timely, focused product. Analysts identify market segments and companies that will provide investors with outstanding investment growth and also work closely with the Corporate Finance Department to guide the evolution and future focus of the firm. Associate research analysts are teamed with senior analysts and are expected to be the leading analysts in their sectors to the institutional marketplace.

Wessels, Arnold & Henderson's Sales and Trading operations are focused on providing deep and liquid markets in the stocks in which we are market makers. This is essential in order to provide efficient stock prices for growth companies. Historically, Wessels, Arnold & Henderson has always ranked highly in making liquid markets for our universe of stocks.

Weyerhaeuser Company

Tacoma, WA 98477
(206) 924-2367

MBA Recruiting Contact(s):
Brian Haun, Director
Investment Evaluation Department
(206) 924-5227

Company Description

Describe your firm's business and the types of clients served by your finance group(s).

Weyerhaeuser is the world's largest private owner of timber, a leader in commercial forest management, and one of North America's largest producers and exporters of forest products. Weyerhaeuser also has significant positions in U.S. real estate development and financial services operations.

Timber Growing and Harvesting
Weyerhaeuser Company owns about 5.8 million acres of timberland in the United States with a merchantable volume of over 8.6 billion cubic feet of timber, the largest of any other private owner. In addition to company-owned lands in the United States, the company has long-term harvest licenses on approximately 12 million acres of productive forest land in the Canadian provinces of British Columbia, Alberta, and Saskatchewan. The company also grows about 300,000 seedlings a year in company-owned seed orchards, greenhouses, and nurseries. Weyerhaeuser supports the management of these resources with the largest private silvicultural and environmental research staff in the world.

Weyerhaeuser Company is unique in the quality of its timber resource and forest management programs. The company began growing timber as a crop in the 1930s. In 1941 it publicly committed itself to sustainable yield forestry with the dedication of lands in southwestern Washington as a "Tree Farm," launching the national Tree Farm movement. The High Yield Forestry program was begun in 1966, which more than doubles annual growth per acre over unmanaged natural stands. These early decisions have provided a relatively stable raw material supply, making Weyerhaeuser less dependent on purchased timber and logs than other companies.

Wood Products Manufacturing
Weyerhaeuser is the world's largest producer of softwood lumber and the largest North American exporter of forest products. Weyerhaeuser manufactures a full range of wood products, including logs, lumber, chips, plywood, oriented strandboard, and composite products at 55 locations around the United States and Canada. The company markets and distributes these products through its own sales and distribution system to industrial, wholesale, and retail customers.

Pulp and Paper Manufacturing
Weyerhaeuser is a leading producer of pulp, newsprint, fine paper, containerboard and shipping containers, liquid packaging board, and chemicals, with 63 manufacturing sites located throughout the United States and Canada. Weyerhaeuser's Pulp Division is the world's largest supplier of market pulp. The Newsprint Division is the largest foreign supplier of newsprint to Japan. Pulp and paper products are marketed through Weyerhaeuser's own sales and marketing organization, as well as through merchant distributors. The company also operates one of the nation's largest wastepaper recycling businesses. Weyerhaeuser's Recycling Division is almost 20 years old and has grown rapidly to become one of the largest paper recyclers in the United States. The company now recycles approximately 1.7 million tons of wastepaper in 20 facilities.

Real Estate Development and Financial Services
Weyerhaeuser Real Estate Company (WRECO), a wholly owned subsidiary of Weyerhaeuser Company, engages in real estate development, residential and commercial building construction, and venture capital projects. These activities are conducted through several operating companies in California, Florida, Maryland, New Jersey, North Carolina, Texas, and Washington. WRECO is one of the largest home builders in the United States. Weyerhaeuser Mortgage Company is one of the nation's largest residential mortgage bankers, with 40 retail branch offices nationwide.

The Finance MBA's Job Description

Describe the career path and corresponding responsibilities for an MBA at your firm.

The Investment Evaluation Department (IED) is the preferred entry point for high-potential MBAs. IED is responsible for providing strategic, financial, and analytical leadership in all acquisition, divestiture, merger, joint venture, and new business evaluations. The group is also responsible for analyzing and forming independent judgments on Weyerhaeuser's major capital investment

119

opportunities. IED is a small group within Weyerhaeuser's finance organization that deals substantially with the company's operating divisions, supporting major strategic and tactical decisions.

The analyst position is the traditional entry point for the department. Analysts typically spend two to three years in IED gaining a broad perspective on Weyerhaeuser's businesses and exposure to senior corporate- and operating-level managers. The department's goal is to provide analysts with a good general understanding of Weyerhaeuser businesses, as well as the opportunity to get to know many of the company's key managers in preparation for long-term careers in the company. The department project directors and manager provide guidance and advice as needed. The analysts tend to move into a business unit of their choice, gaining experience in their areas of interest (marketing, finance, operations management, etc.) to lead them into general management positions.

Weyerhaeuser evaluates many proposals to expand or reconfigure its business groups. They include acquisition and joint venture opportunities within existing businesses, as well as in new business lines. They may also involve divestment or asset redeployment options aimed at upgrading Weyerhaeuser's existing portfolio of assets. The IED analyst is a key member of the team evaluating an opportunity, with primary responsibility for performing the economic analysis. In many instances, analysts help develop the strategic framework for the opportunity. The analyst must also ensure that the presentation of the proposal provides senior management with the key information needed to make the decision. After a decision has been reached, analysts participate in the execution by drafting offering memorandums, working with investment bankers, coordinating buyers' due diligence, advising senior managers during negotiations, and evaluating alternative transaction structures.

Weyerhaeuser competes in highly capital-intensive industries and allocates significant capital resources to its existing businesses. IED brings conceptual and analytical leadership to the capital allocation effort. The analyst is primarily responsible for providing decision makers with independent, thorough, and timely economic analyses of diverse investment proposals. This is accomplished by working closely with business and operating groups, often on site. Some recent projects include the expansion of a joint venture newsprint operation with a Japanese partner, multistage modernizations and expansions at two Weyerhaeuser's largest pulp and paper complexes, and the reconfiguration of our southern sawmill capacity to align better with available raw material and product markets.

The Recruiting Process

Describe your recruiting process and the criteria by which you select candidates. Is prior experience necessary?

IED is looking for MBAs who want to leverage their superior analytical ability, strong leadership, and interpersonal skills into a long-term general management career at Weyerhaeuser. New analysts should have significant prior work experience, good business judgment, and a sense of perspective. They should also be comfortable working independently in a relatively unstructured environment.

How many permanent associates and analysts do you hire in a typical year? How many summer interns do you expect to hire? If you have a formal summer program, please describe it. Please be sure to indicate whether the summer program is in place for all offices or just some.

IED hires one to three analysts a year, primarily through recruiting at top MBA schools around the United States. There is no summer program.

Wheat First Butcher Singer

901 East Byrd Street
Riverfront Plaza
Richmond, VA 23219
(804) 782-3516
Fax: (804) 782-3440

MBA Recruiting Contact(s):
Jack Glover, Associate
Karen Hughes, Recruiting Coordinator

Company Description

Describe your firm's business and the types of clients served by your finance group(s).

Wheat First Butcher Singer is a 100% employee-owned investment bank, headquartered in Richmond, Virginia. Founded in 1934, the company has built upon its historical roots in the mid-Atlantic and Southeastern United States to establish a national-level, full service firm which offers a full range of investment banking products and services including equity and debt origination, distribution and aftermarket support, equity and debt research coverage, and merger and acquisition advisory services. Wheat First employs more than 2,300 people, including 867 retail financial consultants located in 102 branch offices. Wheat First's retail branch system encompasses 12 states and spans from Connecticut to South Carolina. Institutional sales offices are located in New York, Los Angeles, Palm Beach, and Richmond.

Wheat First is organized into three primary operating groups: Capital Markets, Private Client, and Investment Management. Capital Markets is comprised of Corporate Finance, Research, Sales and Trading, Taxable Fixed Income, and Municipal Finance. The Private Client Group includes Retail Branch Offices and Fully Disclosed Clearing. The Investment Management Group includes Commonwealth Investment Counsel, Charter Asset Management, Cambridge Advisors, and Wellesley Advisors.

Discuss changes in your firm's revenues (both domestic and international) and professional staff over the past year; over the past five years.

Wheat First has grown dramatically in the past five years from $204 million in revenues in fiscal 1990 to $320 million in fiscal 1995, an increase of 56%. As of December 1994, Wheat First's Municipal Finance Group ranked fifteenth nationally for lead-managed municipal new issues and Corporate Finance placed seventh in equity underwritings for all non–New York firms. Corporate Finance's Financial Institutions Group ranked eighth nationally for M&A activity.

Since 1992, Corporate Finance has completed 181 transactions valued at more than $14.2 billion dollars, including 71 equity offerings totaling $3.9 billion and 47 strategic advisory engagements totaling $5.4 billion. The department focuses on six industry groups and one product group—consumer and specialty retail, furnishings and textile, financial institutions, health care, communications and technology, general industrial industries, and mergers and acquisitions—and is establishing itself as the industry leader in all of these areas.

The Finance MBA's Job Description

Describe the career path and corresponding responsibilities for an MBA at your firm.

Upon arriving at Wheat First, new associates in Corporate Finance begin a training program consisting primarily of on-the-job projects and classroom sessions covering various finance, accounting, and legal topics. The first 18 to 24 months are spent as a generalist working on a variety of transactions in several of the industry groups. Upon completion of the generalist program, associates join an industry or a product group working directly with a senior banker to further expand industry and product knowledge. The goal of the program is to expose associates to a rich variety of assignments and maximize the level of client responsibility.

Flat transaction teams allow associates to demonstrate their talents and, if capable, provide the opportunity for them to assume responsibility at an accelerated pace. Transaction teams generally consist of three professionals, including a financial analyst, an associate, and either a managing director or a vice president. Advancement is based on demonstrated ability; there are no predetermined time frames for promotion.

Corporate Finance seeks highly motivated individuals with a demonstrated record of achievement who have the ability to work effectively with clients and other professionals within the firm. Wheat First investment bankers have a diverse background, both with domestic and international experience. Common characteristics of Corporate Finance associates include strong initiative, team-oriented attitude, strong work ethic, and excellent analytical and communication skills. Corporate Finance associates typically have prior investment banking experience before coming to Wheat First.

121

The Recruiting Process

Describe your recruiting process and the criteria by which you select candidates.

In the fall, Wheat First begins recruiting at the top business schools in the country. Second and third round interviews are held in Richmond. Wheat First has one or two associate "Super Saturdays"—one in December and another in late January. Prospective associates interview one-on-one in half-hour sessions with associates and senior bankers of the department and selected department heads within Capital Markets.

How many permanent associates and analysts do you hire in a typical year? How many summer interns do you expect to hire? If you have a formal summer program, please describe it. Please be sure to indicate whether the summer program is in place for all offices or just some.

The number of associates hired each year depends on Wheat First's internal needs and the demands of the marketplace. Wheat First typically hires two to four associates per year. Wheat First's summer associate program gives students finishing their first year of business school an opportunity to learn about Wheat First and its various departments while participating in Corporate Finance projects and transactions that span industry groups and transaction types. Wheat First typically hires one to two summer associates.

William Blair & Company

222 West Adams Street
Chicago, IL 60606

MBA Recruiting Contact(s):
Brent Felitto
Corporate Finance
(312) 364-8013

Kent Brown
Debt Finance
(312) 364-8952

David Farina
Research
(312) 364-8918

Robert Newman
Investment Management
(312) 364-8783

Locations of Offices:
Chicago, Denver, London, Liechtenstein, and Zurich

Total Number of Professionals (U.S. and worldwide):
324

Company Description

Describe your firm's business and the types of clients served by your finance group(s).

William Blair & Company is a private partnership offering a full range of investment banking and brokerage services to corporations, institutions, municipalities, and private investors across the United States and overseas. William Blair & Company is the largest full-service investment banking firm headquartered in Chicago with over 550 employees.

The firm was founded over 60 years ago to serve small and medium-sized companies and to participate in their growth through equity and debt financings; research, market making, trading, as well as other forms of after-market support; and financial advisory services such as merger and acquisition advice. To that end, the firm's Corporate Finance and Debt Finance Departments have continued to perform originating, structuring and distributing securities for middle-market companies while also assisting not-for-profit organizations and municipalities with their financing needs. William Blair's Mezzanine Debt Fund, Leveraged Capital Fund, and Venture Cap-

ital divisions also focus on providing capital for and making private equity investments in a variety of middle-market growth companies. The firm's Research Department is widely recognized as one of the industry's best in providing research coverage of small to mid-size growth companies in the United States, following approximately 250 companies and a number of specific industries. Finally, the firm's Investment Management Department currently manages approximately $5 billion for high-net-worth individuals, trusts, foundations, charitable and university endowments, pension and profit-sharing funds, and mutual funds.

Describe your ownership structure.

William Blair & Company is a general partnership registered to do business as a member of the New York Stock Exchange. As of December 31, 1994, the firm's capital position was stated at $65 million. There are currently 118 partners and 569 employees. The firm is entirely owned by the active partners.

How does your approach to finance differ from that of other firms, and what do you consider to be your strengths and distinctive capabilities?

Throughout the history of William Blair & Company, we have held fast to the objectives upon which the firm was founded: to identify money-making ideas for our investing clients and to provide superior execution for our corporate and public issuers. We have accomplished these goals by focusing on identifying high-quality long-term investment opportunities, by providing the highest standards of service, and by being conservative in the way we operate our business and advise our clients. Over the past six decades, we are proud to have helped our clients achieve superior investment returns and attractive financing in both good and bad markets.

Our long-term orientation permeates every aspect of our operations. Our partnership structure provides underlying stability and fosters longevity with the firm. Clients benefit from a continuity of performance and a personal familiarity with their needs that come only from long-standing relationships. Over time, the firm has expanded the scope of its investment banking and brokerage services to ensure our clients' enduring financial growth.

Today, William Blair strives to serve its clients as it has in the past: with prudent judgment, sound advice, and diligent follow-through. We appreciate the confidence our clients have in our abilities. Every day, in all aspects of our business, we work to preserve their trust.

Discuss changes in your firm's revenues (both domestic and international) and professional staff over the past year; over the past five years.

Despite the volatile nature of the securities industry and the downsizing of major wall street firms over the last several years, William Blair has continued to expand. In fact, all of the firm's departments have undergone considerable growth recently. Over the past five years, the Corporate Finance Department has increased from 15 to 24 banking professionals; the Fixed Income Department from 11 to 16 banking professionals; the Research Department has grown from 15 to 21 professionals; and the Investment Management Department has grown from 11 to 22 professionals. The growth in these departments is indicative of the growth of the entire firm.

William Blair & Company has also expanded its international presence by adding offices in Zurich and Liechtenstein to complement our London operations.

The Finance MBA's Job Description

Describe the career path and corresponding responsibilities for an MBA at your firm.

William Blair & Company seeks qualified MBAs who desire to work with mid-sized companies, institutions, municipalities, and investors throughout the country. William Blair & Company recruits these individuals on a continual basis as the firm continues to grow. The firm feels the most effective "Training Program" it can offer is immediate exposure to the industry. New associates do not undergo any outside coursework but rather are assigned to live projects from the start.

Corporate Finance
Associates in Corporate Finance work in small project teams that typically include a partner, an associate, and an analyst. Associates work with multiple teams on a number of assignments simultaneously, including transactions such as equity offerings, mergers and acquisitions, private placements, as well as other financial advisory projects. From the time they are hired, associates act as "generalists" providing them with the flexibility to explore a broad array of industries, clients, and transactions. A decentralized, collegial and results-oriented management style creates an entrepreneurial atmosphere that both encourages and rewards a high degree of initiative. William Blair expects each MBA that it hires as an associate to become a partner of the firm.

Research
William Blair & Company does not employ a system whereby newly hired analysts work as a "junior" to an established analyst. Instead, a newly hired MBA is expected to perform as an analyst from day one, with responsibilities essentially similar to established analysts.

The senior analysts act as mentors to newer analysts, but most training is "on-the-job." Industries and companies followed by the analysts typically are selected by them and often are ones where the MBA has had prior experience. While some analysts have moved to subsequent positions in Corporate Finance or Investment Management, the normal career path is to remain an analyst. Almost half of the analysts are partners of the firm.

Debt Finance
MBAs joining the Debt Finance Department enter as associates with responsibilities that include preparing proposals and marketing materials, assisting in marketing, working with clients on a daily basis, and overseeing details related to the execution of a transaction. Associates work in the fields of corporate debt, financing for not-for-profit institutions, hospitals and higher education entities, as well as for municipalities. This broad exposure provides a thorough understanding of the fixed income industry, the challenges of working on several financings at once, and the opportunity to be a "generalist" rather than an expert in only one facet of the industry. The day-to-day operations of the department and its team approach are similar in structure to the Corporate Finance Department.

Investment Management
The Investment Management Department at William Blair is composed of 22 investment professionals. The bulk of these are portfolio managers, about half of whom have research backgrounds and follow a number of stocks, in addition to their account responsibilities. The balance are full-time analysts. The research function in investment management is designed to complement and supplement the William Blair research product. This is done by following companies that have the following attributes: (1) they meet the William Blair criteria for high-quality growth companies; (2) they are desirable for the construction of well-diversified portfolios and; (3) for reasons having to do with either size or industry affiliation, they are not followed by the William Blair Research department. A new MBA would typically start out as an analyst and be responsible for developing a coverage list of stocks for the department to invest in, over an initial period of at least four to five years. Over the long term, both analytical and portfolio management career tracks are available, with both potentially leading to an invitation to join the partnership. Currently, 13 members of the department are partners in the firm.

Describe the opportunities for professional mobility between the various departments in your firm.

Associates are hired to work within a specific department, although there is open communication between all departments of the firm. The firm addresses the needs of individuals who desire to change their focus and switch departments on an individual basis and after taking into consideration the needs of the firm.

Describe the lifestyle aspects of a career with your firm (i.e., average hours per week, amount of travel, flexibility to change offices, corporate culture, etc.).

A career at William Blair is exciting and rewarding and requires a significant commitment of time and energy. One's average hours and travel schedule will vary depending upon market conditions as well as the number and types of projects on which one is working. People who work at William Blair, however, generally seem to enjoy the lifestyle offered by a career with the firm and fostered by its location in Chicago. In addition, the relatively small size of the firm relative to Wall Street standards tends to encourage close relationships among co-workers, while the firm's long-term commitment to its employees and the broad partnership is representative of the firm's inclusive, not exclusive, culture.

The Recruiting Process

Describe your recruiting process and the criteria by which you select candidates. Is prior experience necessary?

William Blair's recruiting process varies across departments. While Research participates in on-campus interviewing, Corporate Finance, Debt Finance, and Investment Management welcome on-site interviewing through correspondence opportunities. William Blair & Company adheres to school policies in its recruiting practices.

William Blair & Company hopes to attract highly motivated, quality individuals with strong quantitative, communicative, and interpersonal skills. In addition to demonstrating these skills, prior work experience, academic performance, and community service activities are considered in an applicant's evaluation.

How many permanent associates and analysts do you hire in a typical year? How many summer interns do you expect to hire? If you have a formal summer program, please describe it. Please be sure to indicate whether the summer program is in place for all offices or just some.

Hiring is based on the needs of each department. Typically, recruiting goals are set in the fall of the coming recruiting season; however, given the size and nature of the firm and our recruiting process, interviewing occurs on a continuous basis throughout the year. Summer associates are rare across divisions; however, opportunities sometimes present themselves depending on the staffing needs of each department.

The World Bank
The Young Professionals Program

1818 H Street, NW
Washington, DC 20433
(202) 473-0312

MBA Recruiting Contact(s):
Young Professionals Program Administrator

Company Description

Describe your firm's business and the types of clients served by your finance group(s).

The World Bank, which consists of the International Bank for Reconstruction and Development (IBRD) and the International Development Association (IDA), promotes economic and social progress in developing nations by helping raise productivity so people may lead better and fuller lives. This is also the aim of the International Finance Corporation (IFC), which works closely with private investors from around the world in promoting commercial enterprises in developing countries. The principal objective of the Multilateral Investment Guarantee Agency (MIGA) is to encourage the flow of investments for productive purposes among member countries and in particular to developing member countries, thus supplementing the activities of the IBRD, IDA, and IFC.

The IBRD, IDA, IFC, and MIGA (collectively known as the World Bank Group) have three interrelated functions: to lend funds; to provide advice, consulting services, and investment promotion; and to serve as a catalyst to stimulate investments by others. The four institutions are closely associated, with IDA, IFC, and MIGA being affiliates of the IBRD. The same president serves all four institutions. The IBRD and IDA (which are jointly referred to as "the Bank") share the same operational staff, while the staff of IFC and MIGA is, for the most part, separate from that of the Bank.

The IBRD, IDA, and IFC differ in the types of financing that they provide for member developing countries. The IBRD makes loans at interest rates that reflect the Bank's cost of borrowing, while IDA provides concessionary financing for the poorest developing countries. Unlike the IBRD and IDA, IFC loans are not government-guaranteed. Rather, the corporation makes loans to private-sector companies at commercial interest rates. The IFC also takes equity positions in companies.

MIGA, on the other hand, provides guarantees for non-commercial risks and also policy and advisory services to encourage the flow of capital to developing countries and to assist these countries in creating an attractive investment climate.

Describe your ownership structure.

The IBRD, established in 1945, is the oldest and largest of the institutions. It was conceived at the United Nations Monetary and Financial Conference held in Bretton Woods, New Hampshire (U.S.A.) in July 1944. The IFC was established in 1956, and IDA in 1960. MIGA began its operations in 1988.

The IBRD, IDA, IFC, and MIGA are owned by their member governments and controlled by their board of directors. To date, 167 countries have joined the IBRD. Membership in IDA is open to all members of the IBRD, and most countries have joined. The IFC has 147 member countries. As of January 1993, 174 countries had signed the MIGA Convention and 114 had completed the ratification process.

Most of the funds lent by the IBRD come from its borrowing in the world's capital markets. It also receives funds from the capital subscriptions of member countries, repayments on past loans, and sales of loans to other investors. Funding for IDA comes almost entirely from grants provided by its more affluent member countries and from contributions by the IBRD from its net income. The IFC obtains funds from its member governments and from borrowing, mainly from international financial markets. MIGA is financially and legally independent and obtains its funds from its member governments.

The Recruiting Process

Describe your recruiting process and the criteria by which you select candidates. Is prior experience necessary?

The Young Professionals Program (YPP) was established in 1963 as a means of recruiting outstanding recent university graduates. Since then, over 1,000 young professionals (YPs) from over 100 different countries have joined the World Bank Group. The majority of all YPs recruited are still with the organization.

The YPP offers an exciting beginning to a career in the World Bank Group for people under 32 years of age who have strong qualifications in economics, finance, or a related field. We encourage qualified women and men from all member countries to apply. As you consider whether or not to apply, please note the following information.

To apply to the program, candidates must have a master's degree (or equivalent) in economics, finance, or a technical field used in the group's operations, plus a minimum of two years of relevant work experience. The technical fields of particular interest to the Bank Group are education, public health, environment and natural resource management, social sciences, and urban planning and civil engineering.

How many permanent associates and analysts do you hire in a typical year? How many summer interns do you expect to hire? If you have a formal summer program, please describe it. Please be sure to indicate whether the summer program is in place for all offices or just some.

Competition for the YPP is high. Each year, about 20 YPs are selected from a pool of over 6,000 applicants from around the world. Therefore, many candidates whose qualifications exceed the minimum requirements of the program cannot be selected. In fact, in recent selections, successful candidates have generally exceeded the requirements for education and work experience. The average age for selected YPs has been 29. Most economists had training at the doctoral level. Those YPs with master's-level degrees (in economics, finance, or a technical field) had an average of four years of work experience in areas relevant to the operations of the World Bank Group. Most have gained familiarity with the issues facing developing countries, through work experience, focused study, or extended periods living and traveling in one or more developing countries.

The YPP does not recruit individuals whose primary graduate-level training and work experience are in other disciplines (such as computer science, accounting, marketing, linguistics, etc.). Candidates with specializations in those areas should contact the Recruitment Division directly.

Fluency in English is required of candidates to the YPP. It is also beneficial that candidates have a speaking proficiency in one or more of the Bank's other most commonly used languages (i.e., Arabic, Chinese, French, Portuguese, and Spanish). Increasingly, proficiency in one or more languages of Eastern Europe and Central Asia is also being sought in YP candidates.

Applicants must be under 32 years of age as of July 1 of the selection year to be eligible for consideration. Candidates over the age limit should contact the Recruitment Division about other job opportunities in the World Bank Group.

We are now reviewing applications for our upcoming selection (March of next year). Should you be selected to proceed to the second phase of the screening process, you will be required to complete a more detailed application package. For this reason, it is to your advantage to submit a detailed resume *no later than October 31* of this year. Any applications received after the final deadline will be held for review for the next selection.

Glossary

Excerpted from Doing Deals: Investment Banks at Work *by Robert G. Eccles and Dwight B. Crane (Boston: Harvard Business School Press, 1988). The following terms and definitions are intended to explain terms used in* Doing Deals *and do not necessarily cover all possible meanings of the terms.*

Arbitrage: occurs when there is an opportunity to buy one security and sell another security and make a riskless profit. An arbitrage opportunity exists when two securities are mispriced relative to each other, so that it is possible to buy one and sell the other and make a risk-free profit. In the investment banking context, the term *arbitrage* is often used to refer to an activity when an acquisition is announced at a higher price than the current stock price of the target firm. The risk arbitrage department of an investment bank then decides whether to buy the stock to take advantage of the higher offer price.

Asset-Backed Securities: a security backed by a pool of assets, such as automobile loans. The cash flow from the pool of assets is used to make interest and principal payments on the securities.

Asset Valuations: usually refers to the valuation of assets in a merger and acquisition transaction. An investment bank is asked to estimate the value of the various parts of the firm that might be acquired.

Block Trading: trading of a large quantity of securities. The New York Stock Exchange considers a block trade to be equal to ten thousand or more shares.

Bond: see **Debt.**

Bought Deal: in securities underwriting, a firm commitment to purchase an entire issue outright from the issuing company. In recent years this term has been used to mean a firm commitment by one or a small number of investment banking firms.

Boutique: a small, specialized securities firm that deals with a limited clientele and offers a limited product line . . . [e.g.,] with advisory services for issuers.

Bridge Loan: a short-term loan made by an investment bank to facilitate a transaction. It is made in anticipation of a security issue that would repay the loan.

Call Date: the date on which issuers have the right to call in or redeem outstanding bonds before their scheduled maturity.

Capital Markets Desk: a group of investment bankers who typically sit on the trading floor. They provide a direct link between issuing customers and the market.

Collaterized Mortgage Obligation (CMO): a security backed by mortgage bonds. The cash flows from the mortgage bonds are typically separated into different portions (e.g., they can be separated into short-, intermediate-, and long-term portions of the mortgages). Each class is paid a fixed rate of interest at regular intervals.

Co-Manager: works with a lead manager and often a group of other co-managers to manage a security underwriting.

Commercial Paper: a short-term debt with maturities ranging from 2 to 270 days, issued by corporations and other short-term borrowers.

Common Stock: a security representing ownership in a public corporation. Owners are entitled to vote on the selection of directors and other corporate matters. They typically receive dividends on their holdings, but corporations are not required to pay dividends. In the event that a corporation is liquidated, the claims of creditors and preferred stockholders take precedence over the claims of those who own common stock.

Convertible Bond: a bond that can be exchanged for a specified number of shares of common stock.

Credit Rating: typically refers to bond and commercial paper ratings assigned by Standard & Poor's, Moody's, or other credit-rating agencies.

Debt: a security that indicates a legal obligation to a borrower to repay principal and interest on specified dates. It is a general name for bonds, notes, mortgages, and other forms of credit obligations.

Distribution: the sale of a new security issue to investors.

Divestiture: the sale of a corporate asset such as a division.

Due Diligence: a process investment banks undertake to assure that information provided in a security offering is accurate.

Earnings per Share (EPS): the net income of a corporation divided by the number of shares outstanding.

Equity: represents ownership in a public corporation as evidenced by holding of common stock or preferred stock.

Eurobond: bond denominated in U.S. dollars or other currencies and sold to investors outside the country whose currency is used (e.g., a U.S. corporation could issue U.S. dollar-denominated securities to European investors).

Fixed-Income Security: a security that pays a fixed rate of return, such as a fixed rate of interest on a corporate bond.

Floating-Rate Debt: a security with interest payments that vary or "float" in response to prevailing interest rates, such as U.S. Treasuries.

Full-Service Firm: an investment bank that offers a wide range of financial services. The term is also used to refer to securities firms that have both extensive retail brokerage and investment banking services for large institutions.

Hedge: an investment strategy used to reduce risk. It typically involves the purchase or sale of contracts designed to offset the change in value of another security.

Hostile Takeover: an acquisition that takes place against the wishes of the management and board of directors of the target company.

Initial Public Offering (IPO): a corporation's first offering of common stock to the public.

Institutional Investor: an organization that holds and trades large volumes of securities such as pension funds, life insurance companies, and mutual funds.

International Bond: a bond issued outside the home country of the borrowing entity. International bonds can be subdivided into Eurobonds and foreign bonds. Foreign bonds are bonds sold primarily in the country of the currency of the issue.

Investment-Grade Bond: typically regarded as a bond with a credit rating of A or better.

Junk Bond: see **Noninvestment-Grade Bond.**

Lead Manager: works with a group of co-managers to form a syndicate to underwrite a security issue. A lead manager normally "runs the books" (manages the underwriting and determines distribution allocation) and is usually the investment bank that originated the deal.

League Table Rankings: published in various trade magazines that rank security underwriters by the volume of securities underwritten.

Lease: a contract granting use of real estate, equipment, or other fixed assets for a specified period of time in exchange for a series of payments.

Leveraged Buyout (LBO): the purchase of a company, or part of a company, using borrowed funds. The target company's assets frequently serve as security for the loans taken out by the acquiring firm. These loans are then repaid out of the acquired company's cash flow.

Make a Market: trading a security in order to provide liquidity and market prices to investors.

Master Limited Partnership: a limited partnership compromises a general partner, who manages a project and limited partners, who invest money but have limited liability. Frequently, limited partnerships are found in real estate and in oil and gas. A master limited partnership is a limited partnership that is publicly traded to give the investors liquidity.

Merchant Banking: in the context of U.S. investment banking, *merchant banking* refers to activities in which the firm commits its own capital to a transaction, as it does with bridge loans or when it makes equity investments in a company.

Mergers and Acquisitions (M&A): a general term that refers to various combinations of companies. A merger occurs when two or more companies combine; an acquisition occurs when one company takes over a controlling interest in another. M&A groups in investment banks work on these transactions, and they also advise on other kinds of related transactions, such as divestitures and repurchase of significant amounts of corporate stock.

Money-Market Paper: a short-term instrument such as commercial paper that is purchased by corporations and institutions that hold short-term liquid investment portfolios.

Money-Market Preferred Stock: a preferred stock instrument that has been structured to appeal to short-term investors such as investors that purchase regular money-market paper. The preferred stock is repriced every forty-nine days so that it trades like an instrument with a forty-nine-day maturity. From the point of view of the buyer, the advantage of preferred stock is that corporate holders of preferred and other stock only pay income tax on 15% of the dividend.

Mortgage-Backed Security: a security backed by a pool of mortgages. The cash flow from the pool of mortgages is used to make interest and principal payments on the security.

Noninvestment-Grade Bonds: technically, bonds with credit ratings of less than A. They are typically issued by companies without a long track record of sales and earnings or by companies that have experienced difficulty and have questionable credit strength. These securities are often used as a means to finance takeovers.

Origination: obtaining a mandate from an issuer to manage the underwriting and distribution of a new security issue.

Preferred Stock: a class of security that lies somewhere between bonds and common stock. Like interest on debt, dividends are paid on preferred stock at a specified rate, and holders of preferred stock take precedence over holders of common stock in the payment of dividends and liquidation of assets. Creditors, however, are ahead of preferred stockholders in the event of liquidation, and the company does not have a legal obligation to pay preferred stock dividends. Most preferred stock is cumulative, so that if the dividends are not paid for any reason, they accumulate and must be paid before dividends are paid to common stockholders.

Preliminary Prospectus: the first document released by an underwriter describing a new issue to prospective investors. It offers financial details about the issue but does not contain all of the information that will appear in the final prospectus. Portions of the cover page of the preliminary prospectus are printed in red ink, so it is popularly called a red herring.

Primary Market: the first time a security is sold to investors.

Private Placement: securities that are directly placed with an institutional investor, such as an insurance company, rather than sold through a public issue. Private placements do not have to be registered with the Securities and Exchange Commission, so these placements can occur more rapidly and with less information made available to the public.

Recapitalization: a change in a corporation's capital structure such as when the corporation exchanges bonds for outstanding stock. Some companies have been recapitalized in this fashion to make them less attractive targets for takeover.

Refinancing: when outstanding bonds are retired by using proceeds from the issuance of new securities. Refinancings are undertaken to reduce the interest rate or to otherwise improve the terms of the outstanding debt.

Restrictive Covenants: terms in a debt agreement that are designed to protect the creditor's interests. Covenants normally cover such matters as minimum amounts of working capital, maximum debt-equity ratios, and limits on dividend payments.

Retail Distribution: the capability of a securities firm to distribute securities to individual investors through retail brokers.

Secondary Trading: trading of securities which have already been issued in the primary marketplace. Thus, proceeds of secondary-market sales accrue to selling dealers and investors, not to the companies that originally issued the securities.

Securities and Exchange Commission (SEC): the federal agency created by the Securities Exchange Act of 1934 to administer that act and the Securities Act of 1933. The SEC is made up of five commissioners, appointed by the president. The statutes they administer are designed to promote full public disclosure and protect the investing public against malpractice in the securities markets. All issues of securities in the United States must be registered with the SEC.

Shelf Registration (Rule 415): a rule adopted by the SEC in 1982 that allows a corporation to preregister a public offering of securities. That is, they can preregister for up to two years prior to a public offering of securities. Once the security has been registered it is "on the shelf" and the company can go to market with the security as conditions become favorable.

Special Bracket Firm: an investment banking firm that leads the bulk of securities underwritten in the United States. The six special bracket firms [in 1987] are First Boston; Goldman, Sachs; Merrill Lynch; Morgan Stanley; Salomon Brothers; and Shearson Lehman Brothers.

Swap: has two meanings in the context of the securities markets. First, *swap* refers to the act of swapping from one type of security to another, such as an investor who swaps out of bonds into equities. Second, in a more recent use of the word, *swap* refers to debt obligations that are swapped between two borrowers (e.g., a borrower with floating-rate debt may swap its interest payment obligations with a borrower of fixed-rate debt; thus, the floating-rate debt issuer converts its debt into a fixed rate obligation).

Syndicate: a group of investment banks that agree to purchase a new issue of securities from an issuer for resale to the investment public. These investment banks agree to underwrite the securities. That is, they guarantee to purchase the securities. This group of banking firms is normally part of the selling group that distributes the security to the ultimate investors.

Syndicate Desk: coordinates the underwriting function of an investment bank. It helps price the security, works with the other members of the syndicate, and determines the allocation between retail and institutional investors.

Tax-Exempt Bond: a bond whose interest is exempt from taxation by federal, state, or local authorities. It is frequently called a municipal bond even though it may have been issued by a state government or agency or by an entity that is not a municipality. General obligation bonds are backed by the full faith and credit of the issuing entity. These bonds may be underwritten by commercial banks as well as by investment banks. Revenue bonds are backed by the anticipated revenues of the issuing authority. Under present legislation, commercial banks may not underwrite revenue bonds.

Tender Offer: an offer to buy shares of a corporation for cash or securities, or both, often with the objective of taking control of a target company. The Securities and Exchange Commission requires a corporate investor accumulating 5% or more of a target company to disclose the investment.

Thrift Institution: the major forms of thrift institutions are savings and loans and savings banks. These and other organizations receive consumer savings deposits and invest most of their assets in residential mortgages.

Tombstone: an advertisement placed in newspapers and magazines by investment bankers to announce an offering of securities. It gives basic details about the issue and lists the underwriting group members in a manner that indicates the relative size of their participation.

Underwrite: securities firms underwrite a securities issue by assuming the risk of buying the issue and then reselling the securities to the public either directly or through dealers.

U.S. Treasuries: securities issued by the federal government to borrow money.

Wirehouse: a national or international brokerage firm that has a large retail network of branch offices.

1996 Finance Career Guide Questionnaire

Company Description

Describe your firm's business and the types of clients served by your finance group(s).

Describe your ownership structure.

How does your approach to finance differ from that of other firms, and what do you consider to be your strengths and distinctive capabilities?

Discuss changes in your firm's revenues (both domestic and international) and professional staff over the past year; over the past five years.

The Finance MBA's Job Description

Describe the career path and corresponding responsibilities for an MBA at your firm.

Describe the opportunities for professional mobility between the various departments in your firm.

Discuss the lifestyle aspects of a career with your firm (i.e., average hours per week, amount of travel, flexibility to change offices, corporate culture, etc.).

The Recruiting Process

Describe your recruiting process and the criteria by which you select candidates. Is prior experience necessary?

How many permanent associates and analysts do you hire in a typical year? How many summer interns do you expect to hire? If you have a formal summer program, please describe it. Please be sure to indicate whether the summer program is in place for all offices or just some.

What international opportunities does your firm offer for U.S. citizens? For foreign nationals?

Mailing List

This is a mailing list of the firms profiled in the *Harvard Business School Career Guide: Finance, 1996*. Entries are arranged alphabetically and contain the name of the firm, address, phone number, and MBA recruiting contact. Some entries contain alternate contacts. Please refer to the company profile to see if another contact would be more appropriate for you. Before sending letters to the firms on the list, always call to verify the address and the name of the recruiting contact.

Barbara H. Boyle
A.G. Edwards & Sons, Inc.
One North Jefferson
St. Louis, MO 63103
(314) 289-3691

Anne Ford
Alex. Brown & Sons, Inc.
135 East Baltimore Street
Baltimore, MD 21202
(800) 638-2596

Andre Barbosa
Banco Pactual
Av. Rep. do Chile, 230/29° andar
Rio de Janeiro, RJ 20031-170
Phone: (55-21) 272-1100

Debbie Barry
Bankers Trust
130 Liberty Street, 12th floor
New York, NY 10006

Jennifer Rolnick
Bear, Stearns & Co. Inc.
245 Park Avenue
New York, NY 10167
(212) 272-7749

John W. Pollock
Bowles Hollowell Conner & Co.
227 West Trade Street
Charlotte, NC 28202
(704) 348-1092

Wendy Chapman
Broadview Associates, L.P.
One Bridge Plaza
Fort Lee, NJ 07024
(201) 346-9000

Annette Cuttley
Chemical Banking Corporation
270 Park Avenue
New York, NY 10017
(212) 270-7072

Irene J. Melitas
Chevron Corporation
225 Bush Street
San Francisco, CA 94104-4289
(415) 894-2752

Anne Hitchcock
CS First Boston
55 East 52nd Street
New York, NY 10055
(212) 909-2420

J. Morton Davis
D.H. Blair Investment Banking Corp.
44 Wall Street
New York, NY 10005
(212) 495-5000

Elizabeth Derby
Donaldson, Lufkin & Jenrette
140 Broadway
New York, NY 10005
(212) 504-3903

Lucy Marshall
Enron Capital & Trade Resources
1400 Smith Street
Houston, TX 77002
(713) 853-6614

FMC Corporation
200 East Randolph Drive
Chicago, IL 60601
(312) 861-6000

Malcolm Macdonald
Ford Motor Company
World Headquarters Building
11th Floor—East Wing
The American Road
Dearborn, MI 48121
(313) 323-0850

Diane Kopyscianski
Furman Selz, Inc.
230 Park Avenue
New York, NY 10169
(212) 309-8382

Dwaine Kimmet
General Motors Corporation
New York Treasurer's Office
GM Building
767 Fifth Avenue
New York, NY 10153
(212) 418-6193

Chris C. Casciato
Goldman, Sachs & Co.
85 Broad Street
New York, NY 10004
(212) 902-1000

Bill Mitchell
Hewlett-Packard Company
3000 Minuteman Road
Andover, MA 01810
(508) 659-2815

IBM Corporation
IBM Staffing Services
3808 Six Forks Road
Raleigh, NC 27609
(800) 964-4473

Cornelis de Kievit
The International Finance Corporation
1818 H Street, NW
Room I-2193
Washington, DC 20433
(202) 473-7972

Andrea Beldecos
J.P. Morgan & Co. Incorporated
60 Wall Street
New York, NY 10260
(212) 483-2323

Rhonda Johnson
James D. Wolfensohn Incorporated
599 Lexington Avenue
New York, NY 10022
(212) 909-8100

Rita Haring
Lehman Brothers
Three World Financial Center
New York, NY 10285
(212) 526-2000

Roslyn N. Dickerson
Merrill Lynch & Co. Inc.
World Financial Center
250 Vesey Street
New York, NY 10281-1331
(212) 449-8790

Sharon Henning
Montgomery Securities
600 Montgomery Street
San Francisco, CA 94111
(415) 627-2793

Marilyn Booker
Morgan Stanley Group Inc.
1251 Avenue of the Americas
New York, NY 10020
(212) 703-4000

Courtenay Buchan
NationsBank
100 N. Tryon Street
NC1007-21-10
Charlotte, NC 28255
(704) 386-1159

Jeff Watchorn
Nesbitt Burns Inc.
1 First Canadian Place
4th Floor
P.O. Box 150
Toronto, Ontario
M5X 1H3
Canada
(416) 359-4000

Human Resources Department
Nomura Securities International, Inc.
2 World Financial Center
Building B
New York, NY 10281
(212) 667-9237

Lurah Bean
Piper Jaffray Inc.
222 South Ninth Street
Minneapolis, MN 55402
(612) 342-6000

Gary A. Downing
Raymond James & Associates, Inc.
800 Carillon Parkway
St. Petersburg, FL 33716
(813) 573-3800

Douglas A. Guzman
RBC Dominion Securities Inc.
P.O. Box 21 Commerce Court South
Toronto, Ontario
M5L 1A7
Canada
(416) 864-4000

Halsey Wise
The Robinson-Humphrey Company, Inc.
Atlanta Financial Center
3333 Peachtree Road, NE
Atlanta, GA 30326
(404) 266-6000

Stephen L. Shapiro
Rothschild Canada Limited
1 First Canadian Place
Suite 3800
P.O. Box 77
Toronto, Ontario
M5X 1B1
Canada
(416) 369-9600

Maureen Horan
Salomon Brothers Inc
Seven World Trade Center
New York, NY 10048
(212) 783-5924

Andrew J. Frankle
Schroder Wertheim & Co. Incorporated
787 Seventh Avenue
New York, NY 10019
(212) 492-6478

Matthew R. Simmons
Simmons & Company International
700 Louisiana
Suite 5000
Houston, TX 77002
(713) 236-9999

Chip Rae
Smith Barney Inc.
388 Greenwich Street
New York, NY 10013
(212) 816-1764

Robert A. Moll
Teachers Insurance and Annuity Association-College Retirement Equities Fund (TIAA-CREF)
730 Third Avenue
New York, NY 10017
(800) 842-2733

Reginald A. McQuay
Toronto Dominion Bank
31 West 52d Street
New York, NY 10019-6101
(212) 468-0633

Jim Rynott
United Airlines
P.O. Box 66100
Chicago, IL 60666
(708) 952-4000

Frances A. Lyman
Wasserstein Perella & Co. Inc.
31 West 52d Street
New York, NY 10019
(212) 969-2700

Jeremy Hedberg
Wessels, Arnold & Henderson
901 Marquette Ave.
Minneapolis, MN 55402
(800) 955-0920

Brian Haun
Weyerhaeuser Company
Tacoma, WA 98477
(206) 924-5227

Jack Glover
Wheat First Butcher Singer
901 East Byrd Street
Riverfront Plaza
Richmond, VA 23219
(804) 782-3516

Brent Felitto
William Blair & Company
222 West Adams Street
Chicago, IL 60606
(312) 364-8013

Young Professionals Program Administrator
The World Bank
1818 H Street, NW
Washington, DC 20433
(202) 473-0312

Selective Bibliography on the Finance Industry

Sue Marsh
Director of Information Services
Baker Library
Harvard Business School

Some MBAs will want to expand their job search to companies not included in this book. The following bibliography provides additional sources that are relevant to the job search. Directories provide additional companies and company information, rank companies, track industry trends and statistics, and, in some cases, provide key articles on the industry. The journals cited are important to understanding the recent trends and activities. The internet addresses point to a wide variety of related finance job search and industry information.

Directories

America's Corporate Finance Directory. New Providence, NJ: National Register Publishing Company. Focuses on public and private U.S. companies with revenue income and/or pension assets over $100 million per year. Large subsidiaries of foreign companies are also included. For each firm are financial data, key executives, listings of outside service firms, description of business, personnel, and area of responsibility. Indexes include financial responsibility, company, SIC, geographic, who's where, private companies and an integrated company index. (Formerly *Corporate Finance Bluebook*.) Annual companion to the *Corporate Finance Sourcebook*.

Cary, Lucis. *The Venture Report Guide to Venture Capital in Europe.* 5th ed. London: Pitman, 1991. Heavy concentration of U.K. firms, information includes firm history, sources of funds, fees, decision-making process, key management, and profiles of investments.

Corporate Finance: The IDD Review of Investment Banking. New York: IDD, Inc. Reviews the previous year's public offerings completed in the United States, broken out by type of security and underwriter, with a comprehensive listing of the terms of deals done. Organized by industry category, data include U.S. issuers in the U.S. domestic market, highlights of the industry, top managers, financing by type of security, and quarterly financing by type and volume. Excluded are debt-for-debt equity swaps, best efforts deals, private placements, and overallotments. Charts and graphs. Semiannual.

Corporate Finance Sourcebook: The Guide to Major Capital Investment Sources and Related Financial Services. New Providence, NJ: National Register Publishing Company. Nineteen types of capital funding and management firms, including venture capitalists, major private lenders, commercial financiers and factors, lessors, commercial and investment banks and bankers, intermediaries, pension managers, cash managers, corporate and real estate services, business insurance brokers, and CPAs. Data concerning firms vary according to types of activity. Over 3700 firms are covered. Also included is a three-year financing retrospective, listing all corporate public offerings. Annual companion to *America's Corporate Finance Directory*.

Directory of Buyout Financing Sources. New York: Securities Data Publishing. Detailed profiles of more than 600 firms worldwide that provide debt and equity financing for buyouts. Arranged alphabetically within U.S. and foreign sections, information includes addresses, principals, services offered, and the types of transactions. Indexes include a list of leveraged buyout professionals, industry preferences, international activities, and companies. Emphasis is on U.S. firms. Annual companion to the *Directory of M&A Intermediaries*.

Directory of M&A Intermediaries. New York: Securities Data Publishing. Six hundred seventy investment banks, business brokers, law firms, and their intermediaries throughout the world. Contains articles on mergers and acquisitions and leveraged buyouts. The U.S. listing is by state; foreign firms are listed alphabetically. Entries include name and title; type of firm; affiliation; services offered; percentage of intermediary work and other financial services; transaction, geographic, and industry preferences; and types of principal clients. Indexes are by industry preference, professionals, and areas of international activities. Annual companion to the *Directory of Buyout Financing Sources*.

Guide to Venture Capital in Asia. Hong Kong: AVCJ Holdings Limited. Similar in format to *Pratt's*, sections include a history and prospective of venture capital in 16 countries in the Asia Pacific region; details of the industry by country; and profiles of 346 venture capital firms operating in Asia. Indexes include a listing of venture capital associations in Asia. Indexes by location, fund index, management and company. Charts and graphs. Annual.

Major Financial Institutions of Europe. London: Graham & Trotman. Countries covered: Australia, Belgium, Denmark, Erie, Finland, France, Germany, Greece, Italy, Luxembourg, the Netherlands, Norway, Portugal,

Spain, Sweden, Switzerland, and the United Kingdom. Arranged by country, information varies. Listings include directors, board members, principal activities, principal shareholders, number of employees, parent companies, and subsidiaries. Alphabetical index to all companies. Annual.

Nelson's Directory of Investment Managers. Port Chester, NY: Nelson Publications. Two thousand investment management firms profiled, including key executives, organizational overviews, affiliations, specialities, asset allocation, clients, decision-making process, fees, and holdings. Indexes by geography, total assets managed, investment managers by organization, type of investment, specialities, and products offered. Additional index by minority- and woman-owned investment managers. Annual.

Nelson's World's Best Money Managers. Port Chester, NY: Nelson Publications. Comprehensive survey of institutional money managers, Rankings include the top 10, 20, or 40 managers in all areas of financial management including U.S. and international equity, growth, small cap, large cap, fixed income, etc. Ratings based on results of the Performance Presentation Standards of the Association for Investment Management and Research. Annual.

Pratt's Guide to Venture Capital Sources. New York: Securities Data Publishing, Inc. Signed articles on the background of venture capital, how to raise venture capital, and sources of financing and business development. The major index is a geographic listing of U.S. venture capital firms (contact persons; type of firm; type of financing; annual sales; geographic, industry, and project preferences). Separate section of foreign venture capital companies is an expansion of the Canadian indexes, reflecting the growing globalization of venture capital. Indexes by company, professional, industry preference, and stage preference. Annual.

REIT Handbook: The Complete Guide to the Real Estate Investment Trust Industry. Washington, DC: National Association of Real Estate Investment Trusts, Inc. Alphabetical listing of member profiles include officers, stock exchange information, trustees and directors, description of business investments, assets, most recent public offerings and private placement of debt and equity, liabilities and shareholder equity, and investment research companies. Industry statistics included. Annual.

Securities Industry Yearbook. New York: Securities Industry Association. Ranking of 700+ Securities Industry Association members by capital, number of offices, employees, and registered representatives. The major section is alphabetical by firm and includes parent companies;

major subsidiaries; number of offices, employees, and customer accounts; registered representatives; year founded; form of ownership; senior management and department heads; and capital position. Industry trends and statistics. Annual.

Standard & Poor's Security Dealers of North America. New York: Standard & Poor's Corporation. Brokers, distributors, dealers, and underwriters listed geographically and alphabetically. Data include officers, exchange and association membership, type of business, employer's industry number, and number of employees. A separate listing for foreign offices and representatives, new addresses, and discontinued firms. Semiannual.

Periodicals

The Asian Venture Capital Journal
Futures: The Magazine of Commodities and Options
Financial World
Going Public: The IPO Reporter
Institutional Investor
Investment Dealer's Digest
Mergers & Acquisitions
Pensions & Investments
Red Herring
Venture Capital Journal

Internet Sites and Addresses

Business Job Finder. Ohio State University.
[http://www.cob.ohio-state.edu/dept/fin/osujobs.htm]
The most comprehensive site to date for information about finance jobs; use it as a starting place. Covers accounting, finance and consulting. Information is provided about job descriptions, salaries, print resources, future outlook, and leading employers. Areas covered include Accounting, Commercial Baking, Corporate Finance, Insurance and Risk Management, Management Consulting, Management and Financial Planning, and Real Estate.

Finance Sites on the WWW. Ohio State University.
[http://www.cob.ohio-state.edu/htbin/htimage/dept/fin/journal/jf.conf?22]
Points to areas of interest including SEC EDGAR, the S&P 500, *Global Stock Market Report,* and other finance web pages.

Money and Investment Guide. Wall Street Journal.
[http://update.wsj.com/]
Up-to-date coverage of the top stories in business and

finance. News and information from *The Wall Street Journal, The Asian Wall Street Journal,* and *The Wall Street Journal Europe.* Dow Jones Market columns and features available the evening before the print; past articles; and information on investing, taxes, college financing, retirement planning, and other personal finance topics. Available by subscription, free during a trial period.

Other Sites of Interest:

The American Risk and Insurance Association. [http://riskweb.bus.utexas.edu/aria.htm]
CareerMosaic. [http://www.careermosaic.com/]

The Catapult. [http://www.wm.edu/catapult/catapult.html]
The Chicago Mercantile Exchange. [http://www.cme.com/cme/]
Experimental Stock Market Data. [http://www.ai.mit.edu/stocks.html]
FinanceNet. [http://www.financenet.gov/]
FINWeb. [http://riskweb.bus.utexas.edu/finweb.html]
Online Career Center. [gopher://garnet.msen.com:70/11/mcc]
Traders-market. [http://www.traders-market.com/]